THE
DIGITAL
QUALITY
HANDBOOK

GUIDE FOR ACHIEVING CONTINUOUS QUALITY IN A DEVOPS REALITY

EDITION I

A 360 degree view of digital quality with recommendations for Agile & DevOps Practitioners

ERAN KINSBRUNER

DEDICATION

This book, which also received valuable contributions from my brother Lior, is dedicated to my father Marcel Kinsbruner who passed away in 2006. He was a role model for me and my family in terms of perfectionism, dedication, and much more.

PREFACE

As mobile and web technologies continue to expand and drive large organizational business in virtually every vertical or industry, it is critical to understand how to take existing release practices for mobile and web apps to the next level, including software development life cycle (SDLC), tools, quality, etc.

Organizations which are already enjoying the power of digital are still struggling with various challenges that can be related to many factors, such as:

* SDLC and process maturity
* Expanding test coverage to include more non-functional testing, user condition testing, etc.
* Coping with existing limitations of open source tools and frameworks
* Sustaining correctly sized and up-to-date mobile test labs
* Getting proper quality insights upon each test cycle prior to and post production
* Wisely branching cross-platform and cross-feature test suites

The issues above are just a few out of undoubtedly many others existing today. However, in this book, I made up my mind to tackle these and provide working best practices to overcome them.

Each chapter in this book addresses a key challenge and provides practical examples and real life "recipes" to overcome these difficulties and eventually help other organizations who might be facing them.

THE MOTIVATION BEHIND THIS BOOK

Being in the mobile space since the year 2000, I witnessed the rise (and fall) of the J2ME[1] mobile technology. Then Symbian paved the way to the iOS and Android revolution. I am convinced that the market over the past 2 decades is moving much faster than organizations can keep up with when it comes to

---

1   Java 2 Micro Edition (J2ME), Oracle — http://www.oracle.com/technetwork/java/embedded/javame/index.html

SDLC processes, adoption of tools, engineering skillsets, and more.

In the early 2000s, I was managing the J2ME Software Quality Engineering (SQE) teams of Sun Microsystems, which were spread across multiple locations, trying to assure the quality of the SDK tools, the MIDP reference implementation, and other supporting mobile technologies developed by the company at that time. As a manager and practitioner, I felt similar pains that organizations are suffering from today in the Android and iOS era. One of the issues I was facing was related to matching the right test suites to the right devices for target execution. I found out the hard way that not every device was running the same implementation of the MIDP RI, thus causing lengthy and inefficient cycles due to irrelevant tests that were launched against devices that did not actually support some of the features in the tests.

This challenge — only one among many others that I have faced over the past years — brought me to drive the development of an innovative feature that was registered as a U.S patent[2] after being implemented. As noted above, my current role as the Mobile Technical Evangelist at Perfecto gives me the chance to talk to enterprises, as well as small businesses, who are stumbling and falling when trying to juggle between the quality of their digital products and the velocity/ release cadence that they have to establish and maintain.

WHO SHOULD READ THIS BOOK?

This book is aimed at digital teams that are developing and testing mobile and web apps and that are stuck and experiencing such difficulties. It will be particularly useful to organizations looking for guidance on continuous improvement in terms of effectiveness, efficiency, performance, best practices, open source tools and frameworks, and the like. In this regard, it will be equally interesting for developers, testers, managers, product owners, et cetera: everyone involved and interested in the release of high quality digital products.

Since this book is not only bringing my personal experience[3] and practices, but also includes innovative knowledge shared by leading industry practitioners, I

---

2   Mechanism for Graphical Test Exclusion — http://patentimages.storage.googleapis.com/pdfs/
US6980916.pdf

3   Mobile Testing Blog — https://mobiletestingblog.com/

hope that it will allow mobile teams to learn something new and help improve their current processes and best practices.

THIS BOOK IS ORGANIZED AS FOLLOWS:

Section 1 is an introduction to the digital testing space, its challenges, pitfalls, and common mistakes as well as a prescriptive approach for mobile test lab foundation.

Section 2 drills down into more advanced techniques for mobile and web functional test automation, enhancement of test automation frameworks, and some innovative open source tools that can help test automation engineers perform their tasks more efficiently.

Section 3 is fully dedicated to digital platforms testing in the context of Agile workflows, shifting app quality left toward the build cycle, and marching towards enabling a digital DevOps organizational culture using the right tools.

Section 4 is fully dedicated to non-functional, user-experience-based approaches and covers methodologies surrounding performance testing, production monitoring, user condition based testing, and more.

Section 1: Introduction to Continuous Digital Quality

- Chapter 01: Digital Quality: Beyond the Technical Initiative (Chris P. Willis)
- Chapter 02: Digital Mobile Testing (Jonathon Wright)
- Chapter 03: Mobile Space Overview and Tools Landscape
- Chapter 04: Sizing a Mobile Lab for International Mobile Products
- Chapter 05: Guidelines for Common Industry Pitfalls and Test Planning
- Chapter 06: Shifting from Manual Mobile Testing to Automation
- Chapter 07: Optimizing Test Automation through Android & iOS Property Files

Section 2: Advanced Continuous Digital Quality Practices

- Chapter 08: Extending Open Source Frameworks for Advanced Functional Testing (Wim Selles)
- Chapter 09: Advanced Automated Visual Testing (Adam Carmi)

INTRO PROLOG

Digital is one of the biggest business disruptions happening to enterprises today.

This disruption creates new winners and losers in various industries, transforms brand engagement as well as how business models are evolving.

At the core of the disruption is engagement with the end user (customer, employee, partner, vendor), moving from human interaction to digital integration through **APPLICATIONS**.

Applications are moving from supporting business initiatives to BECOMING the business. Think of it: banking apps are not just supporting customer needs; for more and more users they **are** the bank itself.

This change means that application delivery is becoming a critical capability for enterprises. This is no longer a competitive advantage, but vital means to stay relevant.

Delivering applications must happen faster than before and within cost limitations. Quality tends to be at a level higher than ever before, keeping customers engaged and delighted. This means **Quality** and **Quality at Speed** are at the center of successful application delivery pipelines.

Perfecto is investing in research dedicated to the phenomenon of how quality is transformed in this new Digital Era and is bringing you, in collaboration with industry leading companies, this comprehensive guide to walk you through the disrupted new world of **Quality.**

Roi Carmel, Chief Strategy Officer at Perfecto

TABLE OF CONTENTS

1 Introduction to Continuous Digital Quality

Digital Quality:
Beyond the
Technical Initiative

THIS CHAPTER WAS CONTRIBUTED BY CHRISTOPHER P. WILLIS, CMO AT PERFECTO

CHRISTOPHER P. WILLIS brings over two decades of experience in growing technology companies — with a focus on developing high-performance B2B marketing teams designed to generate demand, drive awareness, and propagate companies' brands across the globe. As a mobile industry pioneer, Chris helped set the direction for marketing of mobile applications and mobile application development platforms over a decade ago. Since then, he has remained at the forefront of the industry, propelling companies to leadership positions in a rapidly evolving segment. Leveraging a measured combination of demand generation, marketing communications, media management, online, social media, and multi-media outreach, Chris builds and manages teams focused 100% on expanding awareness of the company while exponentially enhancing the volume and quality of sales leads.

INTRODUCTION

There is a shift occurring in enterprise IT. We are talking about the shift from Mobile and Web to a consolidated Digital strategy for customer interaction. And specifically, we are going to elaborate on how "Quality" is a critical factor to this shift.

When we talk about a "shift to Digital," it is usually in terms of release cycles (more, faster), development approach (Agile), and the consolidation of mobile and web delivery.

These are all valid side effects of the transformation, but we are sort of missing the bigger picture — the one that takes Digital from a technical hiring plan ("We need someone to run our web and mobile delivery... Let's call it digital") to a board-level imperative to change the very face of the business.

RE-ARCHITECTING BUSINESSES IN THE DIGITAL AGE

"Digital" is a shift in business mentality that is putting IT/ Development in the driver's seat in a way that it has never been before. Why a shift? Because 5 years ago your website, and then your mobile app, was primarily brochure-ware, designed as a brand extension into a new medium. IT was tasked with developing a new method of delivering, essentially, marketing material. While it seemed very important at the time, the criticality of the web and mobile delivery channels was low. In corner offices and board rooms across the Fortune 5000, decisions have been made to very literally SHIFT the primary engagement point of the business from the physical world (offices, branches, stores, front desks, and service counters) to what we are referring to today as the Digital World (mobile phones, tablets, laptops, cars, and IoT). And this shift cannot be taken lightly. This is not a classic IT project of yesteryear, where they would have been given 16–18 months to convert from Jana CRM to Siebel, or to upgrade to the most recent version of SAP. No, this is a wholesale shift in the business. CEOs all over the world are placing bets — outweighing by far the value of their businesses — on their ability to deliver an engaging and delighting experience that will serve the ever-expanding needs of their customers, while at the same time drawing new customers to the business.

WHAT DOES QUALITY HAVE TO DO WITH IT?

Good question. When there is a meeting with technical management at F500 companies, one cannot just walk in and say, "There's a shift to Digital," and then define Digital as mobile and web, and talk about velocity and quality. It is not doing the shift justice. Rather, one needs to make the case that Digital represents a "mission-critical, jobs on the line — your world just got way more important" initiative.

QUALITY CANNOT BE AN AFTERTHOUGHT

If *the face of the business* is shifting to Digital, QUALITY CANNOT BE AN AFTER-THOUGHT. Imagine that a bank was going to design and build a new branch. Would they just rush into building it, with little planning and no thought of quality practice? It would be a pretty safe bet that doing such a thing would result in a really crazy-looking building, with missing doors, crooked windows, counters being too high, and stools that are too low. Presumably, we would all agree that no one designed and built customer engagement points like that.

Quality has to be a first class citizen in the development of a business critical digital engagement point. It seems like this should go without saying. So quality has to be built into the very fiber of the software development cycle. The better the code, the faster the deployment of new features. Chances are higher that this way there would be more capacity to add further features in future iterations. Apparently, the higher the quality of early-cycle app code, the lower the cost associated with fixing defects would be.

Beyond slowing down planned software deliveries and time to market, however, app defects hurt businesses in a number of ways.

THE BUSINESS VALUE OF QUALITY (AND THE COST OF POOR QUALITY)

It turns out that the shift to Digital is a shift of engagement points. In the case of many companies, that digital engagement point is now a/the primary engagement point.

DOING BUSINESS IN 2017

Tangerine Bank in Canada is a great example of a company that understands Digital. It has gone all the way towards a full transformation. Tangerine converted their branches into cafes, where customers could drink coffee, access their banking app on supplied tablets, and chat with "café associates", if they have any questions. Tangerine does not have a backup plan in the event their digital strategy does not pan out. This is their business in 2017. It is not a campaign and it is not a marketing program. This is what their bank has become. For Tangerine, app quality is paramount because Tangerine understands what is at stake.

WASTING BUSINESS THE "EASY" WAY

So, if you were in the shoes of an entrepreneur and you went for Digital, you should have been aware that there was a quick and easy way of diminishing great ideas and demolishing bright future plans. Poor quality of digital engagement points may quickly turn into a deal breaker. Amazing features and advanced capabilities would be irrelevant if they never worked right or played nicely together. It is that simple.

The cost of bad quality goes beyond a single customer ranting along the lines of "I'm disappointed that my app doesn't work." There is a hard lesson to be learnt — the impact of bad quality in the hands of consumers can be seen immediately. Sooner rather than later, it will ripple across the corresponding business with measurable financial ramifications.

When critical defects make it into production, we generally see a pattern. Let us explore quickly some of the implied costs for bad quality nowadays. Thus, we will try to measure the respective impact on consumer-facing digital businesses.

INABILITY TO EXECUTE INTENDED FUNCTIONALITY

Take a retail app, for example. What would happen if users would not be able to complete a transaction? That would be actually a pretty good showcase to illustrate the cost of a core application functionality not working. We keep on hearing about this during the holiday shopping season.

"XYZ Retailer's" app crashed and was down for 5 hours. Looking at the pure cost of the outage, forgetting about the costs to fix the defects, or the follow-on costs (explained in a bit), a company like Amazon, which used to bring in $125K/ minute in 2015[1], would be at risk of losing around $37M because of their infamous 5-hour outage this same year.

And what about the following review of a real app?

Update app by WillouL
"You need to change the popup message that says, "You can update this app," you can't close the popup message, and when you click update, it takes you to the App Store where there are no updates available. **So much for buying that TV tonight!"**

Nowadays, this is the kind of feedback that would kill young brands in hours. How so?

REPUTATION AND BRAND DAMAGE

When an app does not work, users react. Their reaction is generally quick and decisive. Go through the following real world examples of customers sharing in the wild about their pain and future plans.

Repeated Authorization Code Requests!!! by subSonic2

"My phone was replaced by Apple due to hardware issues. After receiving my new phone and restoring from backup, by banking app requests an authorization code after login every other day. I've removed app, reinstalled, deleted app data, changed my username and password, removed any iCloud data, but it still keeps asking for authorization codes. Very annoying, and inconvenient especially when need to do a quick check on balance. **If this continues I may just go and do my banking somewhere else."**

Figure 1: Negative End User Review

---

1   Mind blowing facts for eCommerce: https://www.readycloud.com/info/mind-blowing-must-know-ecommerce-facts

One of Largest Banks Lands Pitiful APP by CP101

"One would think that one of America's most prestigious financial institution would extend its prestige to a top-performing APP. Quite the contrary — the app has elementary functionality and is a worthless addition to your smartphone except to see balances and make payments. That's stuff from the last decade! **You've really missed the mark on e-banking and even credit unions exceed APP quality by tenfold!"**

Figure 2: Another Hard End User Review

When you think about it, brand damages are not easily cured these days. There are so many good brands in every field, why would anyone bother trusting one with bad reputation?

LOYALTY AND ATTRITION

People rely on the services provided by apps and websites, for real. When an app does not work and disrupts the journey and experience of its end users, these same users rarely look back or think twice. They make it easy for everyone to get to know how bad it went. If you are not convinced yet, go through the user review below and ask yourself a question: "Would I pay through this app?"

Stole my money!!! by Nugget969

"This app is horrible!! I tried paying with Apple Pay to reload my card, and it charged me but didn't reload the card... Seriously?!? This is why Starbucks is winning. People pay more for Starbucks because they have "customer service". Just in case you were wondering, **that's what you are lacking!!"**

Figure 3: An App Review Ruining a Brand

Switching to new digital service providers has become so easy. People know it and they do it, while business owners are haunted by a troublesome question: "How did it come to pass that this whole thing happened because of a single bug???".

SUMMARY

From a business perspective, the quality of digital products and tools is crucial. These days it has a huge impact on the ability to attract and retain customers. Consumer-facing digital businesses which fail to recognize its importance in time struggle a lot, lose a lot, and bleed a lot: sometimes in irrecoverable ways.

2 Digital Mobile Testing

THIS CHAPTER WAS CONTRIBUTED BY JONATHON WRIGHT, CHIEF TECHNOLOGY EVANGELIST, DIGITAL, DEVOPS & AUTOMATION FOR CA R&D

JONATHON WRIGHT is a strategic thought leader and distinguished technology evangelist. He specializes in emerging technologies, innovation and automation, and has more than 15 years of international commercial experience within global organizations. He is currently Director and Chief Technology Evangelist for Digital, DevOps & Automation for CA R&D based between Silicon Valley and Oxford in the UK.

Jonathon combines his practical experience and leadership with insights into practical usage of the core principles and methodologies underpinning DevOps, Digital Assurance, and Enterprise Digital (Smart Cities, IoT and AI). Thus, he is always in demand as a speaker at international conferences such as Gartner, HPE Discover, CA World, Oracle Digital Forum, Unicom, EuroSTAR, STAREast and STARWest.

JONATHON WRIGHT
DIRECTOR OF DIGITAL ENGINEERING

Jonathon is the author of several award-winning books on test automation as well as numerous podcasts, training courses, and webinars.

INTRODUCTION

In the **Digital Economy,** every business is a software business and the software landscape is changing forever. The traditional Core IT approach to providing business value through lengthy plan-build-test-deploy cycles can no longer deliver value in an increasingly competitive, consumer-centric landscape. Merely compressing these cycles through adopting iterative or Agile methods does not address the challenges organizations face in terms of innovation, speed to market, quality, and value to consumers. Shifting to an Adaptive IT model calls for new practices that require accelerated communication, collaboration, integration, measurement, and automation. Whether you label this as **Digital Transformation,** understanding the detail of this journey is an essential part of every business's journey to enabling **Digital Mobile.**

Here is a definition of **Digital** based on the previous industry experience of the author:

> "The digitalization of processes, behaviors and interactions, resulting in continuously, adaptive, cognitive, innovative, business models."

Expanding the definition provides context behind the key digital terminology:

- Digitalization (digital engineering)
- Processes (digital delivery)
- Behaviors (algorithmic-business)
- Interactions (autonomous-business)
- Continuous (insight-driven (prescriptive and predictive))
- Adaptive (multi-modal delivery)
- Cognitive (adoption of social/ artificial intelligence and machine learning)
    - Value-Driven (Business/ Usage/ Technology)
    - Acceptance-Driven (Expectations/ Tolerance)
    - Goal-Driven (Solution Thinking)

- Innovative (smart and differentiated solutions)
- Business Models:
    - Digital by Default (LeanDX/ start-up)
    - Digital by Design (DesignOps)
    - Digital by Device (Digital Mobile)

In this chapter, the paradigm shift from Digital Mobile to multi-modal channels will be addressed. We will also discuss real-world case studies in Artificial Intelligence, Internet of Things, and Smart Cities as well.

DIGITAL LIFE

Our **Digital Experiences** now define our daily **Digital Lifestyles** and how we consume **Digital Services** every single day. We have unique expectations towards the **Digital Quality** of these services dependent on our **Digital Behaviors.** Current mood, state of mind, stress, or even alcohol levels[1] at any particular time of day or hectic schedules — these are some of the factors which affect us. However, it is not all of them. The combination of internal (location, data, and battery) with external (weather, traffic or events) factors is also key to our **Digital Life.**

DIGITAL PROFICIENCY

"Why?" are our **Digital Experiences** so uniquely different? Could it be related to our varying levels of **Digital Proficiency**[2]**?**

- **Digital Natives** — Comfortable in engaging with all **Digital Channels** (i.e. generation x, y & z).

- **Digital Naïve** — Believe that they are **Digital Natives** based on ownership of technology (i.e. millennials/ Xbox generation).

- **Digital Designer** — Build **Digital Technology** around their lifestyles and living space.

---

1   Drunk Crowd Testers, http://www.theuserisdrunk.com, optimised UX to illustrate the simplicity of the ordering process of a leading digital pizza brand.

2   Disrupting Digital, R Wang, 2016, Constellation Research

- **Digital Savvy** — Self-taught and aware of the **Digital Capabilities** of technology.

- **Digital Citizen** — Someone born into **Digital Lifestyle** who consumes without questions.

- **Digital Immigrants** — Crossed the chasm into the **Digital World,** forced into engagement with **Digital Channels.**

- **Digital Voyeurs** — Recognized the shift to digital but not ready to be active yet themselves.

- **Digital Holdouts** — Resisting the shift to digital, ignoring the impact.

- **Digital Disengaged** — Understand **Digital Technology** but avoiding engagement on purpose, often for privacy reason.

- **Digital Dangerous** — Extremely overconfident in their **Digital Capabilities** to the point they can cause disruption or damage.

So "Why?" do we develop a single-purpose endpoint[3] (i.e. UI) to support all the above **Digital Persona?** When even the same object instance (i.e. UI-matrix) viewed by the same categorization of **Digital Persona** could be interpreted completely differently.

DIGITAL EXPERIENCES (DX)

"How?" we approach the interaction with **Digital** can be described as our approach to **Digital Processes** that represent the unique ingredients (or steps) that we execute as part of the overall recipes which are either value acceptance or goal-based.

Again, this order and sequence of execution of **Digital Processes** will continuously change, morph, and evolve individually or within a crowd. So, can our **Digital Proficiency** categorization be dependent on our **Digital Behaviors** such as our specific goals, values or acceptance of change?

Consumer perception is the only reality!

---

3   Automated Help Interface, Jonathon Wright, 2001, University of Nottingham

Each of the above dimensions will directly affect our unique **Digital Interaction.** This may result in a positive or negative user experience based on our own perceptions at that given moment in time.

Consequently, the perceptions of our pre and post Digital Experiences can be more important than the actual **Digital Interaction** itself: for example, the delivery of a service at a perceived level of quality in relation to cost.

DIGITAL ADOPTION

In this section, three case studies are explored with the goal of "going to the movies" based (loosely) on my personal experiences over three time periods. The **Digital Experience** in the late 90s (when the Internet was becoming mainstream) are compared with current trends such as the Internet of Things (IoT).

The first example in **Figure 4** features portable mobile devices, music streaming, online gaming, and notifications (news, traffic, and messaging). All are **Digital Activities** that we should be at least familiar with or consume one or more on a daily basis. So, what has changed over the last three decades? Firstly, our **Digital Behaviors** have changed over time. Our expectations and tolerance of these **Digital Charters** (objectives or goals) have changed our personal pyramid of needs and, hence, increased our expectations.

Case Study A — Urban 1.0 (1999)	
Digital Proficiency	Digital Savvy
Digital Maturity	Ready
Behaviors (Charters)	Quality (audio/ video), connectivity (burst/ high frequency), and communications (asynchronous/ one-way)
Processes (Blueprints)	Offline synchronization (push/ pull), data scavenger (search/ recover) and data discovery (radio/ newsgroups)
Interactions (Schematics)	1. Pre-booked Tickets via combination of Teletext and Interactive Voice Response (IVR) (Location > Showcase > Date > Time > Payment) (50) 2. Pre-Programmed Alarm via Palm-sized (J680) Pocket PC (Windows CE 2.11) supporting cascading GUI with handwriting recognition (50).

Interactions (Schematics)	3. Prearranged Lift via MMORPG (EverQuest) PC (Windows 98 SE) using Guildchat (100).
	4. Check Reviews via CompuServe Newsgroups (Rotten Tomatoes and WikiWikiWeb) (75).
Number of Digital Interactions = 500 **Duration = 5hrs+**	5. Download Music via mIRC (Q-Bot) and Usenet (Pre-Napster) based on Q-Bot recommendations and then offline push synchronization (ActiveSync (IR) and NOMAD (IEEE 1284)) (200)
	6. Play Music via audio cable connecting MP3 player (CreativeLabs NOMAD™) to BMW Z8 (20)
	7. Receive Notification via Pager (Motorola) (5)
User Story (Context) 	The day starts with my personal alarm waking me up with a reminder that the new Star Wars movie is out today. The excitement was killing me and I had already pre-arranged tickets and selected a viewing time weeks in advance to avoid disappointment on the day. I had also arranged a lift to avoid relying on public transport so I checked the local traffic update on the radio for delays. I left plenty of time to log on, check the movie reviews and spend some online time with my friends before setting off to the cinema and enjoying listening to some new music downloaded from the internet that morning. However, my sister was running late due to missing the tram connection and then having to stop to send me a message. Thankfully, my nephew arrived during the opening credits so we could all enjoy the movie.

Figure 4: Case Study on Digital Life "A": Urban 1.0 (1999)

The second major change is **Digital Maturity.** This change has happened as the **Digital Solutions** have evolved and so have the **Digital Blueprints** and **Schematics** that we apply to complete the related **Digital Processes.** Our attention span has also considerably decreased. For example, hunting around on Napster to find a single track, downloading for 10 minutes, and then transferring onto a portable MP3 player through a third-party application is no longer acceptable.

Importantly in this example, there are several **Digital Interactions** involved with such a **Digital Task,** as each interaction produces a different **Digital Experience** which could be extremely positive or negative. The **Digital Risk** associated with

Digital Tasks featuring high numbers of **Digital Interactions** is related to the potential points of failure along the **Digital Journey**. Consequently, the entry barrier to **Digital Proficiency** has restricted certain **Digital Activities** to **Digital Personas** that have a strong focus on information technology.

Three decades of **Digital Evolution** later, the second example in Figure 5 features a similar **Digital Journey,** so what has changed? The number of **Digital Interactions** is considerably less. With around a 90% reduction in the amount of time/ effort to complete similar **Digital Tasks,** the entry barriers have almost disappeared, enabling these **Digital Capabilities** for the masses.

Case Study B - Urban 3.5 (2016)	
Digital Proficiency	Digital Savvy
Digital Maturity	Capable
Behaviors (Charters)	Streamlined (scheduling/ autonomous), connectivity (always-on/ low frequency), and communications (virtual personal assistant/ AI)
Processes (Blueprints)	Self-synchronization (predictive/ social intelligence) and services consumer (algorithmic/ connected intelligence)
Interactions (Schematics) **Number of Digital Interactions = 50** **Duration = 45 mins**	1. Wake up based on sleep pattern recognition and schedule via Fitness Wearable linked to Virtual Personal Assistant (Alexa Skills > Google Home / BMW Connected / National Rail | Calendar = Google / O365 | Smart Home > Hive / Hue / Smart Devices) 2. Connected Car via BMW (Concierge Services and Connected Services > Amazon Music) 3. Reservations & Ticketing via IFTTT > TheTrainLine > RingGo | Wearable > TheTrainLine > StarBucks (Location-based) 4. Navigation via CityMapper > Wearable (Real time transportation status / Rain safe) 5. Reviews via Wall Street Journal VR and Sky Q VR (suggested downloaded content) 6. Take away via JustEat Robot powered by Starship Technologies (https://www.youtube.com/watch?v=NOCZYcuP9iO)

User Story (Context)	It's cold winter's day in December, I awake gradually to music and to be told that today is the launch of the new Star Wars movie and informed about the weather, news and transport updates and my personal schedule for the day. I start getting ready when I'm prompted with the details of the next train time and that it has turned on the climate control on my car to defrost the windows. My espresso is already waiting for me as I leave the house and enter the car which is warm with the heated seats and steering wheel turned on. The car continues to play the same music from within the house then at this point I decide to contact Concierge Services en route to ask if they could send an engineer to check something on my car whilst I'm in London for the day. By the time I finish talking to the personal assistant, I arrived at the train station and then directed to my reserved car parking space. Whilst approaching the train station I am issued with my train ticket as I approach the gate. My watch flashes scan me through the barriers and notifies me on the best location to board based on seat availability. I sit and enjoy the view whilst continuing to listen to the music selection.
	I arrive in London on time to be directed via the rain safe option to the IMAX via the underground. As I walk past the coffee shop, I'm notified that my favorite coffee is waiting for me. After collection, I head to the underground to catch the tube. Whilst watching the reviews on Sky Q VR, I receive an incoming video call in my headset from my nephew to say that he is running late due to underground works on the Jubilee line. I'm then pushed a notification that congestion at the destination station and recommended to alight at the station before and walk now that the weather has stopped and arriving in plenty of time for the showing. Afterwards we cannot decide on where we want to eat locally so we decide to order take away. Getting off the tube we are greeted by the delivery robot which had kept our food hot and waiting for us based on our return travel plans.

Figure 5: Case Study on Digital Life "B": Urban 3.5 (2016)

DIGITAL FUTURE

The final example is a glimpse into our **Digital Future** based on several **Digital Projects** that the author has been involved in over the last few years. In **Figure**

6, an indicative list of example **Cognitive Adaptive Technology** (that the CA R&D teams had been working on) has been visualized.

COGNITIVE ADAPTIVE TECHNOLOGY				
Virtual Personal Assistants	**Connected Home**	**Multi-Reality**	**Context Brokering Platforms**	**Connected Vehicle**
Smart Advisors	Internet of Everything (IoE)	Brain-Computer Interface	Digital Offers	Autonomous Vehicles (C2X)
Natural-Language (Q&A)	Human Augmentation	Emotion Detection	City Data Exchange	Vehicle-to-Infrastructure
Situation Awareness	Ambient Experiences	Head-Mounted Displays	Complex Event Processing	Mood Recognition
People-Literate Technology	Gesture Control	Virtual Worlds	Mass Personalization (Scale)	Digital Offers (Concierge)
Deep / Machine Learning	**Artificial Intelligence**	**Neural Networks**	**Quantum / Fog Computing**	**Cognitive Reckoning**

The **Urban 4.0** case study, **Figure 7,** may sound such as a story straight out of a science fiction movie like the three mentioned within the case studies: "Star Wars: The Phantom Menace" (1999), "Rogue One" (2016), and the "Forces of Destiny"[4] (2019) respectively. However, it is important to recognize the shifts in **Digital Enablement** that will be the **Digital Challenges** that we will be facing in the next few years. This is represented in all the case studies that feature **Digital Mobile** technology. Therefore, any direct interaction through the UI layer is avoided on purpose.

The typical mobile user touches his or her phone 2,617 times every day, over an average of 145 minutes in duration.[5]

Support for this reasoning comes from a study[6] stating it that the average person checks mobile devices 85 times a day. Although over half or these instances are less than 30 seconds in duration, this is still classified as habitual. "Peeking for a thing" turns out to be an automatic behavior for more people. It could also be referred to as the **Digital Grind,** i.e. simple micro tasks like checking for notifications or continuously checking for messages.

Back in 2013 at STARWest in California, I highlighted why banning e-mail as a

---

4 Keynote, Automation Guild, Jonathon Wright, 2017, (http://www.Forces-Destiny.com)

5 Dscout Research, 2016, Michael Winnick, (https://blog.dscout.com/mobile-touches)

6 Study participants aged 18 to 33, 2015, Dr. Sally Andrews, Nottingham Trent University

legacy unstructured communication method was an essential next step in the **Digital Evolution.** A few years later, by using the Microsoft Bot Framework and when linked to an Office 365 account, the daily **Digital Grind** was considerably reduced (especially when directly linked to VPA). It responds to simple structured message requests by filtering tasks directly onto a Kanban Board, for example, as well as managing meeting requests and travel availability.

Case Study C - Urban 4.0 (2019)	
Digital Proficiency	Digital Designer
Digital Maturity	Enabled
Behaviors (Charters)	Bespoke lifestyle (time/ cost / experience) and value (consume over buy)
Processes (Blueprints)	Dynamic (pricing/ scheduling), communication (predictive)
Interactions (Schematics) **Number of Digital Interactions = 5** **Duration = 5 mins**	1. Wake up via Virtual Personal Assistant connected to Social Networking Platforms (i.e. Facebook) and linked into shared calendars. 2. Multi-Reality (VR/AR) via Google Glasses / Microsoft Hololens devices (https://www.youtube.com/watch?v=vy-1jnA_pLUs) connected to Social VR platform. 3. Flexible Leasing Options via Jaguar / Land Rover with Autonomous Driving (C2X support) 4. Predictive Route Guidance / Traffic via The AA with Connected Car (I2X support) 5. Smart Solution Advisory Services (SSaS) via Hitachi Smart City Data Exchange, QPark Smart Car Parks and Data Brokerage Platforms (Dynamic Pricing)
User Story (Context)	I awake to my personal assistant 'Jarvis' apologizing for waking me, "Sorry to bother you sir, but your nephew's virtual assistant 'Jeeves' was wondering if you fancied meeting up to watch the new Star Wars movie? I have scheduled a provisional appointment based on both of your availabilities? Shall I make the necessary arrangements? (Yes 1)

User Story (Context)	Incoming MR (Multi-Reality (VR/AR) transmission from your nephew. I pick up my glasses which projects my nephew's avatar overlaying in the seat across from me "are we going to see the new movie today?" (2) followed by an invitation to join him in the current interactive gaming session. (3) Jarvis overlays a message "I have sent for the car sir" ETA 5 mins. (4)
	The car arrives and I continue the current interactive MR session whilst getting into the driver seat whereupon the car starts driving to the location of the cinema chosen bon the basis of minimizing our travel times. However, during the journey the C2X detects traffic and redirects to an alternative parking lot, releasing our tickets and renegotiates parking as my nephew is not driving a rental car.

During the booking process, it pushes a private viewing offer with an exclusive after event with dynamic pricing as my nephew had already declined the offer (5). As this reduces travel time and includes a discounted valet rate and unique viewing experience I accept the offer and our cars are diverted to the new location. After the cinema experience both vehicles are waiting for us, however Jaguar had now delivered me an F-Type to enjoy the drive home as the sunshine had come out. |

Figure 7: Case Study on Digital Life "C": Urban 4.0 (2019)

Case Study A	Case Study B	Case Study C
Urban 1.0 (1999)	Urban 3.5 (2016)	Urban 4.0 (2019)
Interactions (500)	Interactions (50)	Interactions (5)
Duration (5 hrs)	Duration (45 mins)	Duration (5 mins)

Figure 8: The Trend of Reducing the Number and Duration of Digital Interactions

The message here is clearly to encourage **Digital Experience** (DX) designers and developers to think about how to considerably reduce the number of **Digital Interactions** and their associated durations. We are expected to "do more with less," i.e. increase productivity without reverting to multi-tasking and accepting the decrease in task effectiveness.

DIGITAL DISRUPTION

The **Digital Evolution** is upon us. The approaches to **Digital Delivery** that may have been successful in the past may not be suitable for the **Digital Revolution** in the age of the app economy. The **Digital Revolution** will be the natural selection for the 2 million+ apps on Apple's app store, with over 150 billion cumulative downloads.

"I will make a prediction that there will be no apps in 5 years' time!"[7]
—James Whittaker, Microsoft, 2013

The **Digital Survival** of the smartest, most innovative and differentiated solutions will become the **Digital Solutions** that we consume on a daily basis as part of our future **Digital Life.** However, it is highly unlikely that they will still be in the same form as standalone applications but more likely represent a collection of organisms (nodes) that form the **Digital Ecology** (ecosystem of ecosystems) of billions of endpoints (which may be represented as simple micro services).

"This time last year, I had an app for that.
This year we now have an AI for that!"
—Theo Priestley, Forbes, 2016

SUMMARY

The **Digital Future** roadmap is still waiting for the next extraordinary idea, the next evolutionary iteration that will shape the industry to go **Beyond Mobile and Digital.** Therefore, **Digital** is highlighted before each key term, as **Digital** is interchangeable with the next big industry trend, i.e. **Cognitive.**

The adoption of **Cognitive Adaptive Technology,** such as Artificial Intelligence, Neural Networks[8], Deep/ Machine Learning and Quantum Computing, will unlock endless new possibilities along with **Cognitive Reckoning & Mutation**[9] to reveal undiscovered algorithmic models that will change our future **Digital Life** forever.

---

7   "How to change the way people think in four easy steps", James Whittaker, Engineer, Microsoft, Agile Development Practices West, 2013, (https://news.microsoft.com/stories/people/james-whittaker.html)

8   Language Understanding Intelligent Service, Microsoft, 2017, (https://www.luis.ai/)

9   Project Oxford — Cognitive Services (Vision, Speech, Language, Knowledge, Search), Microsoft, 2017, (https://www.microsoft.com/cognitive-services/en-us/)

3 Mobile Space Overview and Tools Landscape

INTRODUCTION

As of late 2016/ beginning of 2017 — as this book was being written—the mobile market is quite mature. Most organizations, including its early adopters, such as financial institutions, insurance companies, airlines, health, retail stores, faced Digital Transformation, matured, and either shifted to a complete digital offering or are walking the last steps to get to this stage.

A few years ago, if asked about the biggest challenges and hurdles related to web and mobile, organizations would have described and rated their main issues and productivity blockers as gravitating around the plethora of available devices and wide range of versions of Operating Systems (OS) used, and a lack of tooling for proper test automation and device management/ setup.

Nowadays, the challenges have shifted. From a tooling perspective, we see that mobile device Clouds are the industry standard. Perfecto, AWS, Sauce, and Keynote are just few examples. One could choose from a large variety of commercial and open source test automation tools and frameworks. Selecting the right platforms to test against is still a valid challenge, but, luckily, Perfecto developed a quarterly trademark report that can help and guide organizations with picking up the right set of devices, OS versions, and browsers to test against as well as considering other factors, such as geography.

THE CHALLENGES OF TODAY

So, what would be the most serious challenges today? The answer would inevitably come down to maturing what was already accomplished and sustaining it towards continuous integration and delivery (CI/CD) workflows featuring short cycles for any digital platform, high percentage of automation, and fast feedback loops with no media breaks among Quality Assurance (QA), Software Development (Dev), and business stakeholders.

As already mentioned in the "Introduction" section, these insights translate to the list of challenges below:

SOFTWARE DEVELOPMENT LIFECYCLE (SDLC) AND PROCESS MATURITY

As part of their sprints, organizations are required to innovate faster by bringing in many more features and bug fixes while test engineers/QA need to plan and test as much as possible within short time frames. Testing — as you will learn in this book — is not getting any easier. It requires functional and complex non-functional tests exploring and verifying performance and user conditions, security, accessibility, testing in the wild, etc. Of course, this is all done against a wide range of digital platforms. For this to happen, organizations need to do proper planning, advance the knowledge and professional skills of their staff, establish the right culture, embrace the right tools, and much more.

OVERCOMING THE LIMITATIONS OF THE OPEN SOURCE TOOLS AND FRAMEWORKS

For mobile product teams to move faster and release more frequently, there is a clear and notable trend of adopting a mixture of open source test tools and frameworks. The motivation and factors behind such decisions, i.e. selecting[1], ramping up, and adopting open source testing technologies may be summarized as follows:

- Faster test code development of unit tests and simple validation of test results

---

1   Selection of open source test automation tools — http://www.slideshare.net/perfectomobile/choosing-the-best-open-source-test-automation-tool-for-you-64205474

- First-class support for mobile platform development in programming languages, such as Java, Swift, C#, etc.

- Embedded tools within Integrated Development Environments (IDEs), e.g. XCTest within XCode and Espresso on top of Android Studio

- Ability to define and execute complex functional/UI test scenarios

- Cross platform test automation for mobile and web

In this book, some help regarding this subject will be offered. Real life examples will make it clear how some organizations managed to overcome challenges and limitations of open source test automation solutions.

SUSTAINING AN UP-TO-DATE, CORRECTLY SIZED MOBILE TEST LAB

The most painful challenge for organizations today — and it applies to both mobile and desktop web — relates to the proper sizing of their test labs in order to provide coverage of enough platforms, geographies, user conditions, and more. Organizations may either leverage existing analytics platforms, such as Adobe, Google, Flurry, etc., or try to analyze the market trends in order to figure out a "healthy" mix of their own. Bearing this issue in mind, a couple of years ago the author of this book initiated and developed a "Factors Magazine"[2] report which aimed at easing this pain by providing global guidance[3] for mobile and web.

Organizations need to realize that this is not a one-time, one-shot, fire-and-forget evaluation and validation activity paving their way to success. Regularly analyzing the needs of test labs and bringing in sizing adjustment accordingly needs to be understood as a set of value-added continuous improvement practices, optimizing both efficiency and costs. It often makes sense to organize and schedule quarterly-based reviews of existing test labs, so market changes that may also trigger sizing adjustments can be taken into consideration in a timely manner. The frequency of such reviews shall be perfectly mandated by the nature of business requirements hitting individual organizations.

---

2 Perfecto Factors Magazine Report — http://info.perfectomobile.com/factors-magazine.html

3 Ultimate Guide for Digital Test Coverage — http://info.perfectomobile.com/rs/482-YUQ-296/images/ultimate-digital-test-coverage-toolkit.pdf

A chapter of this book will be dedicated to summarizing the ongoing work and progress over the past two years. In addition, within this chapter you will get to know about the methodology, real life examples, and recommendations about building, sizing, and sustainably evolving a mobile test lab of your own.

GETTING PROPER QUALITY INSIGHTS UPON EACH TEST CYCLE — PRIOR AND POST-PRODUCTION

Independent of how a post execution activity is initiated — e.g. triggered by software developers as part of their CI workflow or by QA as part of post-production functional regression testing cycle — the ability to quickly drill down into any failures, filter out false positives, identify critical defects, and act upon them, remains crucial. It is key to achieving and maintaining agility, efficiency and, of course, customer satisfaction — both internal and external.

Organizations matured to the stage of executing regression test harnesses per commit in their source control systems. Depending on the complexity of applications under test (AUT), these test suites may consist of tens of thousands of automated tests. Meetings with such organizations have revealed that simply reviewing the results after the completion of a test cycle sometimes takes mobile teams 3+ hours. Spending a half of a team's daily capacity on exploring and filtering test reports means that those teams cannot fully focus on delivering value-added features along the SDLC. Teams could benefit and resolve such issues by incorporating faster feedback cycles on test results, using better reporting solutions, getting to certain debugging practices and capabilities, setting up proper target environments reflecting end-users' needs and conditions, etc.

Within the book, this subject will be covered and some examples regarding addressing the described challenge will be provided. Thus, organizations can move faster and gain greater results and satisfaction out of the (often troublesome) communication between software development and quality assurance units.

BRANCHING WISELY BETWEEN CROSS PLATFORM AND CROSS FEATURE TEST SUITES

This challenge somehow flies under the radar of most organizations today, often being ignored and neglected. It basically refers to the growing fragmentation between devices, different versions of the same OS, and, of course, the corresponding tests. The gaps are growing and existing tests used to validate specific functionalities of an app on a specific device are now required to evolve and cover modern devices and newer OS versions while also taking into account emerging features of OSes, such as Touch ID, Force Touch, Doze, Split Window, Sensors, etc. Thus, testing scenarios remain mostly unchanged from a business perspective while, from a testing point of view, they are effectively "branched", i.e. there would be a number of tests emerging in order to verify one and the same app functionality on different versions of one and the same OS.

A whole chapter will be dedicated to this problem. It will reveal some suggestions on how to address and tackle such issues. As long as organizations at least become aware that this issue exists, persists, and is growing into a greater challenge (as a natural consequence of the market growth), these efforts will be definitely worth it.

MOBILE SPACE — TOOLS LANDSCAPE

Now that some of the challenges are clear, what about an up-to-date review of the testing tools landscape and frameworks? This is also very intriguing. Taking apart the open source test frameworks, there is hardly a commercial vendor left today that does not offer a Cloud-based test lab for mobile or both mobile and web. The need for speed, the complexity of maintaining a local device lab as well as ever-growing strict security requirements have quite a market, business, and technology impact. Every day we witness more and more vendors, such as Perfecto, Keynote, Amazon, Sauce Labs, and TestDroid offering mobile device lab in the Cloud.

In the past, the author of this book created some tables and blogged about guidelines for selecting mobile tools[4] suitable for various testing purposes.

---

4 Forrester Wave (Q2 2016) Report — Mobile Front-End Test Automation — https://www.forrester.com/report/The+Forrester+Wave+Mobile+FrontEnd+Test+Automation+Tools+Q2+2016/-/E-RES128536

Now he would like to provide an up-to-date summary of the tools compared by different categories.

Since organizations are either in a state of transition to a more Agile form or have already completed it, there is huge impact, as well as benefits, in selecting the right testing tools for mobile apps. They need to equally serve good developers, test automation engineers, test architects, and manual testers.

To date, there is not a single tool that can entirely and efficiently meet and satisfy the needs of all practitioners. Each tool will have its distinct advantages and disadvantages. Therefore, the selection of testing tools and frameworks needs to allow as many types of practitioners to leverage one, two or even more tools. Note that minimizing the diversity of tools and UIs used as part of the SDLC and quality assurance turns out to be crucial for the success of these processes. Should an organization fail at this point, the risk of ending up with a cumber-some, time-consuming and sometimes redundant practices is very real. The reasons behind this kind of complexity are related to multiple test types that need to be maintained, managed, reviewed, and analyzed, and much more.

The key properties that should be part of organizational selection of test tools are as follows:

- Cloud device lab as a service (Public, Private dedicated)
- Cross platform/app type testing (iOS, Android, Desktop Web Browsers)
- Level of support for test automation frameworks
- Mobile platforms context support — app specific vs. full system level
- Support for Object Repository/Page Objects model
- Support for visual object recognition as part of the UI Test Automation
- Solution embedded within leading IDE's (Eclipse, Android Studio, Visual Studio, etc.)
- Official support by mobile platform vendors
- Record and replay test scenario capabilities
- Level of supported details when it comes to test execution reports
- Community support and engagement

* Continuous Integration friendly
* Support for user conditions and environment simulation (GPS, carrier networks, Wi-Fi, battery, etc.)
* Physical locations for real devices as part of Cloud offerings
* Security, data privacy, and customer support of data centers

Table 1 is an objective and up-to-date overview of some of the most distinguished tools and frameworks in 2016, summarizing the strengths and weaknesses of the leading cloud-based solutions for mobile and web testing. There are many other promising tools that are either not yer Cloud-based or still ramping up. Hence, they are not included.

Category		Perfec-to	Key-note by Dyna-trace	Amazon Device Farm	HPE Mobile Center (Micro Focus)	ExperiT-est	Sauce Labs	Test-Droid
Cloud as A Service		V	V	V	X	V	V	V
Cross platform Mobile and Web Cloud		V	X	X	X	X	V	X
Supported Test Auto. FW	Selenium	V	X	V	X	V	V	V
	Appium	V	V*	V*	V*	V*	V*	V*
	Cucumber	V	X	X	X	V	X	V
	Espresso	V	X	V	X	V	X	V
	XCTest	V	X	V	X	V	X	V
	HP UFT	V	V	X	V	V	X	X
Mobile Context Support	App Context	V	V	V	V	V	V	V
	System Level	V	V	X	V	V	V	V
Visual Object Analysis		V	V	X	V	V	X	V
Embedded Within IDE's		V	X	X	X	X	X	X

Record & Replay Capabilities		V	V	X	V	V	X	X
Rich Reports	App/ Device Vitals	V	V	V	V	V	V	V
	Video reports	V	V	V	V	X	V	X
	De- tailed dash- boards with filters	V	X	X	V	X	X	V
	Cross Plat- form	V	X	X	X	X	X	X
Community Support		V	X	X	X	X	V	V
Continuous Integration Friendly		V	X	X	X	X	V	V
Support Real User Conditions (Loca- tions, Networks)		V	X	X	V	V	X	X
Multiple data centers across geographies		V	V	X	X	V	X	V

Table 1: Mobile and Web Testing Tools Comparison Table

* Simple redirect to a vanilla Appium server with no value-added enhancements, such as visual analysis, for example.

SUMMARY

Within this chapter, the mobile space today and the evolution of the corresponding testing practices were discussed. It provided an objective review of the respective challenges that most organizations face today. A valuable review of the landscape of automation tools that helps tackling these issues was also shared. Keep in mind that tools are just a single compound of the solution. Stay tuned to get to know about the rest in the next chapters of this book.

4 Sizing a Mobile Lab for International Mobile Products

INTRODUCTION

It is no secret that achieving the right mobile test coverage is one of the most complex tasks today. With so many different devices, mobile OS versions, various trends and necessities across different geographies, it could hardly be any different.

For the last couple of years, the author of this book has dedicated most of his efforts and energy to trying to solve this problem. Thus, there is a working solution in place.

From there on, building up a well-sized device lab is a matter of systematically applying good practices. Within this chapter, readers will get to know a whole lot about doing it right and avoiding common pitfalls. Furthermore, sustainable evolution of device labs will be discussed.

THE ULTIMATE SOURCE FOR INSIGHTS ON THE MOBILE MARKET

Have you heard of the "Factors Magazine Report"? It is a quarterly report that sizes various markets and provides data-driven recommendations for getting mobile tests performed against the "right" target environments. Keep in mind that the right target environment for you may very well be the wrong one for many other people; defining and sizing it correctly is often a matter of specific business goals and priorities. The good news is that one can make informed decisions about setting it up adequately. The "Factors Magazine Report" can substantially ease the pain for organizations dealing with the delivery of mobile applications. If followed and reviewed regularly, it would be of equal interest to software development, test, marketing, and many other teams.

THE "FACTORS MAGAZINE REPORT" IN A NUTSHELL

How can a data-driven report help test organizations size their device labs better? Well, it provides test engineers with valuable insights sliced by geographies and related to the usage of different devices, adoption rate of concrete versions of mobile operating systems, often/rarely used screen sizes, and so on. Knowing your go-to-market strategy well and having a prioritized list of target markets is all you need to start. From there on, going through the report every few weeks will give you the confidence that the quality of your apps is verified against the most adequate target environment and under the correct assumptions about it. If you take the time and effort to consistently adjust according to the most up-to-date recommendations within, you may not only reduce costs, but also be relieved that every cent spent on the device lab is actually worth it.

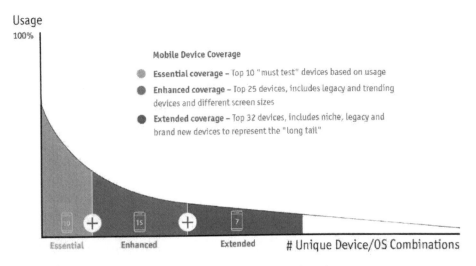

Figure 9: Mobile Test Coverage Method, Source — Factors Magazine

A GLANCE UNDER THE HOOD

The "Factors Magazine Report" is the result of processing and analyzing large data sets provided by research companies (such as comScore, IHS, App Annie, etc.). Based on their data, the notable market trends and other known quality-related incidents the top 32 devices are opted for. Consequently, they are categorized and segmented in three buckets: "Essential", "Enhanced" and "Extended", as depicted in **Figure 9.**

Devices are compared and rated using a common baseline, namely a list of objectives and measurable attributes. As illustrated by the extract of the guide in **Figure 10,** the score of devices depends on both market indicators (e.g. market share, current age, audience demographics) and technical characteristics (e.g. screen size, resolution, chipset, CPU, memory). With each update of the Index, its accuracy and level of detail are increased by extending this list as much as possible.

As part of each group mix, the following attributes should be considered:

- Device and OS popularity (market share)
- Screen sizes, resolution and other screen attributes such as pixel per inch (PPI).
- Device age (launch date)
- New and trending devices and platforms
- Operating system version update rate (e.g. reference devices like Android Nexus get a higher score)
- Unique device properties important for testing purposes – chipset, CPU, memory
- Audience demographics

Figure 10: Attributes and Dimensions for Categorization in the Factors Magazine

Since markets behave differently from a device usage perspective, it is often recommended to merge the results for various countries in order to get to a "golden list" of devices used across multiple geographies. The author of this book released a whitepaper[1] sharing with the public a lot regarding the methodology and logic used for the analysis, preparation, and consolidation of the test coverage report.

---

1   "Digital Test Coverage" whitepaper — http://info.perfectomobile.com/ultimate-digital-test-coverage-ebk.html

MARKET ANALYTICS SOLUTIONS AND BUSINESSES DEVELOPMENT

Organizations utilizing analytics tools (such as Adobe, Flurry, Google) are strongly recommended to validate and compare their insights from app analytics with the information published in the Index. It is sometimes the case that a given analytics report may fail to provide information about an important platform. This might be due to incorrect configuration or technical issues/defects in apps preventing data collection. In other cases, analytics may simply follow the current market trends while not taking into account potential changes in future. Hence, by contemplating and "verifying" the insights from existing analytics solutions with the ones shared in the "Factors Magazine Report," businesses can identify new opportunities for business development and plan for them accordingly.

DEVICE LABS WITH THE RIGHT SIZE

Clearly, the "Factors Magazine Report" helps you to setup a device lab from scratch or continuously optimize an existing one. But to what extent? Is there a structured approach for sizing and planning that could be followed? Success lies in getting to the bottom of these questions.

THE RIGHT DEVICES FOR YOUR APPS

Perhaps the first open question when sizing a device lab would be "What kind of devices will we need?" The Index recommends maintaining a healthy mix of "Reference", "Popular", "Legacy", and "Emerging" devices. As a rule of thumb, you should assume at least one device per bucket. You can learn more by referring to the "Device and Platform Criteria", as extracted by the guide illustrated in **Figure 11.**

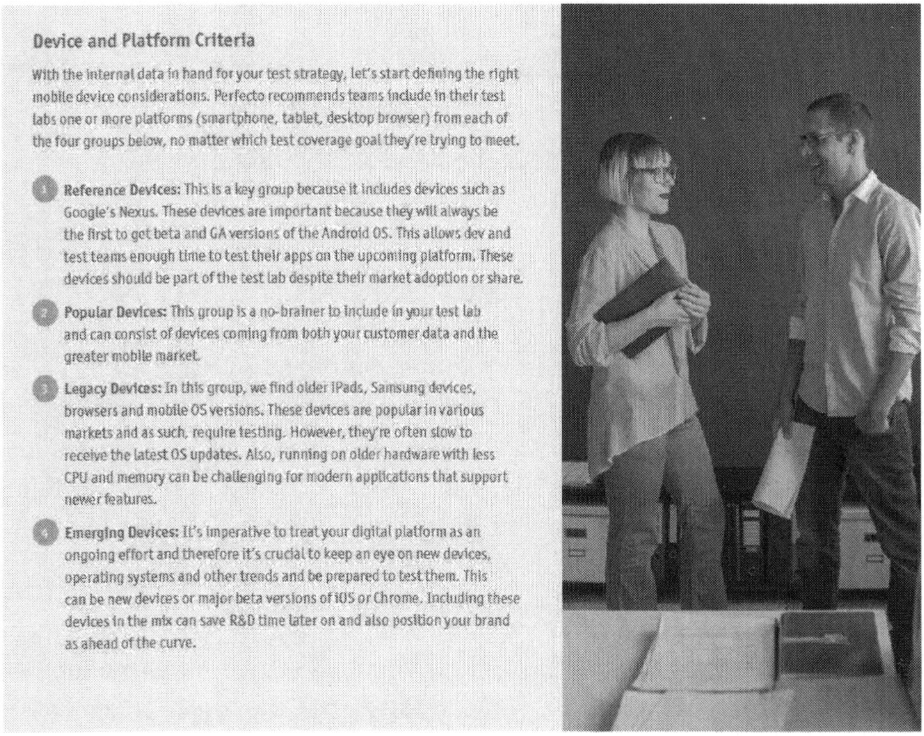

Device and Platform Criteria

With the internal data in hand for your test strategy, let's start defining the right mobile device considerations. Perfecto recommends teams include in their test labs one or more platforms (smartphone, tablet, desktop browser) from each of the four groups below, no matter which test coverage goal they're trying to meet.

1. **Reference Devices:** This is a key group because it includes devices such as Google's Nexus. These devices are important because they will always be the first to get beta and GA versions of the Android OS. This allows dev and test teams enough time to test their apps on the upcoming platform. These devices should be part of the test lab despite their market adoption or share.

2. **Popular Devices:** This group is a no-brainer to include in your test lab and can consist of devices coming from both your customer data and the greater mobile market.

3. **Legacy Devices:** In this group, we find older iPads, Samsung devices, browsers and mobile OS versions. These devices are popular in various markets and as such, require testing. However, they're often slow to receive the latest OS updates. Also, running on older hardware with less CPU and memory can be challenging for modern applications that support newer features.

4. **Emerging Devices:** It's imperative to treat your digital platform as an ongoing effort and therefore it's crucial to keep an eye on new devices, operating systems and other trends and be prepared to test them. This can be new devices or major beta versions of iOS or Chrome. Including these devices in the mix can save R&D time later on and also position your brand as ahead of the curve.

Figure 11: Recommended Mix of Device Categories

Of course, the requirements of different apps imply quite some flexibility regarding device types and OS versions supported. For example, ask yourself whether your application is meant and designed to run on tablets and what percentage of your end-users would find tablet support important. Depending on the answer, you will know whether you need to bring in such devices or not. At this stage, it would be wise to have the list of required OS versions that you need to take into account.

The Index offers a list of unique devices and the versions of the operating systems supported by them. Each device is characterized by a number of attributes, such as screen size, resolution, PPI (pixel per inch), and background apps started by default. Although valuable, this knowledge is not enough to guide organizations on their journey towards complete mobile test coverage. Discovering what types of devices you definitely need is the necessary first step (of two). Which would be the second one?

- · Use market reports like the test coverage Index
- · Make sure to follow the latest 2 iOS/Android versions + Beta's
- · Merge your organizational analytics with the market data
- · Don't forget the user environment angle for extended test coverage

Figure 12: Best Practices as Outlined by the Factors Magazine

HOW TO CALCULATE THE NUMBER OF UNIQUE DEVICES

The minimal number of unique devices satisfying the organizational/ business requirements definitely needs to be determined. Requirements may be about strict timelines for specific test and delivery cycles, execution of both manual and automated tests, and what not. Some of them may be very hard to turn into numbers that you can use for consequent calculations, but you should try to do so. Streamlining and processing these requirements might be difficult, so drawing conclusions from them may be close to fortunetelling.

The thing is that you need to formalize the requirements and turn them into numbers. When you do so, you will often end up with a whole list of parameters. Their values could vary depending on many factors. They affect the total cost of running a device lab. The general recommendation for managing the correct level of complexity is to use or build dedicated tooling.

For example, some organizations use spreadsheets to rationalize the process of sizing device labs. This is a good starting point. There are several good reasons why this is a reasonable investment. First, sizing is a continuous exercise. Second, having this ace up your sleeve, you will be able to play with parameters and ideally observe their impact on required time, money, and effort. One may need to argue, provide reasoning as well as impact analysis on changes related to the size of device labs. It is sad, but true: wide test coverage often collides with organizational and project budgets. Consensus and rational compromises should be found. It is much better to rely on figures and numbers and not so much on gut feelings. You can find an example of a parameterized sizing calculator in **Figure 13.**

	Parallel Platform Execution	Execute in Parallel on mult. Platform sets
Duration (mins)	3	10
Test cases	2,200	2000
Unique Platforms	40	
Parallel Multiplier		9
Effective test cases #		200
Target days	0.5	
Days	5.00	1.39

Prioritized Test Cases		
Critical	75%	1,650
Medium	0%	-
Low	25%	550

Platform Groups		
Primary	75%	30
Secondary	25%	10

Critical + Medium	1,650	75%
Low	550	25%

Figure 13: An Example of a Parameterized Device Lab Sizing Calculator

You know which devices and how many of them you need. You own a weapon more dangerous than a laser sword — a parameterized device lab sizing calculator — and you are not afraid to use it. You may be urged to forget about the hurdles of sizing for the next few months. Well, not so fast.

You will face any number of challenges if you do not bring strong technical expertise to the equation, the sooner, the better. For example, there is a known issue with iOS, namely that it does not allow for incremental upgrades of the OS. This has certain implications with respect to proper sizing of iOS devices.

IMPORTANT NOTE ON MATCHING OS VERSIONS AND DEVICES

The aforementioned limitation means that it is impossible to upgrade a device running an older version of iOS to an arbitrary newer version. You can only upgrade to the latest supported version of iOS for the concrete device, i.e. it is impossible to upgrade from iOS 9.3.5 to 10.0.1 or from iOS 8.4.1 to iOS 10.x. This is the time to employ all possible sources of information like analytics, market research, application roadmap, etc. If you need to support such devices, it would be important to allocate unique Device/OS combinations. Would you like to negotiate on the device lab size and budgeting again? If not, be sure to consider similar constraints at the very beginning, before you have any debates.

This said, the above challenge has its own implications to the normal operations of device labs running iOS devices. If you need to stick to a specific version of iOS already installed on some devices, you should be extremely careful with upgrading iOS. More precisely — you need to make sure that the OS is never, ever upgraded. If you fail to do so, the devices would upgrade to the last possible version, which may not be what you really need. Downgrading iOS to a specific version is painful and officially unsupported by the OS vendor.

THE EVOLUTION — DEVICE LAB ANNUAL GROWTH RATE

Having the right test coverage for a mobile product is great and handy tools like app analytics and the "Test Coverage Index Report" surely help to get to it. However, coverage just reflects a fixed moment in time. Therefore, it needs to be constantly monitored and validated against market changes, while reflecting market dynamics as well.

For instance, the size of a given lab that currently consists of 25 smartphones and tablets will hardly remain the same over the next few years. Organizations need to plan for increasing the size of device labs. As the market matures, new devices and versions of mobile OS are constantly introduced. At the same time, apps evolve as well. They might support new features on specific devices. It might be that new geographies and markets need to be conquered. No doubt, this would bring new requirements towards increasing test coverage, since different geographies use different devices. To wrap it up, device usage in China is very different compared to the USA or Australia.

If you further explore the mobile market over the past few years, you might get the impression that expanding to a new geography would cost 7–10 new devices (smartphones/ tablets). In addition, each year more than 15 key emerging devices are being introduced to the market. Again, annually, old and less popular devices (3.5–4 years old) are being retired. Subtracting 5–7 retired out of the 15+ emerging devices, the predicted YOY growth of a device lab would be 7–10 devices. Knowing this up front could help organizations plan their device lab, their budget, and even head count of testing units better.

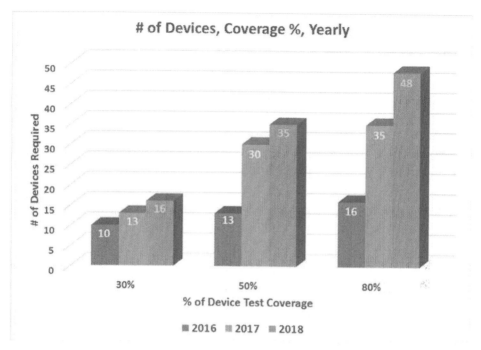

Figure 6: Example of the Annual Device Growth — a 3 Years' Forecast

SUMMARY

Within this chapter, some of the obstacles making device labs hard to size were revealed, as well as proven industry practices which could help you run similar projects successfully. You also got to know about the "Factors Magazine Report" and how you can benefit from it as a single or complementary (when also mapped to existing analytics solutions) source of information and knowledge. Its value as part of sizing exercises also became clear.

Remember that the Index is provided by Perfecto free of charge. Every quarter a new update is released; thus, the report could also be leveraged for continuously sizing a device lab.

5 Guidelines for Common Industry Pitfalls and Test Planning

INTRODUCTION

Being in the mobile space for many years, Perfecto witnessed a wild variety of app defects. At the end of the day, many of them fall into very clear and distinct categories. This allows for smart and structured testing approaches resulting in increased test coverage and superior quality of apps.

Within this chapter, such defects in native apps captured from real devices will be explored. Knowing about common erroneous patterns will make you aware of certain areas and corner cases that you may need to plan for testing with your apps. Test planning for a mobile app can be dangerous. Get to know why and how you can make this whole venture manageable.

An important note for the audience

Testing in general, and mobile testing in particular, is only relevant for a moment in time. Unless you continuously and consciously challenge your app against the latest tests, platforms, versions of operating systems, various user conditions, etc., your tests will be obsolete sooner rather than later.

MOBILE DEVICE/ OS PROLIFERATION FOR EVERYONE

We live in interesting and dynamic times. Technology is driving new business opportunities. Talking about the mobile space, one should not only consider smartphones and tablets anymore. The raise of Internet of Things (IoT) introduced a new wave of wearable devices serving many different purposes. They are constantly getting more and more reach and traction.

While this is great from business, consumer, and geeky perspectives, the current situation imposes huge challenges for test engineers. New devices, platforms/ operating systems (and different versions of these) hit the market and end users literally every day. The test matrix for an app may easily get insanely complex. High test coverage may become impossible to achieve due to increased costs and lack of resources.

The list of unpleasant implications for quality assurance does not end here. Since it is beyond our power to reduce complexity, it is better to embrace it. First things first, let us have a quick tour along common issues in mobile apps. Perhaps knowing some of the potential issues that apps face in general will help us figure out a winning testing strategy.

PERFORMANCE & AVAILABILITY

As a rule of a thumb, mobile apps rely on external and sometimes 3rd party services. Maintaining reliable connections to services and data sources might be limited or not possible at all. Loss of connectivity could be due to different reasons including temporary carrier outages, unavailability of services, defects in apps, and many more. If central to the business purpose of the app, the lack of availability of a certain service may even make an app worthless.

One would think that such a common situation would be handled well, that apps would fail gracefully and to the best interest of end users. If you are convinced of it, please refer to **Figure 14,** which illustrates how different apps fell into the trap of missing availability.

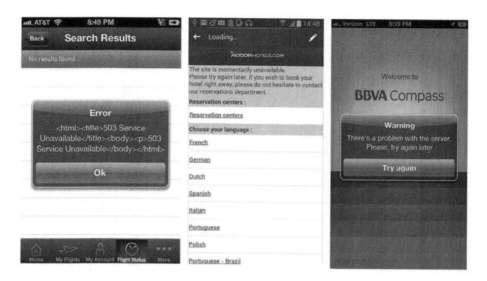

Figure 14: Defects Illustrating Inadequate Handling of Availability Flaws

If an app or a website cannot function properly due to inability to connect to a core service, it would be much better to inform users, prohibit any further usage of the app until the connection is renewed, and prompt users to try using it later. Totally ruining the user experience should never be an option.

Mobile apps are client software that run in very complex, dynamic, and restrictive environments. Thus, availability could be there while performance is poor. Different carrier communication services, such as 2G, 3G, and LTE, imply different bandwidths, download, and upload speeds. Wi-Fi connectivity is just another option for fast (or slow) access to the Internet and other shared resources. Performance in mobile apps can suffer because of services with poor design, excessive payloads, low throughput and scalability, inappropriate geo-location coverage, and so forth.

Issues related to performance flaws of underlying services are another type of defect that somehow easily pass under the radar of quality assurance. However, they have the potential to seriously frustrate end users and decrease the usage of an app; one can easily find examples, like the ones in **Figure 15.**

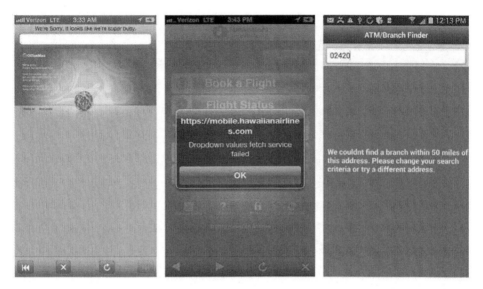

Figure 15: Examples of Poor Performance in Action

APPLE[1] AND GOOGLE (MOBILE OS) RELATED DEFECTS

Mobile operating systems (OS) bring a whole lot of frustration and confusion. Exciting, innovative features and system apps also introduce a number of not so positive consequences for both testers and end users. Every now and then, you read that a particular update for a given OS broke a particular app on mobile device XYZ. Sometimes issues are known and sometimes they are not, but this does not help a lot if your app does not work with the newly released iOS version that is being aggressively pushed by Apple as we talk. **Figure 16** emphasizes on few prominent examples.

---

1 iOS 10.1.1 issues — http://www.gottabemobile.com/2016/10/31/ios-10-problems-5-things-to-know/

Figure 16: Examples of Known Issues with Mobile Operating Systems

If you are not well-prepared, you will risk losing huge number of users in a few days' time. You see, it is not your fault that the underlying OS broke your app, but this does not change things. Lost users are not a herd easily steered around. If you are not there, someone else will be.

You can find official sources for well-known issues with particular releases of mobile platforms. It is good to follow up on these. **Figure 17** illustrates such a troubleshooting guide. You need to be aware that deducing the impact of an upcoming release of an operating system by just reading troubleshooting guides and release notes will not provide you with the right insights about its potential impact on the quality of your apps. Such documents can only give you some direction regarding what you need to test more carefully.

How to Fix iOS 10.1.1 Problems

If you run into an iOS 10.1.1 problem on your device, don't panic. There's a good chance there's a manual fix out there for your issue.

If an iOS 10.1.1 problem problem pops up on your iPhone, iPad or iPod touch, start with our list of fixes for common iOS 10 problems.

This list includes fixes for battery drain, Wi-Fi problems, Bluetooth problems, installation issues, and more.

Figure 17: A Quick Glimpse of the Possible Range of Issues Caused by Mobile Operating Systems

There is no way you can know what is next unless your apps are thoroughly tested against the official beta versions of mobile operating systems. This way, critical issues and regressions can be detected and fixed early enough.

FUNCTIONAL VISUAL DEFECTS AND CROSS-PLATFORM COMPATIBILITY

Fragmentation of underlying mobile platforms does not apply only to different operating systems. It is quite common for different versions of one and the same operating system to bring disruptive changes, often causing unexpected visual defects, discrepancies, and erroneous behavior.

Pay attention to **Figure 18,** showing the main screen of the same app being run on three different devices. Two of them run on different versions of the same operating system. Does it make any difference?

Figure 18: The Same App Screen on Different OS and Versions of OS

While this is bad, some other serious applications provide even more trouble-some experiences. Check out **Figure 19.**

Figure 19: Examples of Severe Visual Defects and Discrepancies

It might be the case that apps are functionally correct, while being completely unusable and messed up from end users' perspective. To make it worse, this may be observed on specific devices, with specific orientation, or with a specific version of the operating system. Another example has been illustrated in **Figure 20.** The video there streams fine. It is just rendered in way that makes it impossible for watching.

Figure 20: Rendering of Video Played on YouTube, Amazon Blu, Android 5.1

There is no way you can guarantee that your app will play nicely with every single device or operating system out there. The only way out is to carefully analyze and identify the business-critical ones. From there on, you can go for regular and thorough testing against them (including beta versions of OS).

SECURITY AND DATA PRIVACY

Apps are now officially the entry points to crucial business interactions. It is not uncommon for companies to invest in one and the same app ported to different mobile platforms. This means that one functionality should behave the same way across all platforms. From a technical perspective, such a requirement is quite challenging. Although there are some technological solutions trying to ease the pain, different platforms are just different. If you need to test any given app for two platforms, you should plan on testing twice.

When you fail to do so, there can be many unpleasant implications related to severe security and data privacy flaws. You could find an example demonstrated in **Figure 21.**

Figure 21: Security Defect in Instagram Across iOS and Android Platforms

The time when security did not matter is long gone. Security flaws and holes are potentially open doors for attackers to get advantage of your system, which might only be a theoretical threat (do not lie to yourself, though: they are not). Disclosing personal and sensitive data as publicly accessible could have an immediate and very serious legal impact.

In order to ensure highest quality and security of mobile apps, one needs to consider conducting security testing on the whole stack. In 2015, we witnessed a number of serious security issues which made it possible for attackers to get to highly sensitive and personal information from the consumers' perspective. This was, in most cases, due to a couple of independent reasons: poorly secured communication channels, i.e. external services, and excessive numbers of permissions requested and granted to the respective apps. Refer to **Figure 23,** which illustrates what this dangerous combination can lead to. Retailer apps used to have access to much sensitive data, such as names, phone numbers, addresses, purchases.

Therefore, vendors of mobile platforms constantly work towards providing more and more secure sandboxed environments for apps. For example, Android Marshmallow introduced a revolutionary fine-grained permissions management concept. Apps were no longer allowed to request all of the permissions that they would theoretically need in advance. The user is prompted and asked for explicit permissions for any given app to use any restricted resource, when this occurs for the first time. Clearly, this means that if an app might be able to use the GPS navigation system, the corresponding permissions would be requested only if this happened. Ideally, this is a much better way to manage application access and permissions.

In reality, this security change brought a lot of sorrow and pain for the existing applications, some of which were not able to start at all, as demonstrated by **Figure 22.**

Figure 22: App Permissions Configuration in Android M[1]

---

1   Source — http://www.androidcentral.com/using-app-permissions-android-m

A smart testing strategy would be to follow up with the major changes in operating systems. Remember, you should not only rely on pure cause and effect theoretical analysis, but also try running and interacting with your apps against beta versions of the respective platforms. You should be extremely careful to discover any security and privacy flaws in advance.

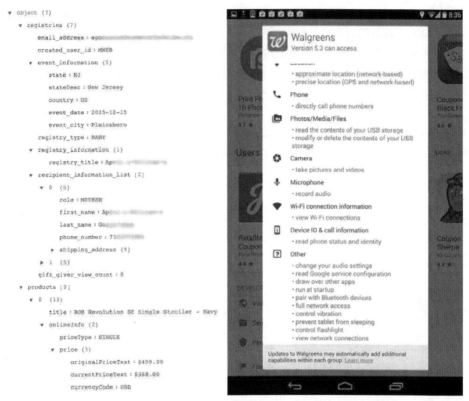

Figure 23: An Example of Compromised End User Privacy in Retail Apps Due to Excessive Permissions

You should also review and question the permissions requested by tested apps. Resource access management is a typical case when less might actually be more. Less permissions requested and granted may easily mean less major flaws that could lead to financial, legal, and business penalties later on. Therefore, this is a topic which definitely deserves high attention and strict governance. From a risk management perspective, introducing a new app permission should be the result of following a clear and streamlined process starting with a well-described request that needs to be assessed and eventually approved or rejected by decision makers. At any rate, they should be aware of the possible harm, as well as benefits, in order to make up their minds in objective way.

MEET "9 BOXES"

The mobile industry faces many challenges. We have gone through some of the most common defects in this realm. To wrap it up, the impact of functional issues is mostly evident while interacting with the user interface (UI) of apps, while non-functional issues either clutter the whole user experience or lead to decreased trust, credibility, and usage of apps. Such issues may be related to poor performance, lack of availability, compliance failures (e.g. compromising data privacy), and security flaws.

RIDE THE WAVE OF INNOVATION

The possible root causes of defects of mobile apps are many. As already mentioned, you need to be extremely careful with adopting new releases of mobile operating systems. While they bring many improvements, enhancements, and badly wanted brand new features, they also tend to break existing apps. Thus, applications are also dependent on the stability of the underlying platform. As a rule of thumb, you would better off to review the release notes of the versions of platforms supported by your app. This way, you could gain valuable insights and get to know what kind of troubles may come out of nowhere. Furthermore, you can plan and spend more time on testing certain scenarios under particular conditions if you know that a certain version of Android has issues with excessive battery consumption on device XYZ, when connected to Wi-Fi, for example. Does this have any impact on your app? This can only be proven right or wrong when tried out.

Talking about potential defects, refer to **Figure 24.** It makes it clear that, in reality, a lot could go wrong. It presents an aggregated summary of various Android release notes. Among different versions of Android, there are multiple known defects that have negative impacts on stability, performance, security, etc.

Android 5.1.1	Lollipop	• Speed improvement • Bug fixes
Android 5.1	Lollipop	• Multiple SIM cards support • Quick settings shortcuts to join Wi-Fi networks or control Bluetooth devices • Lock protection if lost or stolen • High Definition voice call • Stability and performance enhancements
Android 5.0.2	Lollipop	• Performance improvements and bug fixes
Android 5.0.1	Lollipop	• bug fixes, fix issues with video playback and password failures
Android 5.0	Lollipop	• New design (Material design) • Speed improvement • Battery consumption improvement
Android 4.4.4	KitKat	• Fix Heartbleed / OpenSSL vulnerability
Android 4.4.3	KitKat	• Bug fixes • Enable Sprint Spark band 26 and band 41
Android 4.4.2	KitKat	• Bug fixes • Security enhancements
Android 4.4.1	KitKat	• Bug fixes • Enhance the camera on the Nexus 5
Android 4.4	KitKat	• Screen recording • New Translucent system UI • Enhanced notification access • System-wide settings for closed captioning • Performance improvements

Figure 24: Android OS Versions Release Notes Summary

In order to avoid the common situation demonstrated in **Figure 25,** where an app works fine with one version of an operating system and ceases to start with the next one, you need to follow a holistic, structured, and strict approach towards testing your apps. You should also plan for testing your apps against officially released beta versions of operating systems. Thus, critical issues will be discovered and resolved earlier, meaning they will not hit end users.

Figure 25: A Game That Worked Fine on Android 6.0 but Stumbled and Fell on Android 7.0

DEFINE SCOPE OF TESTING

It is clear that, apart from being aware of the innovations, release schedules, and peculiarities of different mobile platforms, test engineers also need to establish and follow a holistic process for planning and performing tests.

The first step is to shape the scope of test cycles. The best way is to have a formal checklist that you go through and cover as much as possible. If you do not have one yet, you are recommended to use the "9 Boxes" presented in **Figure 26.** It can be a great baseline for one of your own. Ideally, you would maintain and stick to a similar test plan describing the scope of testing for each app that you need to test.

When designing your next test plan, try to insure that each box has sufficient coverage across relevant devices and operating systems. Thus, you will sleep better. Obviously, testing app functionality is necessary. Do not forget, though, that testing apps in real environments and under a wide range of conditions is also key to its success. You can explore performance across networks, play with interoperability in cases of incoming events like calls, text messages, pop up screens, etc. Security scanning and verification of usability and accessibility are not wastes of time and resources. Another important testing activity that is so often neglected relates to the life cycle management of apps. Note that if users were unable to install, uninstall or update your app, you would still need to deal with tons of trouble, regardless of whether it functioned well and performed well in a totally secure manner. Therefore, since it is another common pitfall for the industry, the "9 Boxes" checklist contains a dedicated box for "Installation Testing."

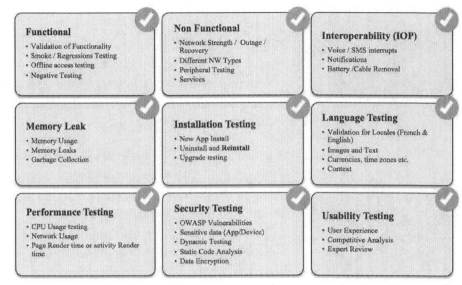

Figure 26: Efficient Test Plan Coverage for Mobile Apps[1]

Last but not least, plan for **negative testing**[2] of application dependencies. For example, if your app interacts with a 3rd party app, such as Facebook or Twitter, in order to share app content with social networks, you are recommended to perform the following tests as well.

1. Test the interaction with the 3rd party app when your app is not installed on the device. It might not be working or this current version may have critical bugs. These may have an impact on your app later on.

2. Test typical interaction (e.g. content sharing) with the 3rd party app before logging in with it. Ideally, end users are presented with a request for authentication with this app. What if this mechanism does not work correctly for some reason?

3. Test the same interaction and deliberately use wrong credentials while authenticating with the 3rd party app. Does your app handle such situations correctly? Would it prompt users that authentication failed or would this lead to a scrambled UI and messed up UX flaws?

---

1   Android OS Versions Comparison — http://socialcompare.com/en/comparison/android-versions-comparison

2   Negative Testing — http://www.guru99.com/positive-vs-negative-testing.html

MOBILE AND INTERNET OF THINGS (IOT)

Quality of apps across smartphones and tablets cannot be compromised, but getting there is tough. Careful and structured test planning starts with the definition of the scope of test cycles. Knowing more about the most widely spread types of defects and getting to a test coverage checklist such as the "9 Boxes" above would be crucial first steps to success.

However, it is not that simple. No, not at all. What if apps sometimes need to communicate with other smaller and even more restricted devices? What if business critical processes were partially performed on mobile devices and partially on some devices under the Internet of Things (IoT) umbrella?

Most seasoned test engineers would probably recommend defining and performing end-to-end test scenarios, taking into consideration all the participants, devices, operating systems, and so on. Well, here is the thing.

Extending testing to IoT[3] is not trivial. One needs to consider additional details. These devices are not only a new form factor to cover, but rather a whole new type of platform. In fact, they represent a huge number of emerging platforms, so standardization should not be a safe and reliable assumption. They vary by battery life, CPU, hardware, and performance. Their screen size is usually very small and often hard to engage with. Interacting with such devices is either done via touch or voice commands. Their connectivity relies on Bluetooth low energy (BLE). The diversity is wild. There are whole books[4] dedicated to testing smartwatches, for example.

That said, IoT and smartwatches impose a whole new unique list of highly specific challenges. Hence, you need a different quality checklist to help you plan the quality of apps running on such devices. **Figure 27** demonstrates a tailored version of the "9 Boxes" that should help you correctly plan such tests.

---

3   Recommendation for testing IOT — http://adventuresinqa.com/2016/02/01/wearables-guest-post/

4   Smartwatch App Testing by Daniel Knott — https://leanpub.com/smartwatchapptesting

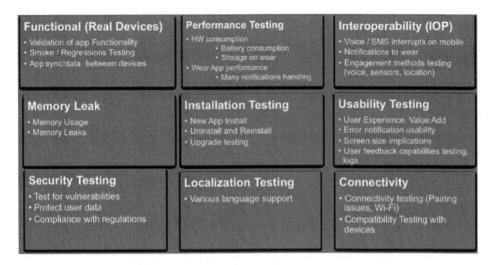

Figure 27: "9 Boxes" for Testing Smartwatches

Although the modified "9 Boxes" checklist now takes into consideration the specifics of smartwatches, the methodology remains the same. The traditional types of app testing were altered in a way that they could satisfy the requirements for testing on smaller devices.

For example, performance testing in the context of IoT devices/ smartwatches would better include tests under limited battery with simultaneous communication between a paired device and smartphone. It also makes sense to enrich such kinds of scenarios with inbound calls that need to be answered and incoming text messages. How will it go? Will you find any serious glitches in user experience or will everything be beautifully handled by both devices? If you think about it, these sorts of scenarios add significant complexity on top of the already troublesome performance testing of mobile apps.

Other testing types should focus on installation and uninstallation of apps on various versions of operating systems for smartwatches. For example, some apps are installed on iPhone and Apple Watch simultaniously, while some are installed seperately. In these cases, the whole application life cycle is now effectively changed. Clearly, updating, reinstalling, and uninstalling such apps should be tried out against both devices. Testing does not get any easier.

It is apparent that the user experience (UX) of such complex apps is an important aspect to consider when planning your testing activities. As already mentioned, IoT and smartwatch devices are quite limited and therefore their UX needs to be consistently great. Apps that fail to satisfy this requirement quickly get removed.

For example, the **TripAdvisor** wearable app allows customers to make decisions right from the TripAdvisor Wear app (as depicted by the screenshot in **Figure 28**). However, from there on, customers need their smartphones to navigate to the places recommended by the app. This is how it works today — each device has its purpose in the digital toolchain. If one fails, the overall UX workflow breaks as well. This is a huge risk that organizations need to consider and plan with respect to a mitigation plan, i.e. ensure that there will be no media breaks whatsoever.

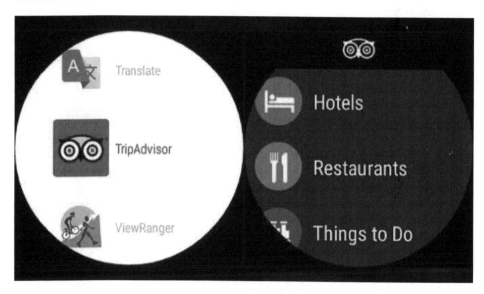

Figure 28: Making Decisions through Trip Advisor Wear App

IoT devices have their unique purposes that drive user adoption and interaction. If these purposes are either unmet or do not provide the highest value from an end user perspective, they will simply be uninstalled. Apps consume memory, battery, and other scarce system resources. IoT testers and developers need to make sure that their apps provide value, convenience, and the lowest possible resource consumption.

SUMMARY

Within this chapter, you had the chance to explore and get to know about the most common industry pitfalls that are likely to bring hard times for every mobile app. They were illustrated by many real world examples. You were also recommended how to plan your testing activities correctly. A handy tool named "9 Boxes" was introduced in order to help you structure and streamline this process considerably.

6 Shifting from Manual Mobile Testing to Automation

INTRODUCTION

Within this chapter, a great challenge that many organizations still face will be addressed — the shift from manual towards automated testing.

Before delving deeper and discussing the merits of the solutions available today, it would be worthy to go through and understand the major blockers dragging organizations behind in terms of automation.

1. **Legacy QA** tools for web being used within organizations are not well-suited to fit mobile and Agile processes.

2. **Existing organizational knowledge and skill matrices** are also subjects of change and evolution as the legacy QA tools employed within organizations right now require a somewhat different type of expertise to be caught up with.

3. The **nature of mobile testing** is quite Agile, meaning that its schedule is dynamic and imposes constant changes over functional and non-functional correctness.

4. **Test flakiness** caused by the underlying mobile platforms as well as the mobile environments that bring to the table virtually all sorts of obstacles, such as unpredictable interruptions, false negatives, unique objects in mo-

bile apps that are hard or even impossible to identify, and many, many more.

5. **Organizational priorities** trading off both quality and velocity of the delivery cycles for mobile apps.

6. Common **myths** around mobile test automation such as "It's hard." ☺

A short disclaimer, though. Within this chapter, not all of the challenges listed above will be resolved. This is simply impossible right now. Completely busting all the myths is a long shot too. Yet, the first steps are always the most important and enlightening ones.

Mobile test automation and mobile testing in general is not easy or simple to get to and start with. It is even more complex to sustain, grow, and evolve a testing solution, so that it would be executed in unattended mode, as part of CI workflows, for example. The key to this kind of transformation is starting with short steps having certain positive impacts on the way organizations operate today, thus increasing their maturity and readiness to embrace and accept such changes. It is a matter of building up trust resulting in strong management support.

The transition also requires evolution of the existing skillset to face the new reality. Most of all, success will be very much dependent on the desire and core understanding of the QA engineers involved as to why these are steps in the right direction. This means that they need to understand "what's in it for them."

We all know that running hundreds of manual test cases on real devices or emulators is not a fun task — not at all. On the contrary, it is time-consuming, error-prone, lacks coverage, and so forth. Often, being performed regularly makes it even more so. This is where mobile test automation helps practitioners to invest their time and effort in a smarter way.

BDD AND OPEN-SOURCE AS CATALYSTS — SETTING IT ALL UP

Do you know that there is a new open-source, behavior-driven development (BDD)[1] test framework[2] that can ease the pain of shifting from manual (or low

---

1 Behavior driven development (BDD) — https://en.wikipedia.org/wiki/Behavior-driven_development

2 Quantum — open source tool, Git repository- https://github.com/Project-Quantum/Quantum-Starter-Kit

skill-set based) test tools to an IDE-based approach? This framework was developed by InfoStretch. It was adopted and tuned to the mobile Cloud by Perfecto.

Think about shifting away from Microsoft Excel/Word or another manual test management tool towards an IDE such as Eclipse or IntelliJ. There, QA engineers can write human readable test scenarios in English, record application flows and objects in a simplified manner, create and populate their own object repository. In addition, it would take advanced manual testers just a few extra steps to regularly run these BDD (Cucumber) tests from within CI, such as Jenkins.

Let us iterate over the basics and get to know how this would look like, work, and do well for us.

1st Step — Setup of Test Development Environment

* Download the Java Standard Edition (Java SE) Java Development Kit (JDK) from Oracle's website and install it.

* Download and install Eclipse IDE for Java Developers or IntelliJ IDEA and the following plugins:

  * Cucumber

  * Maven

  * TestNG

  * For Cloud testing download the Perfecto plugin

2nd Step — Execution Framework Installation

* Clone the GIT repository of Quantum to obtain the framework in a local folder on your computer.

* Modify the file named **application.properties** located within the resources folder as part of your local copy of the Quantum framework in accordance with the guidelines of the project documentation, i.e:

  * Choose type of the tested app (Web, Native)

  * Set device properties and/ or environment parameters for the Cloud

THE FIRST AUTOMATED SCENARIO TO EASE UP THE TRANSITION

After going through these steps, the environment will be ready for test case development and execution. As can be observed in the architecture diagram **in Figure 1,** Quantum offers scripting in BDD terms or Java/Appium. One can execute the developed tests using TestNG and Maven. From there on, Jenkins CI is a no-brainer. After a test run is complete, results may be explored either by using the built-in reporting features of the TestNG framework or as part of a custom-tailored test reporting solution.

This is another important point in the diagram in **Figure 29.** It illustrates the unique reporting capabilities of the Perfecto technology stack integrated within the architecture of a Quantum-based automated test solution.

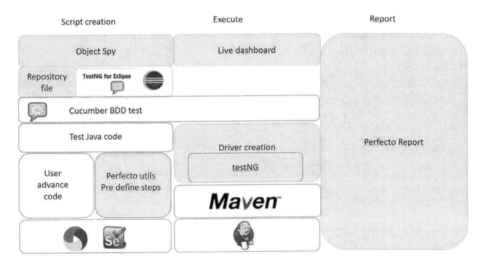

Figure 29: Quantum — An Example of BDD Open-Source Test Automation Framework Architecture

Going through the mapping example in **Figure 30,** you can understand how identification of UI objects may be parameterized through the use of object locator files (in a format pretty much defined by the framework).

Figure 30: An Example of an Object Locator File

The sole purpose of having an Object locator file is to fully separate the implementation of test scenarios from their configuration which naturally results in automated test scenarios that are easier to maintain. They are also much more resilient to changes introduced by software development units. As part of this concrete example, a set of objects (via key-value pairs) is defined. Whenever the native Android app is under test, UI objects can be looked up and identified by the underlying framework either by XPath expressions or, alternatively, by their unique Object identifier (ID).

Figure 31: BDD Test Scenario Example for an Android Native Application

Now, having defined the way relevant test Objects are about to be looked up, it is prime time to quickly develop a behavior-driven test scenario, similar to the one in **Figure 31.** Later on, our BDD scenario will be tagged as **"Android-TestApp"** in the TestNG configuration file, so that the test can be executed by the framework.

```
 1  <!DOCTYPE suite SYSTEM "http://testng.org/testng-1.0.dtd">
 2
 3⊖ <suite name="PerfectoBDD" verbose="0" parallel="tests"  data-provider-thread-count=":
 4
 5       <parameter name="driver.capabilities.platformName" value="Android"/>
 6       <parameter name="features" value="src/test/java/com/perfectomobile/quantum/featur
 7       <parameter name="glue" value="com.perfectomobile.quantum.steps"/>
 8       <parameter name="driver.retry.times" value="3"/>
 9       <parameter name="driver.retry.wait.sec" value="15"/>
10       <parameter name="dryRun" value="false"/>
11
12⊖      <test name="Android_S5" enabled="true">
13           <parameter name="driver.capabilities.deviceName" value=""/>
14           <parameter name="tags" value="@AndroidTestApp"/>
15⊖          <classes>
16               <class name="com.perfectomobile.quantum.runners.MyCucumberTestsRunner"/>
17           </classes>
18       </test>
19⊖      <test name="Nexus_Device" enabled="false">
20           <parameter name="driver.capabilities.deviceName" value="|"/>
21           <parameter name="tags" value="@AndroidTestApp"/>
22⊖          <classes>
23               <class name="com.perfectomobile.quantum.runners.MyCucumberTestsRunner"/>
24           </classes>
25       </test>
26  </suite>
```

Figure 32: TesNG Sample File Used for Execution of the BDD Test on Physical Devices

Eventually, TestNG needs to be configured. This is done as part of the TestNG. XML file, as illustrated by the example in **Figure 32.** Here, QA engineers would typically specify the following parameters:

- **DUT** (Device Under Test) — it can be specified to run the test in parallel on multiple devices
- **Path** to the files containing BDD test scenarios to be executed (similar to the one just created)
- Define **tags** such as the *"AndroidTestApp"*

This is what it takes for any QA engineer to walk the baby steps towards mobile test automation. It is just a matter of editing a small number of configuration files with valuable support built into your IDE. As you can see, not even a single line of source code is necessary to get the automation scripts ready for execution. Instead, we managed to elegantly hook into the underlying frameworks and harness their special powers through configuration. Thus, we ended up with a fully functional and robust mobile automation test solution that naturally plugs and plays with the common mobile development environments.

That said, benefitting from this approach will not take that much of an investment for most mobile development organizations, at least to the point of running a quick proof of concept project to explore the opportunities first hand.

CONTINUOUS INTEGRATION (CI) AND JENKINS AS A CI PLATFORM

Could the sample above be easily extended, so that Jenkins would automatically run the produced test solution? This is the next step on the road to CI/ CD, remember? Fortunately, it is just a matter of configuring a local Jenkins server to run the ready-made POM.xml file (bundled with the framework) as part of a build job upon some triggers.

For example, a build job could be run automatically after code changes for the app pushed by software developers to the source control system, thus also running our test solution. Some may need to establish scheduled regular test execution for the sake of automating transparent nightly builds. This is all easily done with Jenkins. Of course, to quickly get to execution results, the new job will be manually triggered and will only point to the location of the test solution POM. xml file on the file system, similar to the example configuration in **Figure 33.**

Build

Invoke top-level Maven targets		x
Goals	clean test	▼
POM	C:\Users\erank\Documents\Quantum\Quantum-master\BDDSample\pom.xml	
Properties		

Figure 33: Configuring Jenkins CI to Run the POM.XML File of Quantum

From here on, the newly created build job just needs to be triggered. In **Figure 34,** the sound execution log of this first automated test solution for mobile apps can be reviewed.

Figure 34: An Example Console Log within Jenkins CI after Test Execution

Note that only the sky (or the Cloud?!) is the limit for evolving such automated test suites.

Jenkins is an incredibly powerful and robust CI platform. Its huge community keeps contributing to the availability of an astonishing number of easily install-able plugins that makes it a solid foundation for mobile test automation against every major mobile platform.

SUMMARY

The whole domain of mobile test automation can hardly be presented within a single chapter. Many complex questions that you could come up with may not have been considered or mentioned at all. Keep in mind, though, that this is just the beginning and by no means the end of the journey towards robust and scalable mobile test automation. Rather, it starts with a practical and easy to follow approach that you can try out and, if satisfied with the results, share as pure knowledge with others.

The benefits are huge:

1. A practical and easy to follow approach for Manual testers to improve their professional skills

2. Which clearly leads to increased Manual testers' satisfaction

3. Because they can do less error prone manual testing

4. While achieving faster testing cycles

5. Experience faster feedback cycles with development teams and all interested parties, including stakeholders, due to unified, detailed and understandable reports common for all. And why not regular ones?

6. Leverage the power of defining BDD test scenarios as the means for getting to a common agreement about detailed functional specs among QA, software development teams, stakeholders, and other involved parties.

7. At the end of the day, this is a solid foundation for evolving more sophisticated test solutions with a robust object repository in place.

7 Optimizing Test Automation through Android & iOS Property Files

INTRODUCTION

The mobile space is highly dynamic, fragmented and challenging — this is not breaking news, right? However, if you think about the general impact of any new major mobile OS release on testing activities, well, this can be a bit scary.

Within this chapter, readers will dive deeper in this topic. The first step towards overcoming fears requires proper understanding of the fear factor and the root causes. It is often the case that new obstacles relate to issues that test engineers have already faced and resolved before. A glance back may help with working it out in the present. Perhaps, a solution leading in the right direction already exists. Read on.

INNOVATION IS COOL, ISN'T IT? WELL, THINK TWICE (IF TESTING)

A look at some of the innovative features introduced as part of the new Android OS and iOS releases over the last couple of years will definitely illustrate this point to the best. Please, keep in mind that this is by no means a complete list or release notes for each corresponding OS.

Android 6.0[1] (Marshmallow) introduced features such as:

* Doze for battery saving purposes

* A new app search bar

* Finer granular and stricter controls over the permissions of apps featuring a new mechanism that prompts users to grant specific permissions upon apps' actual usage of shared system resources, e.g. Camera, Location, etc., i.e. not in advance during app installation

* Fingerprint scanning capabilities

Android 7.0[2] (Nougat) steadily built on top of its predecessor(s) and brought in:

* Split-screen mode

* Enhanced battery performance by extending Doze

* More changes to system notifications

* Quick system settings

The iOS platform is no different. Its fast pace of innovation brings a lot value added features and enhancements as part of recent major releases, i.e. iOS 9 (2015) and iOS 10 (2016).

iOS 9[3] introduced great improvements in terms of:

* User Interface (UI)

* 3D Touch

* Searching for content on the cell phone is now way more powerful and, well, different

* Apple Wallet is here to stay

* Support for new devices, such as Apple Watch Series 2

* Improvements relevant to specific devices like multitasking for iPad

* A brand new major release of Safari

---

1   Android 6.0 (Marshmallow) — https://www.android.com/versions/marshmallow-6-0/

2   Android 7.0 (Nougat) — https://www.android.com/intl/en_uk/versions/nougat-7-0/

3   iOS9 Info https://developer.apple.com/library/content/releasenotes/General/WhatsNewIniOS/Articles/iOS9.html

* Xcode features, of course

* Enhancements in Maps, Siri and much more

iOS10[4] release had a substantial impact on User Experience (UX) of the platform in general and this apparently triggered a bunch of changes, such as:

* Enhanced notifications, messaging, maps, and voice commands

* New major Safari release

* Xcode development also seems to be on track considering its new releases

* Apple's own UI automation framework (UIAutomation) was replaced by a new one called XCTest

With such an aggressive pace of innovation, few things are very clear. While mobile developers have greater opportunities for using more and more app capabilities facilitating a rich user experience and improved engagement models, testers have to deal with the consequences, namely supporting multiple OS families, test tools and still managing to do app and feature testing right.

A fearsome question arises: "How is this complexity managed?"

THE LESSONS OF THE PAST

The answers of open questions today can sometimes be found in the past. This time a real life story about an existing U.S. patent (owned by the author of this book) may come in handy. The implementation of the aforementioned patent offers a solution named *"Mechanism for Graphical Test Exclusion"*. A great deal about it is revealed by **Figure 35** and **Figure 36** below.

Not so long ago, the world of mobile test engineers was ruled by a monster with many faces — namely J2ME. This was the reference specification of the ultimate mobile platform, as published by Sun Microsystems (later acquired by Oracle). Many device manufacturers were implementing J2ME on their own and in different ways.

You are probably already asking yourself whether this would mean different J2ME implementations for different devices, aren't you? Well, this was exactly

---

4   iOS10 page — http://www.apple.com/ios/ios-10/

the case. Thus, testing of a full reference implementation was pretty much a nightmare across devices manufactured by Nokia, Samsung, LG, Sony, and more. A full run of the MIDP suite against different devices used to result in huge number of errors and failures that had to be carefully analyzed, processed and followed up. These were mostly due to incomplete and defective implementations of the same features (as specified by J2ME) coming from different sources.

The essence of the patented solution was to provide a dynamic mechanism for scanning through the capabilities of any connected devices in order to iden-tify the supported and unsupported features for any of them. Based on this information, test solutions could automatically enable and disable certain test suites, so that the "noise" from tests destined to fail was considerably reduced.

Apparently, such a technology solution — as part of the Java test framework offered by Sun Microsystems at that time — enhanced testing productivity and sped up release cycles.

Figure 35: Test Exclusion Flow Diagram, Source — U.S. Patent US 6980916

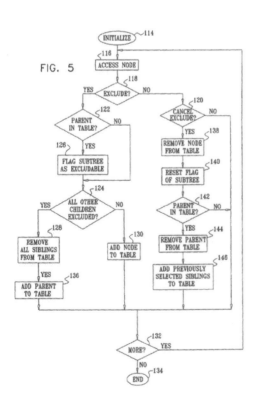

FIG. 6

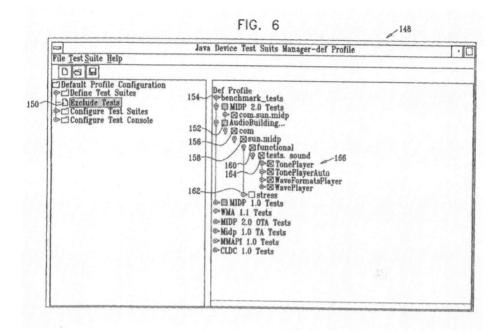

Figure 36: Test Framework GUI, Implementation Example, Source — U.S. Patent US 6980916

THE CHALLENGES OF TODAY

While J2ME is fortunately gone for good, mobile test engineers still face precisely the same issues with modern mobile platforms and apps. It is just a bit more serious now. How so?

Think about a native iOS application that used to run well on iOS 8 and now has to be tested on iOS 9 and iOS 10. If you would like to have the Android perspective, you could imagine an Android 5.x app that has to be tested on Android 6.0 or 7.0. While the underlying OS and hardware are different, the conceptual issues that you would face would be pretty much the same.

The native Facebook app for iOS would be a great example. **Figure 37** below demonstrates how the functionality of this app varies across different devices and versions of mobile OS. Hence, when planning a test, this should be taken into consideration, i.e., depending on different target environments, the app needs to be tested in different ways (taking into account certain features, while filtering out the ones unsupported for the current target environment). In this example, the Force Touch capability is used (though you could pretty much use the Touch ID one) to login to the app on iPhone 4S vs. iPhone 6 or vs. iPad Mini.

What does this mean if you are an automation test engineer and you need to maintain existing test suites/solutions that are run against target devices from different OS families and generations (similar to the Facebook app example below)? Keep in mind that this is a pretty common situation. At first glance, you are out of luck. Usually such situations cause unnecessary "branching" within test suites and thus add an unnecessary layer of complexity.

Test Scenario	iPhone 6/iPhone 5S	iPhone 6S/6S Plus	iPad Tablets
Login	YES	YES	YES
Write Post (FB UI)	YES	YES	YES
Write Post (FB **Force Touch**)	NO	YES	NO
Upload Photo/Video (FB UI)	YES	YES	YES
Upload Photo/Video (FB **Force Touch**)	NO	YES	NO
Take Photo/Video (FB UI)	YES	YES	YES
Take Photo/Video (FB **Force Touch**)	NO	YES	NO

Figure 37: Facebook Native App — Feature Support Matrix Example

If a concept for dynamically probing the available capabilities (similar to the one explained above) is applied, branching can be avoided or at least reduced. In order to do that, one needs to establish a smart logical connection among test cases, target devices, and applications under test, as proposed by the chart in **Figure 38.**

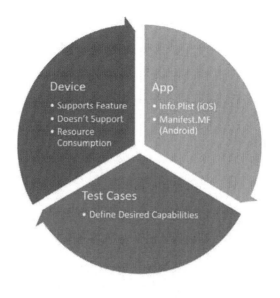

Figure 38: Connecting Three Mobile Layers as Part of Test Automation Optimization

LEVERAGING APP METADATA AND APP PROPERTY FILES

For both iOS and Android platforms, mobile developers use application-wide property files (AndroidManifest.XML for Android, Info.Plist for iOS) to define sets of supported features, required permissions and other app related metadata. Such files are one good source for dynamic analysis at runtime — usually prior to test execution. Keep in mind that knowing what a tested app supports in terms of functionality and user interaction may be crucial to the success of the whole test cycle. Therefore, these Application resources can also be statically analyzed during test planning phases.

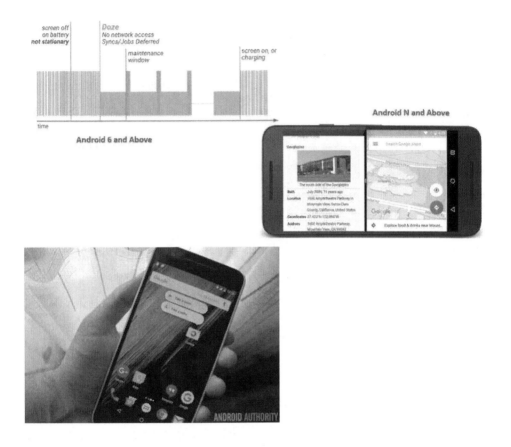

Android 7.1 App Shortcuts Example

Figure 39: More Examples of Unique Features for the Android Platform

Getting back to the example of testing the Force Touch feature in iOS, one may open and go through an Info.Plist file for any app supporting the discussed capability. The property called ***UIApplicationShortcutItems*** is easily found, as also depicted in **Figure 40.** It provides the menu options available for end users when working with this app and performing a Force Touch (3D Touch) on the iPhone. In the case of the Facebook native app, the menu items defined by this property are **Search, Write Post, Upload Photo/Video, Take Photo/Video.**

A lot can be learned when an iOS IPA (a deployable archive containing iOS apps meant to be run on real devices) or an Android application package (APK) file is unpacked by experienced test automation engineers. Introspecting application properties can be a very quick, easy, and rewarding exercise. It reveals what you can test the app for, i.e. which of its features will be available across different devices.

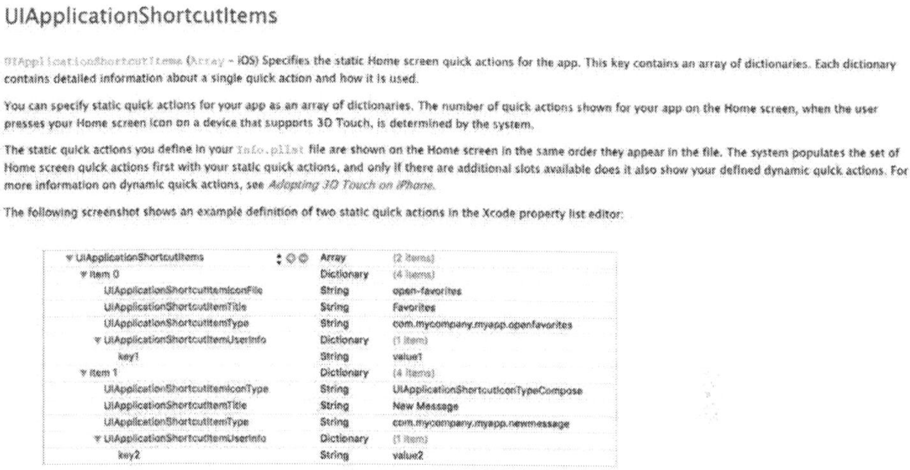

UIApplicationShortcutItems

UIApplicationShortcutItems (Array - iOS) Specifies the static Home screen quick actions for the app. This key contains an array of dictionaries. Each dictionary contains detailed information about a single quick action and how it is used.

You can specify static quick actions for your app as an array of dictionaries. The number of quick actions shown for your app on the Home screen, when the user presses your Home screen icon on a device that supports 3D Touch, is determined by the system.

The static quick actions you define in your Info.plist file are shown on the Home screen in the same order they appear in the file. The system populates the set of Home screen quick actions first with your static quick actions, and only if there are additional slots available does it also show your defined dynamic quick actions. For more information on dynamic quick actions, see *Adopting 3D Touch on iPhone*.

The following screenshot shows an example definition of two static quick actions in the Xcode property list editor:

▾ UIApplicationShortcutItems	Array	(2 items)
▾ Item 0	Dictionary	(4 items)
UIApplicationShortcutItemIconFile	String	open-favorites
UIApplicationShortcutItemTitle	String	Favorites
UIApplicationShortcutItemType	String	com.mycompany.myapp.openfavorites
▾ UIApplicationShortcutItemUserInfo	Dictionary	(1 item)
key1	String	value1
▾ Item 1	Dictionary	(4 items)
UIApplicationShortcutItemIconType	String	UIApplicationShortcutIconTypeCompose
UIApplicationShortcutItemTitle	String	New Message
UIApplicationShortcutItemType	String	com.mycompany.myapp.newmessage
▾ UIApplicationShortcutItemUserInfo	Dictionary	(1 item)
key2	String	value2

Figure 40: Sample Info.list File Listing Supported Application Properties[5]

Figure 41 demonstrates the same ability when it comes to reading Android OS application configuration files. There, capabilities are defined in XML format within the file AndroidManifest.XML file.

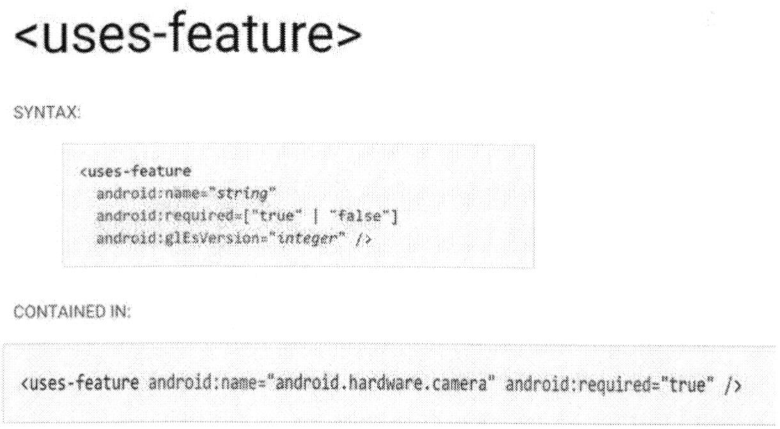

<uses-feature>

SYNTAX:

```
<uses-feature
  android:name="string"
  android:required=["true" | "false"]
  android:glEsVersion="integer" />
```

CONTAINED IN:

```
<uses-feature android:name="android.hardware.camera" android:required="true" />
```

Figure 41: Examples of Feature Definitions within the Android AndroidManifest.XML File

5 Source – Apple Developer Website

Before we dwell on some viable options for dynamic analysis of Application metadata, keep in mind that it is utterly important to make up your mind which scenarios you need to automate and which are not worth it.[6] Selecting the wrong test to be part of an automation suite could turn out to be very problematic and time-consuming.

If you often find yourself of "branching" your test suites, sooner rather than later you will feel the pain of continuously maintaining and evolving constantly diverging test cases. The investment required to handle such situations could be immense depending on the complexity of the apps under test and the size of the existing test solution. Do not forget that there is often pressure related to release dates and test cycles. Always think twice and try to assess the projected value before automating concrete scenarios.

PROPOSED SOLUTION FOR ANDROID OS

Now that static analysis of application capabilities and other metadata can be conducted by using simple text editors and dedicated tooling (Apple support their own format and tools for dealing with plist files as part of XCode), how can this be done at runtime?

Perhaps a library or utility that could be referred to as a dependency by test solutions would facilitate the dynamic analysis of supported application features. It should be able to:

1. Open a packaged app.

2. Load its application metadata in memory.

3. Provide the means to query/introspect application metadata with regard to some interesting capabilities.

Thanks to Dror Kedem[7] there is already an open-source solution for Android OS and it is publicly available on Github.[8] In order to get started quickly with

---

6 Manual to Automation Challenges — http://www.softwaretestinghelp.com/manual-to-automation-testing-process-challenges/

7 Dror Kedem (Senior Software Engineer, Perfecto) LinkedIn Profile — https://www.linkedin.com/in/drorkedem

8 AndroidManifestReader code sample on Git — https://github.com/ek121268/AndroidManifestReader

the tool, you just need to follow the steps below.

1. Create a Java project in your Java IDE of preference.
2. Add the Java files that you will find in the aforementioned Git repository.
3. Modify the "main" method in "AndroidManifestReader.java" so that it points to the correct path of your APK.

Running this file as a Java application will dump into the "Console" view of the IDE everything that can be retrieved from the Android manifest file bundled with the APK.

If you need to embed this utility as part of an existing test suite, you could also refer to the implementation of the "main" method. It clearly illustrates what is currently supported in terms of metadata handling. Below you will find a similar example.

```
"String filePath = "C:\\apps\\Android APK File Path.apk";
AndroidManifestReader reader = new AndroidManifestReader(file-
Path);
List<String> usesFeatures = reader.getUsesFeatures();
System.out.println("Features:" + usesFeatures);
List<String> usesPermissions = reader.getUsesPermissions();
System.out.println("Permissions:" + usesPermissions);
List<String> activities = reader.getActivities();
System.out.println("Activities:" + activities);
Map<String, String> usesSdk = reader.getUsesSdk();
System.out.println("SDK: " + usesSdk);"
```

Running this tool against an existing APK (e.g. an old version of the Angry Birds app) would most likely best reveal its value. The respective output is captured in **Figure 8.**

Mobile app Game - Angry Birds:

Features: [android.hardware.touchscreen, android.hardware. touchscreen.multitouch, android.hardware.touchscreen.multitouch.distinct]

Permissions: [android.permission.INTERNET, android.permission.ACCESS_NETWORK_STATE, com.android.vending.BILLING, android.permission.WRITE_EXTERNAL_STORAGE]

Activities:[com.rovio.rcs.RovioUnityActivity, com.unity3d.player.UnityPlayerActivity, com.unity3d.player.UnityPlayerNativeActivity, com.facebook.unity.FBUnityLoginActivity, com.facebook.LoginActivity, com.facebook.FacebookActivity, com.facebook.unity.FBUnityDeepLinkingActivity, com.rovio.fusion.VideoPlayerActivity, com.jirbo.adcolony.AdColonyOverlay, com.jirbo.adcolony.AdColonyFullscreen, com.jirbo.adcolony.AdColonyBrowser, com.facebook.ads.InterstitialAdActivity, com.rovio.rcs.socialnetwork.SocialSharingViewWrapper, com.google.android.gms.ads.AdActivity, com.rovio.skynest.channel.ChannelPromoViewActivity, com.prime31.EtceteraProxyActivity, com.prime31.WebViewActivity, com.prime31.P31VideoPlayerActivity, com.google.games.bridge.NativeBridgeActivity, com.unity3d.ads.android.view.UnityAdsFullscreenActivity, com.google.android.gms.common.api.GoogleApiActivity]

SDK: {minSdkVersion=16, targetSdkVersion=24}

Figure 8: Android SDK, Features, Permissions, and Activities Supported by a Game App

Thus, one quickly gets to know that the analysed application requires billing permissions, external storage write permission, multitouch screen, Internet connection, etc. The relevant activities[9] that are used or implemented by the app are listed as well.

Such information can be leveraged in many ways. Some prominent examples can be found below.

▪ Fine-tune test coverage to assess and verify the expected application be-

---

9 Android Manifest File Activities — https://developer.android.com/guide/topics/manifest/activity-element.html

havior in case of missing permissions for the tested app.

- Define the correct list of supported devices for testing. For instance, if an app does not support versions of the Android SDK older than version 16 (Android 4.1), you would need to enlist the suitable testing devices accordingly.

- Derive new test cases out of similar restrictions; for example, you could try installing such an app on a device running an older version of Android SDK. What will happen then? Will the installation go fine or will it be prevented (the preferred behavior)? You get the point, right?

SUMMARY

Knowing what application features are supported for any given version of a tested mobile app is essential for better planning and test execution in a way that unnecessary "branching" of test suites is minimized or avoided.

In the diverse and fragmented target mobile environments, analysis of supported capabilities and the relevant constraints help us manage our test effort much more efficiently. The knowledge and awareness one can extract out of it also unleashes the potential for better coordination, understanding, and agreement among testing and software development units. It also allows for more thorough and focused testing.

2 Advanced Continuous Digital Quality Practices

8

Extending Open Source Frameworks for Advanced Functional Testing

THIS CHAPTER WAS CONTRIBUTED BY WIM SELLES, TEST AUTOMATION ENGINEER AT RABOBANK, NETHERLANDS

WIM SELLES, Test Automation Engineer contracted by Rabobank since 2010, lives in the Netherlands and works for a small company called deTesters. Wim has been using Perfecto since 2014. In March 2015 he started with the implementation of an automation framework with Protractor + CucumberJS to automate a hybrid app based on Angular. Before Perfecto introduced support for Protractor in October 2015, Wim and a colleague of his managed to set up an on-site device lab for Rabobank.

In his spare time Wim likes to make websites and tries to learn more and more about test automation. He is fond of sharing and contributes to a few open-source projects on GitHub.

INTRODUCTION

One of the key benefits of using open source testing tools is having the flexibility of customizing them for unique use cases and complementing them to meet special app testing requirements. There are plenty of examples on the market where organizations positioned test frameworks, such as Selenium WebDriver/ Grid and Appium, as technology foundation for custom tailored test solutions satisfying special requirements.

Within this chapter, a similar example of extending the Selenium WebDriver test framework will be provided. The value of this approach will be illustrated through a powerful open source test framework named Protractor.[1]

As part of mobile web, responsive web or hybrid app testing, it is necessary to deal with either unique objects or dynamic objects changing upon an event or other triggers. Sometimes Selenium cannot fully detect and provide the means for addressing such state changes and transitions. For this reason, the community developed Protractor which runs on top of Node.js and has been specially designed for testing AngularJS applications.

Protractor uses Selenium WebDriver and supports BDD frameworks like Jasmine[2], Mocha[3] or Cucumber[4] to execute tests on real browsers and devices.

FIRST STEPS WITH PROTRACTOR

What would a typical test solution based on Protractor look like? It merely consists of a small number of plain text files that need to be understood and authored accordingly.

The Spec.js file is the place for test automation engineers to develop their scripts or test scenarios. Conf.js is the file where configuration of the underlying Selenium WebDriver/ Grid is done. The Spec.js describes the targets for testing, e.g. mobile devices, browsers.

1   Protractor project page — http://www.protractortest.org/#/
2   Jasmine test framework — http://jasmine.github.io/
3   Mocha test framework — http://mochajs.org/
4   Cucumber framework — https://cucumber.io/

Figure 42 provides the example source code (**spec.js**) of a test that uses Protractor.

```
// spec.js
describe('Protractor Demo App', function() {
  var firstNumber = element(by.model('first'));
  var secondNumber = element(by.model('second'));
  var goButton = element(by.id('gobutton'));
  var latestResult = element(by.binding('latest'));

  beforeEach(function() {
    browser.get('http://juliemr.github.io/protractor-demo/');
  });

  it('should have a title', function() {
    expect(browser.getTitle()).toEqual('Super Calculator');
  });

  it('should add one and two', function() {
    firstNumber.sendKeys(1);
    secondNumber.sendKeys(2);

    goButton.click();

    expect(latestResult.getText()).toEqual('3');
  });

  it('should add four and six', function() {
    // Fill this in.
    expect(latestResult.getText()).toEqual('10');
  });
});
```

Figure 42: A Sample "spec.js" Protractor File[5]

Last but not least, the test execution environment needs to be configured. This is done by modifying the **conf.js** file. With this particular example in **Figure 43** a typical execution environment for web apps is defined and configured to use both Chrome and Firefox browsers.

Once a Protractor test solution has beens developed and the environment has beens setup, a test execution could be initiated through Jenkins CI or by manually typing ***"protractor conf.js"*** on the command line.

---

5   Source — Protractor Project Website

```
// conf.js
exports.config = {
  framework: 'jasmine',
  seleniumAddress: 'http://localhost:4444/wd/hub',
  specs: ['spec.js'],
  multiCapabilities: [{
    browserName: 'firefox'
  }, {
    browserName: 'chrome'
  }]
}
```

Figure 43: A Sample "conf.js" File for Protractor

HOW RABOBANK WENT HYBRID WITH PROTRACTOR

Rabobank develops and maintains a hybrid[6] banking application. More than 75% of its implementation is based on WebView. The rest is native. The main reason for creating a hybrid banking application is to have a common platform powering up all use cases related to mobile, web, and mobile web.

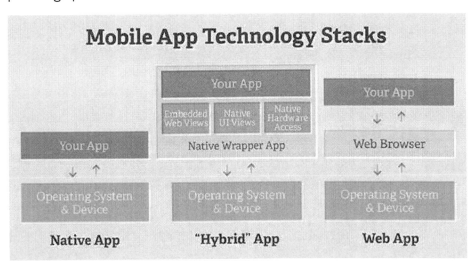

Figure 44: "Hybrid" Apps as Part of the Mobile App Technology Stacks

---

6   Example of Hybrid app architecture — https://myshadesofgray.wordpress.com/2014/04/15/hybrid-applications-and-android-native-browser/

WHY PROTRACTOR

A couple of years ago Rabobank tried to solve a set of problems. Keep in mind that in 2014 the market was way more immature in regards to offering the proper means for testing hybrid mobile applications. This said, after a careful analysis of the pain points the team got to the list of high level requirements towards the soon-to-come technical foundation for test automation.

1. The test automation solution needed to support the following capabilities:

   a. Test the app in parallel natively, in web and in mobile web modes

   b. Efficiently serve 15 different teams that are involved in the SDLC of this app

2. The solution should have easily provided mocked app data..

3. By supporting multiple teams, it needed to be accessible and shared among all of the aforementioned teams — both testers and developers.

4. The maintenance of the test environment should have been very easy and seamless for all of the teams.

5. Tests would have to be written in Gherkin.[7]

Of course, there were also other challenges, but taking the above into consideration, Rabobank decided to turn to Protractor as the shell framework for their solution.

SPECIAL REQUIREMENTS OR EXTENDING PROTRACTOR

A framework, all by itself, is not enough, at least not enough to fully support teams with automating the features they build. Take the following as an example.

The test toolset used by Rabobank included Protractor and CucumberJS. In order to test any given feature for (mobile) web, one needed to login to a secure environment and navigate to this feature. Testing the same feature within a native app actually imposed a number of extra steps, such as install and open the app, navigate to an entry point for the secure environment there, login, and navigate to the feature of interest.

---

7   Gherkin: https://github.com/cucumber/cucumber/wiki/Gherkin

If there are 15 teams, the wheel should not be reinvented 15 times (and even more, taking into account how creative developers could be). Especially when the goal for each team is to create, deliver, and contribute **their feature** instead of "wasting time" with test tools/ authentication methods. This was the starting point for laying the foundations of an utility library called "protractor-utils".

Rabobank wanted a common place for dependency management of their test tools. It should have also boosted sharing test automation knowledge throughout the organization. Thus, each team should have used the very same version of the test toolset to prevent technical tool depths. From one hand side, Protractor was evolving really fast. On the other, Selenium WebDriver was aggressively striving to support the fast release cycles of modern web browsers.

By using "protractor-utils" the authentication mechanism required for testing resulted in a single method called "logon()", as illustrated in **Figure 45.** Based on the capabilities passed to the Selenium WebDriver, the method itself is smart enough to determine if it needs to logon to (a mobile) web or a native version of the app. Well, in fact "protractor-utils" takes care of the heavy lifting part and automation engineers just need to provide credentials. Note that the documentation of the method is generated automatically.

Methods

`logon()`

Exposes a promise to logon as a customer to the teamserver. When the baseUrl contains 'localhost' logon is not needed, the promise is resolved and the given baseUrl is loaded.

Returns

`promise` The promise is resolved as soon as the login has been executed

Example

```
1.    // Example of the params
2.    {
3.        customerID: 110800000000,
4.        redirectUrl: '/path/to/your/feature',
5.        securityLevel: 3,
6.        showTour: false,
7.        siteContext: '/secure/environment'
8.    }
9.    //Feature-file
10.   Given I logon with valid credentials
11.
12.   //Stepfile:
13.   this.Given(/^I logon with valid credentials$/, givenILogon);
14.   function givenILogon() {
15.       var params = {
16.           customerID: '110800000000',
17.           redirectUrl: '/path/to/your/feature',
18.           securityLevel: 3,
19.           showTour: false,
20.           siteContext: '/secure/environemt'
21.       };
22.       return protractorutils.logon(params);
23.   }
```

Figure 45: Login Functionality Based on "protractor-utils"

From that point on, this useful library evolved into a npm module for Protractor that has being used by multiple teams for the past two years. They found it useful for developing Cucumber-based test automation and for performing parallel testing on both mobile and web platforms. Last but not least, the library also helps with producing standard test execution reports for all teams.

"protractor-utils" now contains:

- All of the dependencies (the underlying test frameworks), such as Protractor, CucumberJS, etc.
- "Default" configurations for Protractor and CucumberJS
- Utility methods to ease the testing of frontend projects
- Means facilitating reporting (hooks and basic test execution report generation)
- Configuration files
- Examples

In addition, as part of "protractor-utils" extra npm-modules were developed to bring in value added capabilities for:

- Re-running of flaky tests with "protractor-flake"
- Filtering in the device lab to retrieve the correct Selenium WebDriver capabilities
- Image comparisons (screenshots/ elements) created with (mobile) web or native apps (based on a fork of "pix-diff").

Support for Cucumber, Firefox, Internet Explorer, Microsoft Edge and Safari was introduced gradually

As you could see in **Figure 46,** "protractor-utils" is fully documented. Each method has its own automatically generated and well-structured description.

Figure 46: An Extract from the Documentation of "protractor-utils"

Furthermore, the usage of "protractor-utils" is explained in multiple markdown README.md files provided as part of the module. The contributors maintain them as clear and understandable guides for getting started with the basics really quickly, as also evident in **Figure 47.**

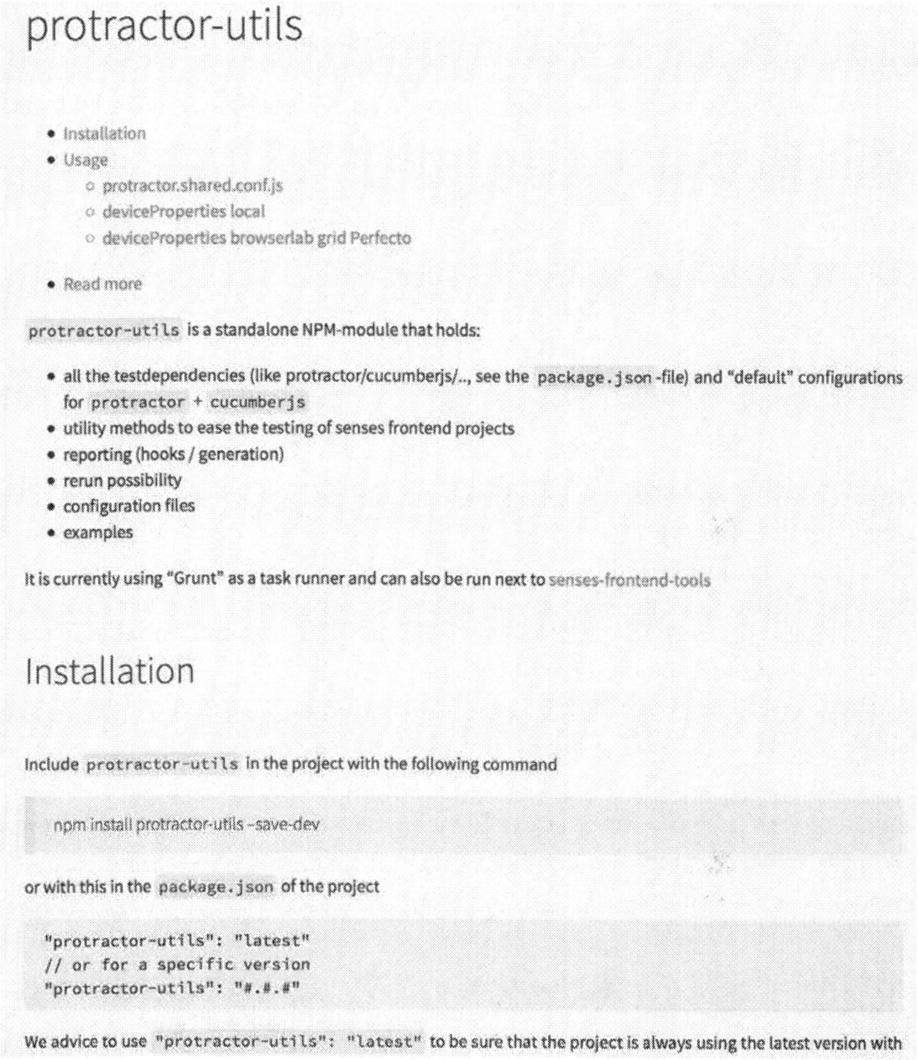

protractor-utils

- Installation
- Usage
  - protractor.shared.conf.js
  - deviceProperties local
  - deviceProperties browserlab grid Perfecto

- Read more

`protractor-utils` is a standalone NPM-module that holds:

- all the testdependencies (like protractor/cucumberjs/.., see the `package.json` -file) and "default" configurations for `protractor + cucumberjs`
- utility methods to ease the testing of senses frontend projects
- reporting (hooks / generation)
- rerun possibility
- configuration files
- examples

It is currently using "Grunt" as a task runner and can also be run next to senses-frontend-tools

Installation

Include `protractor-utils` in the project with the following command

```
npm install protractor-utils --save-dev
```

or with this in the `package.json` of the project

```
"protractor-utils": "latest"
// or for a specific version
"protractor-utils": "#.#.#"
```

We advice to use `"protractor-utils": "latest"` to be sure that the project is always using the latest version with

Figure 47: Installation Procedure for "protractor-utils"

PROTRACTOR AND FLAKY TESTS[8]

Whoever is in the business of assuring the quality of mobile and web applications understands that testing against such dynamic platforms often returns false negatives or failures. While some of the reasons might be due to incorrectly

---

8   Protractor flaky tests mechanism repo — https://github.com/NickTomlin/protractor-flake/blob/master/README.md

implemented tests, others directly relate to changes of the target environment or its availability, more precisely, to its lack of availability.

For example, a target device may malfunction or the installation of a native app may fail, or probably a browser session could not be initiated as desired. Keep on using your imagination and you will get to a long list of potential glitches that may (and will) cause test execution failures at some point. Thus, it is hard to think of mobile target environments in very friendly terms. What is even worse, one needs to count on them to get the job done. Tricky, isn't it?

This is why Nick Tomlin developed a NPM-module that would re-run potentially flaky Protractor tests before they would be announced as "failures". Initially "protractor-flake" did not meet the requirements of Rabobank, because it only supported Jasmine and Mocha tests. Therefore, CucumberJS parser and CucumberJS documentation[9] were introduced next, so that the NPM module could be adopted and used by Rabobank as well.

By bringing in this into "protractor-utils" flakiness could be reduced significantly by just appending a single command line option.

```
protractor:subtask --rerun-flake --attemps=amount
```

Apparently, this feature enhances efficiency, saves debugging time, and even more so, if you consider the large number of Rabobank teams working on this project.

FILTER ON THE DEVICE LAB TO RETRIEVE CORRECT CAPABILITIES (PERFECTO CLOUD)[10]

This NPM module has two clear goals:

* Always request devices with a standard/ controlled set of capabilities.
* Target specific device capabilities, such as device model, OS, browser (name), etc.

An internal NPM-module for introspecting and filtering the device Cloud of

---

9   https://github.com/NickTomlin/protractor-flake/blob/master/docs/cucumber.md

10   Querying a Cloud for specific devices — https://community.perfectomobile.com/posts/1072813

Rabobank was developed. Thus, the module returns the desired capabilities to be used by the test code.

With "protractor-utils" one could select all iOS devices by appending a single command line option, just like this.:

```
protractor:subtask -capabilityFilter='[{"platform-
Name":"iOS"}]'
```

What if selecting more than one specific devices would be necessary? No issues here, since the capability filter is able to accept any number of filtering criteria.

```
protractor:subtask -capabilityFilter='[{"model":"i-
Phone-6S"}, {"model":"Galaxy S6"}]'
```

Running some of the commands above will produce a JSON-formatted file describing all of the desired capabilities needed by Rabobank in order to start a device in the Cloud. It is based on a predefined template. One could refer to the extract in **Figure 48** to get the full picture. This way multiple implementations for starting devices will be prevented and there is no need for all of the feature teams to keep and maintain this kind of knowledge.

The above NPM module is the central place for:

* Maintaining and evolving the knowledge for managing all of the devices used
* Ensuring the same device conditions for every test, i.e. a more stable target environment
* Updating the version of the tested app without notifying each team in advance

```
deviceTemplate = {
    applicationName: '<% var applicationName = environment +\'_\'+ manufacturer +\'_\'+ model: %><% applicationName.toLowerCase().replace(/ \/g. \'_\') %>',
    appPackage: '',
    app: '',
    autoInstrument: true,
    available: '<%= available %>',
    browserName: '',
    bundleId: '',
    deviceProperties: {
        appType: '<%= appType %>',
        deviceId: '<%= deviceId %>',
        deviceType: '<%= deviceType %>',
        environment: 'pm',
        inScope: '<%= inScope %>',
        os: {
            name: '<%= os.toLowerCase() %>',
            version: '<%= osVersion %>'
        },
        resolution: '<%= resolution %>'
    },
    fullReset: true,
    inUse: '<%= (status === \'Not Connected\' || status === \'Ready to connect\') ? false : inUse %>',
    logName: '<%= manufacturer %> <%= model %> app',
    manufacturer: '<%= manufacturer %>',
    model: '<%= model %>',
    password: '',
    platformName: '<%= os %>',
    platformVersion: '<%= osVersion %>',
    reserved: '<%= reserved %>',
    screenshotOnError: true,
    status: '<%= status %>',
    user: '',
    useHybridAppAsBrowser: true,
    windTunnelPersona: 'Empty'
}}
```

Figure 48: An Example of a Device Template File

IMAGE COMPARISON (SCREENSHOTS/ UI ELEMENT SCREENSHOTS)

Rabobank also needed the ability to compare screens/ UI elements with each other. Researching the topic on the Internet in 2015 they found the library Pix-Diff. The core of Pix-Diff[11] could not be used for testing the hybrid app of Rabobank with browsers different from Chrome. Hence, they forked Pix-Diff and added Cucumber, hybrid app and additional browser support. Screens/ UI elements could now be compared during the "normal" test runs with just a single line of code.

Compare a screen:

```
expect(browser.imageComparison.checkScreen('exampleP-
age')).toEqual(0);
```

Compare an UI element:

```
expect(browser.imageComparison.checkElement(element(By.
id('title')), 'examplePageTitle')).toEqual(0);
```

---

11   Pix-Diff repository — https://github.com/koola/pix-diff

For example, one could compare a baseline UI element image with the actual UI element image as it would be faced by anyone exploring this version of the app manually. In the particular example depicted in **Figure 49,** the actual UI element screenshot deviates from the mandatory color for alerting messages. This is detected and reported by the tool as a substantial difference.

- **Baseline:**

  Danger message   ✕

- **Actual screenshot:**

  Danger message   ✕

- **Difference:**

  Danger message   ✕

Figure 49: An Example of Detecting Deviations against Baseline Requirements

As a consequence, in 2016 the following framework features were contributed to the Pix-Diff open source project.

- CucumberJS
- Multiple browser sessions
- Appium as the backbone for image comparison on mobile devices

At the end of 2016 Wim announced and published his own open source NPM module "protractor-image-comparison"[12] with even more functionality that Rabobank and others could benefit from.

THE TEST AUTOMATION STRATEGY OF RABOBANK

The way the app has been developed within Rabobank requires a well-defined

---

12   NPM: https://www.npmjs.com/package/protractor-image-comparison, GIT: https://github.com/wswebcreation/protractor-image-comparison

process, constant alignment and discipline amongst all of the involved teams. Since each of them would contribute a specific component to the app while utilizing a common framework and infrastructure, it is important for each team to take care of its own tasks without neglecting dependencies that would be the foundation for other teams to perform their near future activities.

A prominent example for such a dependency would be the "constantly" and rapidly changing HTML code. Within the timeframe of a week the HTML code for a date field might change from three input fields (denoting day, month, and year) to three select options. Such a change would definitely break all of the tests relying on this specific date field.

In order to mitigate and manage this risk, Rabobank agreed that each team would create PageObjects with a consistent API that other teams could also reuse for testing their own features. As long as the API would not change, dependent tests would not break when the new version of the aforementioned date field would be introduced.

SUMMARY

At the end of the day, by extending the Protractor framework Wim managed to offer a robust framework satisfying the needs of 15 feature teams consisting of both developers and testers. It was designed from ground zero to seamlessly integrate within the target environment and IDEs used on daily basis by the developers at Rabobank. It was also easily connected with the Jenkins CI workflow as well.

Open source, best practices, and industry standards (such as PageObjects, Cucumber, and a number of open source modules) allow testing teams to develop and deliver test automation code and enhancements in a friendly and easy, yet controlled, manner without any worries about the underlying test engine.

9 Advanced Automated Visual Testing

THIS CHAPTER WAS CONTRIBUTED BY ADAM CARMI, CTO AND CO-FOUNDER OF APPLITOOLS

ADAM CARMI is the Co-founder and CTO of Applitools — a Cloud service provider for automated visual testing. Prior to Applitools, he held management, research, and development positions at Safend, IBM, and Intel. He regularly talks about software testing at conferences around the world. Last but not least, Adam also manages the Israeli Selenium Meetup group.

INTRODUCTION

Visual software testing is a quality assurance activity aimed to verify that the User Interface (UI) of an application renders correctly in all the different execution environments it is expected to run on. In recent years, it has become increasingly difficult to be performed manually for two reasons. On one hand side, the number of popular devices, browsers, screen resolutions, and operating systems is rapidly growing, thus imposing an

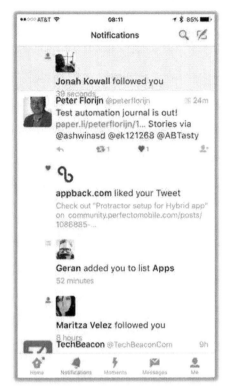

Figure 50: A Visual Bug in the Twitter Mobile App

impossibly huge test matrix. The second one relates to the constant pressure to shorten release cycles which leaves little time for testing.

Within this chapter, one will get to know about the importance of automating visual tests, as well as the respective challenges. Some great automation solutions for increasing visual test coverage will be proposed.

VISUAL TESTING IN A NUTSHELL

In today's digital world, applications and websites are the face of the business and the primary means by which businesses interact and engage with their customers. User experience (UX) plays a key role in the adoption or abandonment of apps and directly affects business economics. Thus, UX and visual testing is becoming a mandatory phase of every software release. When it comes to mobile applications, pre-release testing is even more critical. Unlike websites, you cannot push daily updates to the app store, which means that if you have a bug in production, your users are stuck with it for a while. Even when you do push a fix, users can opt-out of the update and never get the fixed version.

Figure 50 shows a visual bug found in the Twitter mobile app, where the notification details overflowed downwards on top of the notifications below them due to lack of horizontal screen space. As typical for many other forms of visual bugs, this issue would not reproduce on devices with a slightly wider form factor. But even when these defects do reproduce, it is unlikely that they would be detected by your automated functional tests. This is because all of the expected content is available on the page and all the links and buttons are active and clickable. The app is fully functional. It just looks bad.

VISUAL TEST COVERAGE AND AUTOMATION, DO THEY PLAY WELL?

Of course, one may believe that automating visual tests could be a solution. So, think about what it would take to implement an automated test that would provide visual test coverage by only using a traditional functional test automation tool, such as Selenium or Appium. For each element appearing on the screen we would need to acquire a unique locator to access it and write multiple assertions that verify its position, size, visibility, z-order, text, font, image, color, transparency, and style. Some of the expected values for these assertions would be applicable to all execution environments, while others (such as position and size) would have to be environment specific. Last but not least, we will also have to handle the usual synchronization and page stabilization issues when accessing elements.

For a standard application page, we may end up writing hundreds of lines of code. What's more, we may easily end up having to write more test code than was required to implement the app itself. Do not forget that even modest apps consist of dozens of pages and UI states. Moreover, when the app (or a 3rd party library that it depends on) has been changed in an incompatible way, there might be literally thousands of failed assertions and object locators to be investigated and fixed. Clearly, this is not the way to go.

AUTOMATED VISUAL TESTING TOOLS TO THE RESCUE

This is where automated visual testing tools come in handy. There are dozens of them available, both open-source and commercial, and they all share the same simple workflow:

1. **Navigate the application under test and take screenshots of your app.** You can use just about any test framework in any programming language to accomplish that. For example, Applitools Eyes — a leading commercial tool — provides over 20 different SDKs that allow you to add visual test coverage to your existing tests in any test framework including Selenium, Appium, Espresso, XCUI, UFT, LeanFT, CodedUI, and many others.

2. **Compare the screenshots with baseline images.** They define the expected appearance of your application at each point of the test. In most cases, baseline images are screenshots of your app that were taken in previous

test runs and were found to be valid. Naturally, the first time you run a test there is no baseline to compare against and the screenshots are simply set as the baseline. Starting from the second run onwards, you always have a baseline to compare with. The comparison is done by the tool.

3. **The tool generates a report** that consist of all the screenshots, baseline images, and any differences that were found.

4. **Manually inspect the report** and decide for each difference (if there are any) whether it is a defect or a valid change. If it is an issue, you reject the new screenshot and open a bug. If it is a valid change, you accept the new screenshot, so that it will be used as a baseline image for subsequent test runs.

There are many differences between the capabilities of the different tools. They range from naïve implementations that perform pixel to pixel bitmap comparisons and produce test results in the form of diff image files to premium services employing advanced image matching algorithms that emulate the human vision and can scale to run tens of thousands of tests a day with a negligible test maintenance overhead.

ADD VISUAL TEST COVERAGE TO EXISTING FUNCTIONAL TESTS

Independent of what tool for visual test automation you choose, there is a good chance that you could quickly ramp up with improved visual test coverage by combining your existing functional tests and the respective tool in efficient way.

THE EXISTING TEST

Figure 51 represents an existing functcional test. In order to maintain strong focus on visual testing, it has been oversimplified.

```
1:  [Test]
2:  public void TestMobileGithub()
3:  {
4:      var cap = new DesiredCapabilities();
5:      cap.SetCapability("platformName", "Android");
6:      cap.SetCapability("deviceName", "192.168.116.101:5555");
7:      cap.SetCapability("browserName", "Chrome");
8:
9:      var driver = new RemoteWebDriver(new Uri("http://127.0.0.1:4723/wd/hub"), cap);
10:
11:     try
12:     {
13:         driver.Url = "https://github.com";
14:
15:         driver.FindElement(By.ClassName("octicon-three-bars")).Click();
16:         driver.FindElement(By.ClassName("nav-item-personal")).Click();
17:
18:         driver.FindElement(By.ClassName("octicon-three-bars")).Click();
19:         driver.FindElement(By.ClassName("nav-item-opensource")).Click();
20:     }
21:     finally
22:     {
23:         driver.Quit();
24:     }
25: }
```

Figure 51: A Simple Appium Test of Github.com

The code snippet above is a simple C# Appium test for github.com running in a Chrome browser on an Android device. In **lines 4–9** we identify the target device and browser and start a remote web driver to control the browser via the Appium server running on the local machine. In **line 13,** we navigate the browser to the Github home page. In **lines 15–16,** we click the hamburger button to open the navigation menu and then click the "Personal" item to navigate to the "Personal" page. In **lines 18–19** we open again the navigation menu and navigate to the "Open Source" page. Finally, in **line 23** we close the browser and end the test. Basically, the test visits three pages of the Github. com website and performs no assertions.

AUTOMATICALLY INCREASE VISUAL TEST COVERAGE

Next, we will add visual coverage to our test using the Applitools Eyes C# Appium SDK, as shown in **Figure 52.**

```
 1:  [Test]
 2:  public void TestMobileGithub()
 3:  {
 4:      var cap = new DesiredCapabilities();
 5:      cap.SetCapability("platformName", "Android");
 6:      cap.SetCapability("deviceName", "192.168.116.101:5555");
 7:      cap.SetCapability("browserName", "Chrome");
 8:
 9:      IWebDriver driver = new RemoteWebDriver(new Uri("http://127.0.0.1:4723/wd/hub"), cap);
10:
11:      var eyes = new Eyes(new Uri("https://demo.applitools.com"));
12:      eyes.ApiKey = Environment.GetEnvironmentVariable("DEMO_APIKEY");
13:      eyes.ForceFullPageScreenshot = true;
14:
15:      try
16:      {
17:          driver = eyes.Open(driver, "Github", "MobileGithub");
18:
19:          driver.Url = "https://github.com";
20:          eyes.CheckWindow("Home");
21:
22:          driver.FindElement(By.ClassName("octicon-three-bars")).Click();
23:          driver.FindElement(By.ClassName("nav-item-personal")).Click();
24:          eyes.CheckWindow("Personal");
25:
26:          driver.FindElement(By.ClassName("octicon-three-bars")).Click();
27:          driver.FindElement(By.ClassName("nav-item-opensource")).Click();
28:          eyes.CheckWindow("Open source");
29:      }
30:      finally
31:      {
32:          eyes.Close();
33:          driver.Quit();
34:      }
35:  }
```

Figure 52: A Sample Visual Test of Github.com with Applitools Eyes

In **lines 11–13** we initialize the SDK. In **line 11** we create an instance of the Eyes class and point it to the URL of the Eyes server which will store the test results. In **line 12** we specify the API key that identifies our Applitools account (in this case taken from the environment variable "DEMO_APIKEY") and in **line 13** we instruct the SDK to capture full page screenshots of website pages. This is necessary, because the Chrome browser only provides screenshots of the visible browser viewport. To capture a full page, screenshot the SDK will take multiple screenshots while scrolling the page and then stitch them together to produce a simulated screenshot of the entire page.

Once we are done initializing the SDK, it only takes three lines of code to add 100% visual coverage for the 3 web pages visited in our test. Each call to *eyes. checkWindow* (in **lines 20, 24 and 28**) waits for the page to stabilize, captures a full page screenshot of the page, and validates it. In addition, the SDK automatically detects the details of the execution environment (device, browser, operating system, and screen resolution). It locates the proper baseline to compare against as well. It is also possible to compare against a different baseline in order to perform a cross-device or a cross-browser test. Any scaling (a.k.a. "device pixel ratio") differences between the screenshots and the baseline images are automatically normalized.

In **line 32** we conclude the test by calling the close method which informs the Eyes server that the test has been completed. If any differences are found between the screenshots and the baseline images, eyes.close would fail the test by throwing an exception that includes a direct URL to the test results in the Applitools Eyes test manager. This URL will end up listed in the test report of your Continuous Integration (CI) server or any other tool that was used to run the test.

AUTOMATED DETECTION OF VISUAL DIFFERENCES IS REAL

As shown in **Figure 53,** any visual differences between the baseline images (on the left-hand side) and the screenshots obtained during the test (on the right-hand side) are clearly highlighted in the generated test report.

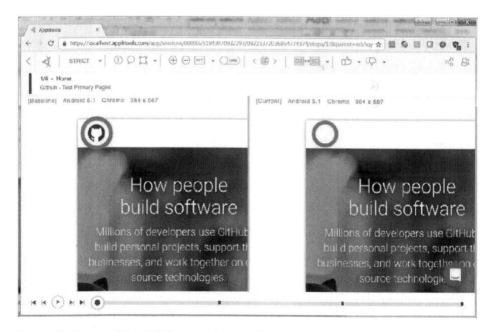

Figure 53: Report of Visual Differences Produced by Applitools Eyes

Furthermore, if the same difference appears in multiple checkpoints across different tests and execution environments, the Applitools Eyes test manager will only show a single representation of the difference.

For example, the report shown in **Figure 54** consisted of 19 tests which ran on 4 different mobile and desktop browsers to cover the different layouts of the Github.com website.

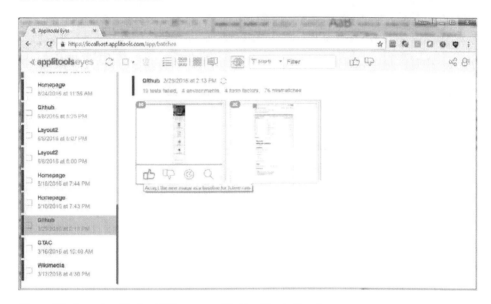

Figure 54: Grouping Similar Differences with "Applitools Eyes"

In total, the test detected 76 mismatching images that represent multiple occurrences of 2 unique differences, as clearly indicated in the report. While reviewing the two representative images of each unique difference, the test engineer inspecting the report could easily accept or reject the entire set of screenshots with two clicks.

SUMMARY

Visual test automation tools allow for automated validation of the visual correctness in your apps. This is a critical test activity that can no longer be effectively performed manually.

Such test automation solutions are extremely useful for automating a wide range of testing activities, including:

* Functional testing of deterministic graphical output
* Cross-device and cross-browser tests
* Localization testing
* Accessibility testing
* Responsive design testing
* Printed form validation
* Production monitoring to detect site defacements by hackers.

To learn more about visual testing visit the Applitools website.[1]

To see additional visual analysis testing tools, please read through this post[2]

---

1   Applitools website — https://applitools.com

2   Top visual testing tools — https://www.joecolantonio.com/2017/02/02/top-21-free-visual-valida-tion-tools-testers/

10 Eliminating Mobile Test Flakiness

THIS CHAPTER WAS CONTRIBUTED BY PAUL BRUCE, DEVELOPER EVANGELIST AT PERFECTO

PAUL BRUCE currently works with the Perfecto's team as a Developer Evangelist helping development groups to improve their velocity and quality throughout the software delivery process. Previously, he served as an advocate for API development and strong testing practices at SmartBear Software. With more than 15 years of work as a full-stack developer of front-end apps and backend solutions in non-profit, enterprise, startup, and small IT business organizations, Paul now uses his experience to help other developers to save time, build really cool and useful software, and encourages open source contribution wherever possible. Paul writes, speaks, listens, teaches about software delivery practices in key industries worldwide.

INTRODUCTION

Early user interface (UI) testing provides critical feedback to development teams about how changes in code will affect user experience (UX). Unfortunately, it is often plagued with reliability issues that undermine the value of these insights.

You could improve the reliability of your continuous delivery process by working on a sustainable strategy towards minimizing the so called "flakiness" of UI test suites. Eventually, you will go down to some very basic needs like having a clear definition of test stability. Then you will likely make the next one and create guidelines to help you maintain and sustainably evolve a suite of stable tests.

Now, if you are ready to dive deeper, there is a single open question left: "How to get there?"

In this chapter, a number of proven industry practices will be shared. They will hopefully make it easier for you to get to the bottom of it. Just keep in mind the complexity behind flakiness of tests, i.e. you should be aware that this issue could hardly be tackled by technology, processes, or people alone. It is a matter gluing them all together and this is where culture comes into play.

KEEPING QUALITY IN SYNC WITH NEW WORK

The software delivery process is constantly evolving to meet market and economic demands, as visualized by the chart in **Figure 55.** New technologies allow developers to build software faster which requires equal improvement of practices in other areas of delivery (such as testing) to avoid creating gaps in quality or velocity.

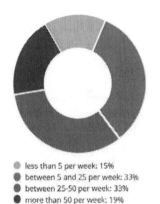

A modern approach of top performing teams for tackling this challenge is to adopt testing as part of short iterative development cycles rather than treat software quality as a separate phase of the delivery chain. Incorporated into shorter timelines, testing therefore has to be fast, resilient to changes, and reliable in execution.

● less than 5 per week: 15%
● between 5 and 25 per week: 33%
● between 25-50 per week: 33%
● more than 50 per week: 19%

Figure 55: Release Frequency of Mobile Teams

As a key component of their continuous delivery pipeline, organizations increasingly adopt automated testing earlier into their development process to minimize the downstream impact of defects and their multiplied cost at later stages of delivery.

THE GOAL: NO "FLAKY" TESTS EVER!

"Flaky" automated tests throw a monkey wrench into the software delivery process. Tests that tend to fail inconsistently block the process of integrating changes into a build that is always "green". They are ultimately hindering software teams from deploying on an as-needed basis. In this way, test flakiness represents a tangible barrier between downstream[1] development and delivery activities.

Test flakiness occurs due to several common reasons:

* **Test execution environment** is inconsistently managed or unreliable
  * Resources used by UI testing are not reset or are in an inconsistent state
  * External dependencies propagate unreliable behavior into tests
  * New requirements reserve testing resources, thus blocking existing requirements
* **Code changes** are not reflected in test design
  * Modifications to workflows are not communicated between team members
  * Development and QA release activities do not operate on the same schedule
* **Rigid UI element locator strategies**
  * XPath and other selector patterns are rigid or based on dynamic data
  * Tests duplicate steps required to select element or navigate through the app
  * Locator patterns are incompatible between platforms and various device models
* **Test data is out of sync** with environment under test
  * Restriction on data due to security or privacy inhibits timely testing
  * Inability to obtain latest data leaves gaps in test plans, i.e. apps in the wild may behave in unexpected manner

---

1 Brian Dawson, CloudBees http://www.slideshare.net/collabNet/linking-upstream-and-down-stream-agile/23https://www.youtube.com/watch?v=uGquTO7GIVA

- Distribution of responsibility for managing test data does not match team needs

Needless to say, a feedback mechanism that provides inconsistent or incorrect information is bad news, particularly in rapid development cycles. Not only you do have to pause development, but you also have to investigate whether the code under test caused a failure or it was the test itself. The more often a test fails erroneously, the further trust in the validation system is reduced.

What does a "rigid" element locator strategy look like?

Below is a classic example of "fragile" test code, highlighting a specific problem in element locator strategy:

```
driver.findElement(By.xpath("//device/view/group[1]/
group[1]/group[1]/group[1]/group[1]/group[1]/view[1]/
group[1]/viewpager[1]/group[1]/group[1]/scrollview[1]/
group[1]/group[3]/text[1]"));
```

These kinds of verbose XPath expressions are often the result of using GUI tools to find an element in an app, typically resulting in brittle tests because they break with even the slightest change to the style or layout of your app.

When you see a test that contains code like this, you have one of two choices:

1. Fix it to use a more robust selector.

2. Set a reminder to do so at a more convenient date and stick to it (see above).

Considering that most elements have a unique ID, a classification attribute, or some other distinguishing data characteristic, it is far more suitable to use a pattern that looks more like this:

```
driver.findElement(By.xpath("//android.widget.Edit-
Text[@resource-id='io.perfecto.testapp:id/etOccupan-
cySpec']"));
```

In the second example above, the element is identified on the screen using the unique identifier of the object, making automation of this element resilient to aesthetic changes.

Figure 56: Rigid Element Locators and Ways to Fix It

WRITING STABLE TESTS TO INCLUDE IN DEVELOPMENT CYCLES

To improve test flakiness, coding and testing activities need to be synchronized appropriately through good practices. The less gap exists between coding and testing activities, the more ownership over improvements to quality will show their merits as part of the work being delivered.

Developers, who are familiar with how app code is tested and how realistic the test environment is compared to the one in production, write code that ultimately conforms to real-world expectations in a much easier fashion. Similarly with test code, no one likes when their test fails because of a resource left in an improper state by a prior script execution or a fellow co-worker.

Make sure that "setUp" and "tearDown" methods are properly implemented within tests, so shared resources are dismissed and left in a healthy state. Deleting temporary files, resetting sensors, rolling back incomplete database transactions, and closing network connections whenever possible is a prerequisite of maintaining a stable testing environment.

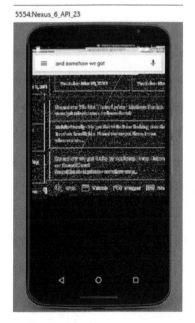

Figure 57: Rendering Errors on Android Emulator under Low Memory

The shared tenancy of a test environment could also cause unexpected failures of test cycles, which is why many organizations are making a switch to automate the management of all environments through container deployment and artifact management technologies. Nevertheless, changes to network configuration and domain administration can have negative impact over test execution, so it is important to carefully manage and buffer these changes from your development process until they can be adequately addressed.

CODE AND TESTS: TWO SIDES OF THE "QUALITY" COIN

Automation has driven testing to become a code-oriented discipline in order to meet the complexity and the quick pace of innovation which are typical side-effects of app development. Fortunately, this means that you could apply a number of well-known coding practices and improve the stability of your tests. Essential techniques are described below.

TREAT YOUR TESTS AS EQUAL CITIZENS TO APP CODE

This allows your testing strategy to inherit positive aspects of principal project assets, such as versioning, traceability, and ease of distribution. In terms of importance, using a source control system like Git to maintain your test scripts positions them on the same level with the rest of the app. This is a tangible step towards including quality in development.

"Just as good code is worth writing tests to cover, good tests are worth committing to the project source."

REDUCE TECHNICAL GAPS BETWEEN APP AND TEST SOURCE CODE

Writing tests in the same language as the app and importing app resource dictionaries into your test scripts encourages healthy coupling between these assets. Test failures at compile/ build time are much easier for troubleshooting and resolution than issues detected during regression cycles later on.

A practical example of this kind of coupling could be found in the the Espresso test framework for Android applications. It uses the same resource dictionary to identify objects in both app and test code, as explained in **Figure 58.** This is facilitated by Java as the common programming language in between.

BE AS HERMETIC AS POSSIBLE BUT NOT OVERLY SO

The more elaborate or resource-dependent the test, the flakier it could get. Unlike code-level unit testing, validation at the UI level often requires an interactive session or simulated environment to run these tests. While this is execution overhead from the perspective of unit and some integration testing, a real-time reflection of how the app works exposes many defects that code and service level testing cannot. Therefore, make sure that your UI tests are executed in realistic environments, but do not rely on 3rd party or other external services that have previously proven themselves as flaky.

SOAK TEST NEW TEST SUITES IN ISOLATION BEFORE ADDING THEM

This helps you to "put your tests to the test" by exercising them in advance, thus avoiding uproars with your team and slowing down progress. At first, new tests that are included in code commits can easily be run in a way that only the corresponding contributors would be notified of errors and failures. Once run successfully in the time span of a "graduation" period, tests could be tagged as "ready for further incorporation". Determining how this actually works in your development process is unique to each team. In any case, the isolated tests should meet a minimum accepted level of reliability that development, testing, operations, and product ownership teams all agree upon.

How does Espresso rock element identification?

In every Android UI project there is a dynamically generated R.java file which contains information about resources, their IDs and other useful bits of metadata. Therefore, you can write code like this:

```
findViewById(R.id.my_text_box);
```

This is a powerful feature from a test authoring perspective, as it provides rich detail on the inner context of the application under test, including drawables, strings, layouts, and animations. When app code and tests share a common source for this reference metadata, it is far easier to note and understand which tests break due to a recent code change because it is not based on static strings which is often the case with XPath expressions.

Localization (i.e. support for multiple languages) is also dramatically simplified by the "R" class under the "string" package, since you could use the same resource string key in your code, yet provide multiple locale-specific dictionaries with your app. For more information, visit the Android Developer API Guide on Localization.

Figure 58: Espresso for Android — Element Identification under the Hood

REAL DATA IS PART OF THE REAL WORLD

For automated testing to cover important conditions, representative data must be integrated into the test plan. The easiest way to overcome restrictions on this data is to create a representative data set and regularly incorporate new data from defects as they are discovered and fixed. Vigilance is the key here. Defects exposed by data are notoriously hard to catch early in the development process.

To make sure that all testing incorporates the correct data, each test should be considered as a candidate for using an existing or new test data set when it is first checked in. Since this is a responsibility of the team member who checks it in, it is by definition a shared activity across the entire development team. This further distributes the concept of upfront thinking about quality into group culture and collaterally into the product of group work.

SUMMARY

Stable tests allow teams to more confidently validate and improve the quality of their work. The faster developers receive complete feedback on their current work, the less time they spend fixing bugs later down the line. This translates to greater productivity and bandwidth to ship better code and improve the delivery process.

11 Testing Bots in the Context of Mobile Apps

THIS CHAPTER WAS CONTRIBUTED BY YORAM MIZRACHI, CTO AND CO-FOUNDER AT PERFECTO

YORAM MIZRACHI — the Chief Technology Officer and founder of Perfecto — brings wealth of experience in networking, security, and mobile telecommunications. He founded Perfecto after serving as the CTO of Comverse Mobile Data Division. In this capacity, he dealt with a variety of technology challenges in mobile applications, WAP, and location-based services. In 1999 Yoram was the CTO (and founder) of Exalink, which was later acquired by Comverse for $550 million.

Prior to founding Exalink, Mr. Mizrachi held several technology-related positions in the fields of communication and cryptography.

INTRODUCTION

The app is dead, long live the chatbot![1] Yeah, well, not so fast... Bots are nice, but

---

1 Chatbot definition — https://en.wikipedia.org/wiki/Chatbot

have you tried any before betting on them being the new "face" of your brand?

Some experts are arguing that it is impossible to automatically test bots because they are using extremely complex neural network (to achieve intelligence) borrowed directly from Star Trek. Hence, their output is completely unexpected. We shall agree with "unexpected", but for very different reasons. For years, complex testing scenarios have pushed testing to be manual, but Agile practices mandate automation. Bot or not, this should not be an exception.

STATE OF THE "ART"

Whether we are actually talking about an art might be a subjective topic. Read on and decide for yourself. Below you will find some examples which you could try for yourself. Fun is guaranteed.

Open a chat with CNN on Facebook Messenger. Start easy with "What's the weather?" and get a "Here are some weather stories". Hmmm... Not exactly up to some reasonable expectations. Even if you go a bit more into details, as depicted in **Figure 59,** you are getting the same.

Figure 59: CNN Chatbot in Facebook Messenger Promotes News Stories When Asked for Weather

By the way, CNN does offer weather services[2], even in Berlin. However, the bot does not know about it. Perhaps it is not well informed. Try typing in "news in my area". The outcome is captured on the screenshots in **Figure 60.** We hope that this would be quite relevant to a news service such as CNN. If you also get in response something about Dolly Parton and you also share nothing in common with her (at least location-wise), you are definitely not alone.

---

2   CNN Weather services http://edition.cnn.com/weather

Probably this bot is not the sharpest pencil in the artificial intelligence (AI) drawer. Try "What can I ask you to do?". Did you also receive a "Sorry, try again" reply?

Playing super nice and typing what the reply prompted us to type (Who is the bot now?), it actually worked (**Figure 61**).

If you are tired with getting the "news", how about arranging for a nice weekend in London? Let us try another chatbot and use Expedia for that purpose.

So, if you go with "Any good deals for weekend in London?", you will end up with a sorry message. What if you get smart and type "wakka wakka wakka London"? The friendly bot will eventually understand your intentions to travel to London.

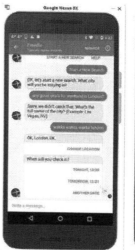

Figure 60: CNN Bot Also Misbehaving about Local News

Figure 61: Playing Nice Makes the Bot Provide Basic Hints on Its Usage

TESTING 101

When it comes to testing, the underlying "product" technology is not that important. Think about what you need to verify. In this regard, the basic question of "What are you actually testing" is the core for anything and should help you test your chatbots in the exactly same way as websites or your mobile apps.

The general requirements towards sane bot implementations could be described in user stories.

For example, as a chatbot user:

1. I want to see that I am getting an answer (any) in a timely manner.

2. I want to see that asking "happy path" questions will result in relevant answers (we will define "relevant" shortly).

3. I (might) want to see that the bot can handle context over several messages. This really depends on the flow of the conversations.

4. I want to see that "bad" (ill-defined from the bot's perspective) questions are getting the right error message.

If you look at the above, this is likely the type of service you would expect from your travel agent. The fact that it is a human and not a super complicated (Star Trek) chatbot is not that important. Let us explore the potential of this assumption.

When calling a travel agent...

1. Any questions would get some kind of a response within a reasonable timeframe (1–2 seconds). This could be "Hey George, what's up?" and getting a "Good, and you?" or "I need a flight plan for next week" in response. "Where are you traveling to this time?" might be an alternative or a follow up question on the other side. This is still a "reply" within a reasonable timeframe.

2. If asked about time for flight to London on next Wednesday, a travel agent would return a "time of day" type of answer.

3. Assuming that one would reply with "I'm traveling next week", a "where to" follow-up question would be received in response.

4. If asking for the airspeed velocity of an unladen swallow, you would presumably get a "what?" type of reply.

A QUICK GUIDE TO THE WAY CHATBOTS WORK

Like all machines in the world (including humans) chatbots are working in 3 steps:

1. Collect information

2. Digest it

3. Reply with an answer and engage end users

COLLECTING THE INFORMATION

This is where most of the magic happens. Instead of working with menu-based applications or structured input, chatbots analyze "free style" sentences – much like human beings do. At first they try to match it to a given intent and then turn the sentence into structured input for a well-defined function.

For example, "I'm flying to San Francisco next weekend" would map to "flight search" intent because of the "flying" word. Next the sentence will be decomposed and mapped to the following:

* Who: this user. "I'm" (meaning user who is engaging the conversation)

* Type of travel: flight. After lemmatization "flying" gets mapped to the verb "fly", so that the noun "flight" is eventually "understood".

* From: your current location (e.g. Boston)

* Destination: San Francisco

* Depart date: Dec 30th. Today is Dec 21st which means that "next weekend" will be Dec 30th.

* Return date: Dec 31st. "Weekend" is assumed to mean a single night.

This is also reflected by the response of the Expedia bot, as visualized in **Figure 62.**

Getting to this kind of "understanding" is not that easy for machines. Internally a whole lot of preprocessing and fuzzy logic is done. Machines need to "sanitize", "normalize", and tag in a language-dependent manner ("part-of-speech tagging") sentences just to to filter out some "irrelevant" words and get to know about others with "special meaning". These could be locations, names of people, i.e. persons, organizations, and many more. These are then bound to each other and meaning is deduced, so that the data structures similar to the above are filled in. Based on missing pieces, bots ask follow-up questions. This said, there is a whole branch in Computer Science — very much related to and utilizing AI — dealing with this kind of problems. It is named Natural Language Processing (NLP).

Now you understand that most chatbots will create a conversation if some of the information required to provide service of value is missing. For example, "I

Figure 62: Searching
for Flights Using the
Expedia Bot

want to fly next weekend" will/ should trigger a follow-up question of "where to". Ideally, its response will provide the missing piece of information.

In some cases, bots could ask questions or respond in a manner which can be learnt over time. For example, given the above question, a follow-up question might be "Are you traveling alone?" to make sure that "I'm" means "exactly one traveler". Bots could create a "short-cut understanding" over time and assume that when "John Smith" says "I'm", what he really means would be "I'm traveling alone to."

Note that once all contextual information is gathered, the next steps are very much similar to submitting a standard form in the web by clicking "Search" or "Submit" buttons.

DIGESTING THE INFORMATION

There is no secret sauce here. As the information is now structured, we are talking about plain old "system of record" type of operation. There is a great chance that it is not even related to the chatbot experience, not at all. Testing wisely, there is no difference in the way processing is done, no matter the engagement type — chatbot, web or mobile app.

ENGAGING END USERS VIA OUTPUT

Depending on the medium and channels used, the output formats vary. If this is an audio only channel (such as Alexa), the system will most likely pre-select the best (according to some logic) option and engage with a confirmation or negotiation phase. For example, "The cheapest option is departing at 16:00 PM with United..." If the output format is visual (such as Facebook Messenger), the rest of the engagement journey may be pretty much similar to the existing web interface. Refer to **Figure 63** to get to know how it works.

Figure 63: Chatbot Engagement Journeys Still Resembling Traditional Channels

CHATBOT TESTING

Going back to the aforementioned requirements. As a chatbot user:

1. I want to see that I am getting an answer (any) in a timely manner.

2. I want to see that asking "happy path" questions will result in relevant answers.

3. I (might) want to see that the bot can handle context over several messages. This really depends on the flow of the conversations.

4. I want to see that "bad" (ill-defined from bot's perspective) questions are getting the right error message.

Let us try to understand what it would take to satisfy them.

VALIDATING "IN A TIMELY MANNER"

Collect several straightforward sentences that require no additional information from the bot, each of them effectively resulting in a distinct pieces of information or actions offered by the service.

For example, let us use "Tommy Hilfiger" bot as a reference and ask a couple of fair questions?

1. "Do you have a store near me?"

2. "What are the opening hours?"

Both questions should result in an answer within a short time period. Automating this is quite easy making sure the "..."on the screenshot in **Figure 64** disappears after X seconds (likely 2–3). Note that this test does not check the content itself, just the response time. As always, the key question for testing is "What are you

Figure 64: Unexpected Delays in Answering Due to Unknown User Input (Tommy Hilfiger Chat Bot)

testing?" Make sure you do not mix two (or more) answers, i.e. intentions and validations, into a single test.

Specifically (at the time of writing this chapter), Tommy answered the first question within 2 seconds and it took "him" about 30 seconds to answer the second question.

HAPPY PATH VALIDATIONS

Bots are trained to handle intents. The more intents are defined by the bot, the more natural the conversation with it will be. For example, CNN might deliver weather forecast as a service, but unless there is a bot intent mapped to "what's the weather", you will be likely to receive the wrong answers, as the analysis will fall into another defined intent — an incorrect one. In the example above, the "news on topic" intent handled the "what's the weather" question which made the bot looks a bit dumb.

Switching to "The Weather Channel"[3] and typing "01803" should result in "Ok, Burlington, MA".

Typing "Just check weather" should result in the actual weather for "Burlington, MA".

If the accuracy of the result needs to be validated, one could navigate to the weather web site, type "01803" and get comparable results.

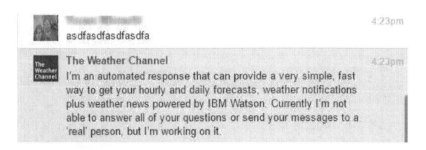

Figure 65: Typing Gibberish Should Trigger Adequate and Timely Reactions in Chatbots

---

3   Weather channel — www.weather.com

Normally, intents in bots are just another method to get the information which could be obtained through other channels, such as web, or mobile apps, or even direct API to backend servers.

BAD QUESTIONS

Theoretically speaking, there are no bad questions to bots, since they all lead to a conversation. Thus, all inputs are valid. Obviously, if you type gibberish (like in the example in **Figure 65**), you will get some kind of an error message. Seasoned test engineers know that obvious behavior needs to be constantly questioned and validated. Some bots might wait for too long while trying to decide which intent should handle the junk.

INTENT CONFLICTS

All of the above testing can easily be automated for almost all types of bot channels, such as Facebook, Slack, and even Alexa (given your testing lab can handle audio in/ out). They all answer the basic requirements of the automated testing paradigm, namely — "Given a known input, I'm expecting a specific output repeatedly." If anything, since the engagement type is narrow and well-defined (input is always the same field, output is the last message), implementing automation tests for bots can be extremely easy and the script can look more or less like a conversation.

When designing tests for intents, you should consider what the sentences for triggering each intent would be. The more intents a chatbot has, the more the chances of intent conflicts there are, meaning the engine deciding which intent should handle the request will decide on the wrong one. This is where automation is a must have. Projects with dozens or even hundreds of intents, each with few possible matching sentences, are quite common. Consider a data-driven approach for guaranteeing "sanity." It would include all intents, each with few activating sentences, and a "happy path" result. This should probably be executed at the build level, as changes are inserted into your bot project. API level testing will likely be easier.

SUMMARY

Chatbots might rely on complex algorithms but when it comes to testing, they should be treated much like any other testing project exploring end user engagement channels. In addition, bot projects should add automated testing to them from day one.

Like other engagement types, combinations between API level and functional UI testing are important for the overall user experience validation. That said, we are pretty much ready to bring the quality of bots to the next level by harnessing the power of existing tools and frameworks for testing mobile, web, and service API. All it takes is asking the right questions and adhering to the functional and non-functional requirements, as we did above.

12 Robust Mobile Test Automation Using Smart Object Identification

THIS CHAPTER WAS CONTRIBUTED BY UZI EILON, CHIEF TECHNOLOGY OFFICER (US) AT PERFECTO

UZI EILON is the Chief Technology Officer (US) at Perfecto. He joined Perfecto in 2010 after a fifteen-year career as a software developer and manager at IDF, Netrialty, Comverse, and SanDisk. Over the past seven years, Uzi has grown the company by managing expanding R&D teams and leading Sales Engineering teams. His fields of expertise includes mobile application testing, automation tools, defining customer projects, and on-boarding, plus bringing Agile methodologies into the equation. Uzi Eilon speaks regularly on behalf of Perfecto at events, such as AnDevCon, StarWest, HP Discover, and ongoing technical webinars.

INTRODUCTION

It is clear that getting native objects identified properly as part of the test automation process is key to successful continuous test automation. Selenium allows test automation engineers to identify objects[1] by 7 different locators such as XPATH, CSS, ID, Text, Class, etc.

Within this chapter, we will go through some of them and we will introduce a brand new tool[2] that could help you improve the reliability of object identification in Selenium tests. The tool was developed and open-sourced by the Office of the CTO at Perfecto. Think about it as an object analysis grader where the highest score would mean that the test engineer found/identified the best-matched object name to be used in the test code. It also provides valuable recommendations on how the corresponding expressions could be improved in a way that they would identify objects well across different platforms.

OBJECT ID AND AUTOMATION

Getting the most accurate object as part of any automation test code delivers several key benefits, such as:

- Test code that is easy to author and debug
- Highly maintainable test code which is more resilient to changes in the app under test
- Reusable automated tests across different versions of the app under test
- Cross-platform automated solutions (mobile and desktop web) can be built
- Reduce false-negative errors

Stable test code is not the only prerequisite for a continuously working automation. It is also a matter of a well-defined process and collaboration between the various teams. Before diving into the technical talk about XPath, it will be worth it to discuss a process used successfully by agile devOps teams. It will help testers write better automation code that can be easily integrated in the

---

1 Selenium object locators — http://www.testinginterviewquestion.com/p/object-identification-in-selenium.html

2 XPath Validator tool — http://xpathvalidator.projectquantum.io/

early stages of CI workflows.

Both mobile and web developers will typically define the identifiers of UI objects as part of their application code.

In a mobile web/ HTML app, it will be through adding the ID attribute to HTML elements, as also depicted in **Figure 66.**

```
<input type="text" placeholder="ZIP Code" maxlength="5"
id="zip" name="zip">
```

Figure 66: An Example of a HTML Text Field That Could Be Located By Its ID

In a native mobile app, it would be through adding the ID to the UI control object (Android and iOS), as one can observe in **Figure 67** and **Figure 68.**

```
<TextViewandroid:textAppearance="?android:attr/textAppear-
anceMedium"
    android:text="My ip"
    android:id="@+id/my_ip"
    android:layout_alignStart="@+id/btn_cam"
    android:layout_marginTop="35dp"
    android:layout_below="@+id/mimageView" />
```

Figure 67: An Example of Defining Text Field That Could be Located by ID in an Android App

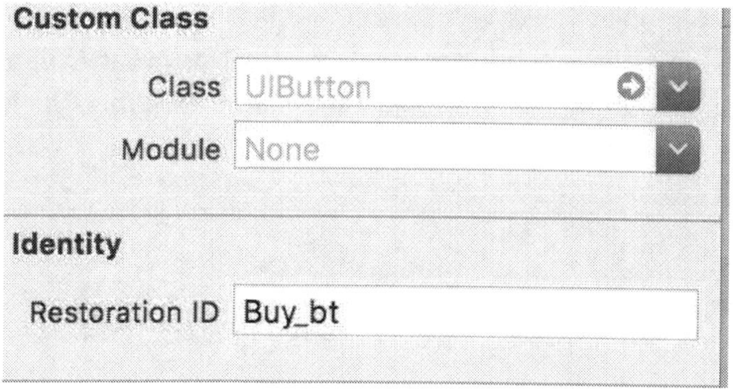

Custom Class		
Class	UIButton	
Module	None	
Identity		
Restoration ID	Buy_bt	

Figure 68: An Example of Defining UI Control That Could be Located by ID in an iOS App

At the beginning of each sprint, both **developers and testers** would define the UI objects together (including the corresponding objects IDs) and create a joint repository that will be used once by the developers while writing the code and, later on, by test engineers during the test automation development.

Both the code and the tests will be committed together into the main source code management system (SCM) and will be executed as part of the CI cycle.

The process of defining the objects jointly by developers and testers is critical for writing robust automation code. In addition, this process helps developers understand the testing requirements and code with testing in mind which is clearly a win-win situation for the entire mobile team.

XPATH IN A NUTSHELL

The process described above requires developers and test engineers to work together. Unfortunately, in many projects this is not the case and testers usually receive the app under test without any metadata about UI objects, i.e., their IDs are not defined. This is where XPath locators come in handy.

XPath is a syntax of defining parts of an XML objects tree. In Selenium and Appium tests, the structure of the displayed page/screen is described by a hierarchy which is accessed as an XML document in memory. For automation purposes, XPath expressions can be defined and run against this document object in order to locate specific UI objects (often represented as sub-trees in the corresponding XML object trees). Selenium and Appium make object identification through XPath expressions very easy, so you will not need to deal with any in-memory representations of XML object trees. However, this is how it works under the hood and this is why XPath is a relevant tool for all mobile test automation engineers.

XPath structure:

```
//object_type_n1/ object_type_n2[@attribute =value … ]
```

XPath expressions can be very powerful object locators. Table 2 lists three typical examples of identifying certain HTML UI elements (objects) in web pages rendered by web browsers.

Xpath Expression	Definition
//button[@type='submit']	Matches any button element of type "submit"
//input[@name='zip']	Matches any input element named "zip"
//div[@dir='ltr'] /input	Matches any input field element within a div with an attribute "dir", which has a value of "ltr"

Table 2: Sample XPath Expressions Used in Web Apps

The ability to locate any given UI object in the tree model is invaluable. However, sometimes test automation engineers fail to recognize the true beauty of XPath, that is, its impressive set of built-in functions. This way, test engineers can make their automated test solutions much more robust and even smarter.

This said, XPath supports functions for working with:

* Strings[3]: e.g. **start_with, contains,** and many more.
* Direction[4]: e.g. **following, preceding,** etc.
* Standard conditional operators[5], such as **and, or,** and others.

XPath and Automation

As described earlier, XPath has been used by automation frameworks such as Selenium and Appium as a means to identify the UI objects of web apps (DOM), native mobile app (Object trees), and hybrid mobile apps (objects tree containing DOM). DOM stands for Document Object Model and every web page has its own instance of it created by web browsers when pages are loaded.

XPATH WARS — WELL DEFINED VS. POORLY DEFINED EXPRESSIONS

Let us start with a practical definition of well and poorly defined XPath expressions by using the web and mobile apps for Bank of America.

Figure 69 shows the login area of the website bankofamerica.com.

---

3   String functions — http://www.w3schools.com/xml/xpath_operators.asp

4   Direction functions — http://www.w3schools.com/xml/xpath_operators.asp

5   Xpath operators — http://www.w3schools.com/xml/xpath_operators.asp

Figure 69: The Sign-in Area of the Bank of America Website

An excerpt from the corresponding DOM can be found in **Figure 70.** Note the marked password field.

Figure 70: The Input Text Field for the Password in the DOM

We mentioned earlier that XPath expressions can be an extremely powerful weapon for identifying every single UI object on the screen in both web and mobile apps. However, XPath locators could be also used to shoot yourself in the leg.

That said, let us get back to our example above. If you go through the list in **Table 3,** you will find out that there are at least eight different XPath expressions matching the **passcode field.** Do you already get it? All of them will work and match our query. However, some of them would prove to be poor decisions during the evolution of the app. They would need to be modified too often and would bring inefficiencies in the maintenance of the automated test solution.

1	//*[@id='passcode1']
2	.//*[text()="Passcode"]
3	//input[@name="passcode1"]
4	//body/div[4]/div[2]/div[1]/div[1]/div[6]/div[1]/form/div[2]/input
5	//form[@id="idForm"]/div[2]/input
6	//form[@id="idForm"]/descendant::input[2]
7	(//input)[25]
8	(//input[@type!='hidden'])[4]

Table 3: Eight XPath Expressions Matching The Password Field in the Login Area

So, now the challenge would be to assess and evaluate each and every one of them in order to filter out the ones which would bring more damage than value. Let us digest the list and briefly discuss the options.

XPath expressions #1 and #3 are the ones mostly recommended to use. They both use a stable attribute ("ID" or "name") to identify the field. Its value will be the same across all platforms or versions of the app. In addition, **XPath expression #3** also specifies the type of the UI element (**"input"**), which increases the accuracy of the expression looking up one specific object.

XPath expression #2 may look like a good candidate, but the text value can be changed and the XPath will stop working as it used to. **Figure 71** illustrates how easy it is to break this one. Once a password is entered by an end user/automated test script, the value of the field would be already changed to many dots.

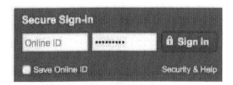

Figure 71: Normal App Interactions Breaking Poorly Authored XPath Locators

XPath expression #4 is based on absolute path which is very hard to maintain and very fragile. Any change in the page will break this XPath. Therefore, automation engineers should never use this type of XPath expression.

XPath expression #5 relies on identifying the *form* object which contains the creational fields. In this regard, it is better than expression #4, but it will not work as expected when the form is changed.

Xpath expression #6 is an interesting one. It looks up the parent object (in this case the "form") by its "ID" because it is defined and known. From there on, the built-in XPath function *"descendant"* is used to get access to the child elements filtered by their type ("input"). Of course, this is precisely the list of text fields representing the username and the passcode. XPath provides access by index to the elements in such lists. This way, the "passcode" text field is picked as the second element in the list. When you have no ID or good attribute to identify your object, try to make use of its "relatives" as stable anchors to locate your object in a more reliable way.

XPath expression #7 pinpoints the input field in the list of "input" objects on the whole page, while **XPath expression #8** does almost the same in a very cryptic manner. It looks for the fourth hidden "input" element available on the page. Both of them will not work if a new text field is added. In addition, #8 is also vulnerable to scrolling in the web browser.

Good	Medium	Never use
Expressions #1 and #3 stand out for their robustness. You should ideally use similar XPath expressions when automating test scenarios.	Expressions #5 and #6 identify the first parent with ID and as a next step select the needed "object". Expression #6 is more robust than expression #5.	Expression #2 will not work in any scenario when the value of the field is changed. Expression #4 will constantly give you hard times because it is based on a full path expression. Expression #7 will be broken many times when text fields are added or removed to the page. Expression #8 is a last resort.

Table 4: A Summary of the Analysis of XPath Expressions

ASSESSING GOOD AND POOR XPATH EXPRESSIONS IN THE SMART WAY

There are rules that can be used to differentiate between well- and poorly-defined XPath expressions. To help you test your XPath expressions, the Office of the CTO at Perfecto built a web tool that checks the quality of any XPath expressions passed through it. It conducts static analysis of the expressions so that the Object trees/DOM are not needed, i.e. it pretty much does what we have covered in our comparison of XPath expressions above.

The tool takes into account certain rules and heuristics in order to analyze XPath expressions and assess their quality. You can find some of them below.

* Does the XPath expression contain attributed definitions and, if yes, which ones?

* What is the length of the expression and how many indexes [n] does it contain? XPath expressions with large number of indexes are weak and can be easily broken across versions and platforms.

* How many tree levels ("/") does an expression contain? Too many levels may indicate "full-path" type of expression.

* How strong is the selected identifier (ID)? For example, in the case of mobile apps, some automation tools generate automatic IDs and name them after numbers that get changed with every build run. This makes certain XPath expressions relying on specific values of identifiers very weak.

* The quality of the XPath expressions is decreased when many words or too many XPath operators are used to get to an object identifier. Complex XPath locators could become troublesome across different platforms and lead to different (and often) unexpected results.

* The number of special characters has an effect on the quality of XPath expressions. In many cases, an excessive number of such symbols indicates that the identifier is generated automatically. Of course, this also means that the corresponding value will most likely be changed with the very next build. For example, the following xpath (//span[@id="ext-element-140"]) [1] contains a couple of minus (-) symbols which should make automation engineers think twice before using it.

The tool analyzes XPath expressions and generates a quality score. It also highlights any detected issues. This tool is built based on knowledge collected from customers' test automation results. It is the result of analyzing the success rate of thousands of different XPath expressions over time in the context of different versions, platforms, and executions.

Let us quickly illustrate the value of the tool by analysing one of the XPath expressions that we used for the sake of understanding well designed and poorly designed expressions. The result has been displayed in **Figure 72.**

Figure 72: Quality Analysis of a Poorly Written XPath Expression

As you can see, there are four critical issues discovered. Each of them is described and the general score of the expression is by no means impressive.

If we do the same and pass one of the expressions that we assessed as a "good" one, the tool confirms our understanding of XPath, as evident in **Figure 73.**

Figure 73: Quality Analysis of a Well Written XPath Expression

XPATH FOR MOBILE TEST AUTOMATION

The XPath expressions used for the sake of automating tests for mobile apps are a bit different from the ones used to look up objects in the DOM in web browsers. This certainly affects the way automation scripts are implemented.

Let us demonstrate these differences through a practical example, so that they may be more easily understood. This time, we will give the mobile app of United a spin. We will search for a flight. There is a ready-made, behavior-driven test illustrated in **Figure 74.**

```
@united @search_flight
Given I start application by name "united"
Then  I enter "91" to "Sreach_flight_field"
Then  I click on "Search_BT"
Then  I validate results
```

Figure 74: Behavior-driven Scenario for Searching a Flight in United

Right now, you can safely disregard the validation step. We will get back to this topic later in this chapter. Other than that, the flow is the same for both iOS and Android devices. Even the UI of the corresponding apps looks the same, as also confirmed in **Figure 75.** However, the two object trees are different and consequently the XPath locators used to identify UI objects will differ.

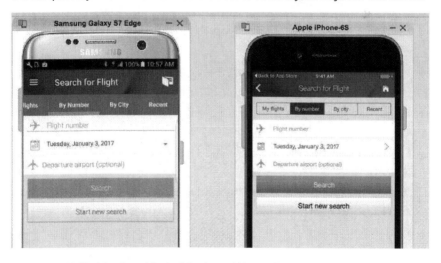

Figure 75: Unified Look-and-feel of the App of United for Both Android and iOS

Objects in Android are identified by ID, while in iOS they are not. The iOS objects contain few attributes.

The difficult part for automation engineers is to write and maintain one test script (and with the same flow) with different locators used for object identification across platforms.

There are two ways to address such a challenge:

* Build two external object repository files (one for iOS and one for Android) and provide them as parameters to the test script.

* Find common XPath expressions for both iOS and Android by using advanced functions like "contains" and **"starts-with"**. You could also make use of logical operators (*"AND", "OR"*) to enhance the lookup logic in terms of platform adaptability.

Keep in mind that the differences are substantial, as depicted in **Table 5.**

Object	Android	IOS
search_field	//*[@resource-id="com. united.mobile.android:id/ flightNumber"]	//*[@value="Flight number"]
Search_BT	//*[@resource-id="com. united.mobile.android:id/ searchButton"]	//*[@label="Search"]

Table 5: XPath Locators for Android and iOS — Comparison

That said, it will pay off to list the major differences between the models of the object trees in iOS and Android. The implications to the respective XPath expressions will become clear as well.

* Android objects contain a unique identifier ("ID"), while the corresponding UI elements in iOS do not.

* The names of the types of UI objects have absolutely nothing in common. Take, as an example, text fields. In iOS they are instances of the *"UIATextField"* class, while in Android they would be instances of *"android.widget.EditText"*.

* Each type of UI object has a different set of attributes that can be queried.

* The hierarchy of composing UI objects, i.e. the object trees, have different structures.

In order to explore how both approaches work for United's app, let us try to come up with an XPath locator that is able to look up objects on both platforms. It is much better to work a bit more on a smarter query than parameterizing the whole scenario, isn't it?

At first, we need to figure out how to look up the "Search" button. The only common attribute between the iOS and Android apps turns out to be the label/text of the corresponding buttons. The label cannot be changed by end users as it is static for the corresponding resources. Thus, the only expression which works has been illustrated in **Figure 76.**

```
//*[@text="Search" or @label="Search"]
```

Figure 76: The XPath Locator for Looking Up the "Search" Button for Android and iOS

There are at least a couple of limitations relevant to this locator. If the app supports different languages, the expression will not work in languages different from English. The query is too generic and it basically describes any object labeled "Search". What would happen if a text field with this placeholder (i.e. search bar) would be introduced? That is right, there is no guarantee whatsoever that the button would be returned and not the text field.

If we quickly do the same exercise in order to identify the field where the flight number needs to be entered, we get the results shared in **Figure 77.**

```
//*[@value="Flight number" or @text="Flight number"]
```

Figure 77: XPath Query Looking Up the Field for Flight Numbers in the App of United

The aforementioned issues are applicable to this expression as well. Even worse, the value of this field is modifiable by end users, so when they enter a flight number, our expression will be unable to locate anything.

These expressions look good, but they are not stable and can be quite restrictive. In this particular case, we cannot not find good XPath locators which work flawlessly on both platforms. Therefore, we need to figure out different expressions that will bring better results when run against the corresponding platform-specific objects tree.

Let us start with Android. The first rule in UI automation is: if there is an ID, use it. The resulting expressions are listed below.

Flight number:

//*[@resource-id="com.united.mobile.android:id/flightNumber"]

Search button:

//*[@resource-id="com.united.mobile.android:id/searchButton"]

When it comes to iOS, the solution will be a bit more complicated. As you probably remember, there is no notion of strictly defined object IDs in iOS. There is a convention of using the accessibility label of UI elements as an object ID, but this is totally optional. Some development organizations do not become aware of it until it is too late. That said, the resulting expressions for iOS could be found below.

Flight number:

(//UIATextField)[1]

The concrete screen of the United app contains only one text field and the only attribute that could be used for automation purposes is its value. However, we have already discussed the downsides. This attribute turned out to be useless in terms of object identification. Therefore, it would be safer to fall back to the index of the text field in the corresponding list in the objects tree.

Search button:

//UIAButton[@label="Search"]

This is a good example of having the chance to benefit from the accessibility label of the field which was pre-set during the development of the app. It is stable and cannot be changed by end users. The type of the UI element is also clear, which makes it impossible for the underlying XPath implementation to look up and pick an incorrect element in the hierarchy.

In this example, we could not find a good common base for aligning the object identification for our automated solution on iOS and Android. The best implementation will rely on different expressions for object identification. They could be injected as a parameter in the script describing the flow of the scenario. There is a good chance that your automation framework already supports this automation use case. If not, you could implement it on your own.

For example, the open-source framework Quantum supports parameterization of object identifiers, as illustrated in **Figure 78.** In the testNG example, you can see how to pass the parameter **env.resources,** which points to different objects.

```
<test name="Web Scenarios Android Test" enabled="true" thread-count="10">
<parameter name="driver.capabilities.model" value="Galaxy.*"></parameter>
<parameter name="env.resources" value="src/main/resources/android"></parameter>
<classes>
    <class
        name="com.qmetry.qaf.automation.step.client.gherkin.GherkinScenarioFactory" />
</classes>
</test>
<test name="A1" enabled="true" thread-count="10">
<parameter name="driver.capabilities.model" value="iPhone-6 Plus.*"></parameter>
<parameter name="env.resources" value="src/main/resources/ios"></parameter>
<classes>
    <class
        name="com.qmetry.qaf.automation.step.client.gherkin.GherkinScenarioFactory" />
</classes>
</test>
```

Figure 78: Quantum and TestNG Descriptor Featuring Parameterization of Object Identifiers

Note that the parameter named "env.resources" is defined twice in the scenario definition descriptor. This way, different XPath expressions could be injected and used in a test script, while the automated user flow would stay the same.

XPATH FOR VALIDATION PURPOSES

As part of a test script, we would typically like to validate certain requirements by analyzing and asserting the intermediate results of different interactions. Unlike flow objects, validation objects are more complicated to define, because:

* User interactions may have more than one valid and acceptable result.

* Results can vary between different executions.

▪ Most of the time the elements do not have an ID defined.

If we continue with our flight search scenario, after entering the flight number and pressing the "Search" button, the script will need to validate the results. However, most of the results can change over time and different executions. Flights tend to be delayed all the time, so:

▪ Flight status may be "On Schedule" or "Delayed".

▪ Time, dates, and gates may be different during different executions.

This is also depicted in **Figure 79.**

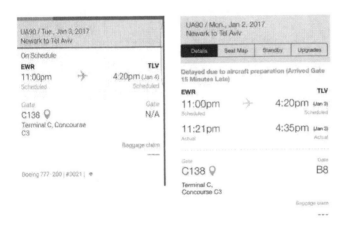

Figure 79: Different and Dynamic Results Between Different Scenario Executions

There are means for automation engineers to introspect the object trees of apps while running on different platforms. Using basic tooling, one can reach the right conclusions about how a certain UI object could be looked up. You can pinpoint the flight status field during such introspection, as also illustrated in **Figure 80.**

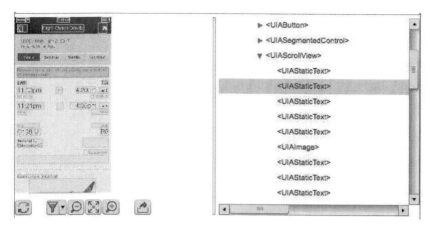

Figure 80: Introspecting the Objects Tree of the iOS Version of the United App

Thus, one will learn that the status field is the second instance of *"UIATextField"* within a concrete "UIAScrollView".

There are a few ways to validate the results after interacting with these fields. They have been explained and discussed in more detail below.

Option #1

Identify the element with the expected string or strings. If it is not found, catch the exception and raise an error, as also done in the code snippet in **Figure 81.**

```
@Test
public void checkFlightsStatus()
{
    String xpath = "//UIAStaticText[contains(@value,\'Delayed\') or @value=\'On Time\']";
    try {
        getDriver().findElement(By.xpath(xpath));
    } catch (NoSuchElementException e) {
        // Raise an error
    }
}
```

Figure 81: Raising an Exception When an Element Is Not Found

Option #2

Get all the elements by calling the method "findElements" of the Selenium/ Appium driver instance. If iterated upon and checked, the results can be verified and an error can be raised when an unexpected value is found. Such an approach has been illustrated in **Figure 82.**

```
@Test
public void checkFlightStatusLoop()
{
    String xpath = "//UIAStaticText";
    List<WebElement> elements = getDriver().findEleme
    nets(By.xpath(xpath));
    Boolean found = false;
    for (WebElement element : elements) {
        if (element.getText().equals("Delayed")) ||
            element.getText().equals("On Time")
        {
            found = true;
        }
        if (!found) {
            // raise an error
        }
    }
}
```

Figure 82: Iterating over Text Fields on Screen to Validate Flight Status

Option #3

A third option would be to use automation tools supporting means of visual validation. In this case, you will not need XPath expressions at all.

If it is not possible to use a visual validation tool, Option #1, described above, is superior, because:

- The validation done by the XPath expression and the Java code is very simple and easy to understand.

- It is easier to maintain, since only the XPath locator would need to be modified, in cases of UI changes.

- The script queries the relevant field and not all the elements on the screen. This is how execution time is reduced, while the accuracy of the interaction results is increased.

SUMMARY

To wrap up and summarize this chapter, we have prepared a list of industry-proven good practices that you can find below.

- Use an ID whenever you can.

- Build processes inspiring the collaboration between developers and automation engineers at a very early stage during the creation of scripts.

- If your objects do not contain IDs, but the objects' parents or siblings have such, use them as anchors in conjunction with built-in XPath functions, such as:

  - "following-sibling"

  - "parent"

  - "descendant"

- Use automation frameworks that support external object repositories. Add and maintain all of your XPath locators within a set of external resource files (refer to **Figure 83** as an example) that can be injected within test scenarios depending on the context/ platform.

```
# search
search=xpath=//*[@id="search"]
searchClear=xpath=//*[@id='searchReset'] [1]
searchGo=xpath=//*[@id='searchReset'] [2]


#item managment
details =xpath=(//*[contains(text(),'view details')]) [1]
add_to_list =xpath=(//*[contains(text(),'add to registry/list')]) [1]
add_to_cart =xpath=(//*[contains(text(),'add to cart')]) [1]
approve_to_cart =xpath=(//*[contains(text(),'add to cart')]) [2]
view_cart=xpath=(//*[contains(text(),'view cart & check out')]) [2]


 ## log in page
user =id=logonIdMain
password=id=logonPasswordMain
SignInBT=id=signin-btn
# can be login or account (if already logged in)
firstLogInElement=xpath=(.//*[@id='rightNavigation']//following-sibling::a) [1]
```

Figure 83: An Example Object Repository

- For **mobile** app/web, add the object repository as **parameter** to the script to execute one test/flow on all platform (iOS, Android, web).

- Try to add the **validations** to the XPath expression, build XPATH with the expected results, and look for the element as part of the script.

- For mobile apps, try your XPath expressions on all platforms. For responsive web, try it on three different screen sizes (desktop, tablet, and phone) before you commit your tests in the source control system.

- Try to limit expressions to a depth of two levels. For example, //o1/o2/o3 is not a good XPath.

- If an XPath locator contains more than one index id [n] and n > 1, the XPath is not strong enough and can change between different versions of the app under test or platforms.

If your XPath expressions still look like this, please re-read this chapter again:

```
//body/div[4]/div[2]/div[1]/div[1]/div[6]/div[1]/form/
div[2]/input
```

13 Complementing Mobile UI Functional Testing with API Testing

THIS CHAPTER WAS CONTRIBUTED BY LIOR KINSBRUNER, TEST AUTOMATION MANAGER

LIOR KINSBRUNER brings more than 17 years of experience in the QA area. He has held several roles and experienced various technologies. Lior has been leading and managing testing teams for web and data mining applications and client-server systems consisting of both software and hardware units. Mr. Kinsbruner has vast technology expertise in .NET, Java, SQL and Oracle-optimized queries, QA and QA-automation, XML, HTML, JavaScript as well, shell scripting

using Python and Perl are among his core competencies. Lior holds a "black belt" in leading test frameworks, including Selenium, JSystem, UFT, Appium, and many more.

INTRODUCTION

As mobile application automation becomes more and more complex and expensive, Return on Investment (ROI) becomes a factor to consider before any automation effort. Since most logic and functionality lies in the back-end and within the in-use APIs, it makes sense to cover as much functionality as possible via API testing, thus allocating less time and effort to UI tests.

Within this chapter, you will get to know what API testing is all about and how you can perform and automate it in the right way.

Note that this approach does not replace the need for UI testing. It is just a better alternative in terms of test coverage. UI testing must be still performed to eliminate all types of UI related bugs and failures.

For some teams, it might take time within the development cycle to get access to specific API that needs to be used for testing. In other cases, there might be missing API endpoints, i.e. ones that were not exposed yet. A working solution is the notion of MOCK API.[1] These APIs can mock the pre-developed or missing ones and "cover" for them until they get implemented and used. Obviously, there are other challenges related to the robustness of API[2], their flakiness having an impact on dependent teams. These are truly interesting challenges, but they will go way beyond our current scope.

API AND MOBILE-RELATED API USAGES IN A NUTSHELL

An application programming interface, or API[3], is referred to as the set of routines, protocols, and tools necessary for building software applications. An API specifies how software components should interact. It is a set of clearly defined methods for communication between various software components.

COMMON APPROACHES TO API TESTING

When talking about API testing, we actually refer to the testing effort dedicated to measuring and verifying the correctness "under the hood" (from the perspective of UI). This kind of testing is more focused on testing functionality rather than app behavior or user experience. Some might even argue that API automation testing is much more valuable than UI testing in terms of ROI, since API is much

---

1   Mock Rest API's — https://jsonplaceholder.typicode.com/

2   Web API's Fragility — http://www.st.ewi.tudelft.nl/~zaidman/publications/espinhaMobileSoft2015.pdf

3   API definition — https://en.wikipedia.org/wiki/Application_programming_interface

more stable than the UI, which changes rather quickly.

So, where should you start from? There are three principal strategies for different types of API testing. Below you will find more about each one of them.

1. **Input argument values** focuses on all types of values and their boundaries to validate that specific API endpoints can handle both expected and unexpected input values in a sane manner.

2. **Error validation** has a strong emphasis on exception handling, verification of proper error codes, and such kinds of corner validations related to the robustness of the tested endpoint in terms of correct and reliable error handling.

3. **Scenario testing** requires performing end-to-end flows, similar to real-life business cases.

API TEST DESIGN OBJECTIVES

Independent of the testing strategy, API tests require certain execution phases to be considered and implemented, so that the test solution will be able to scale well and continuously bring value. The most common test design objectives are listed below.

1. **Setup** requires the ability to initialize the System Under Test (SUT), create necessary objects, start up services, etc.

2. **Execution** is all about running the relevant test scenarios.

3. **Verification** and evaluation of test results is a "must-have" requirement.

4. **Reporting** for passing/failing/blocked types of test results needs to be provided.

5. **Cleanup** is essential in terms of bringing the SUT back to its initial state for subsequent testing activities.

Keep in mind that these are the basic design objectives that you need to take into account. Complex automation tasks could add up in specific phases. Make sure to take care of the listed ones with the highest priority. Then you will have the foundation to enhance the design further.

THREE-TIER ARCHITECTURE OF MOBILE APPLICATIONS

From the perspective of software architects, mobile apps usually make use of the Three-Tier system architecture. Each layer, as well as its technical meaning, is shortly discussed below.

1. **Data Tier** represents the storage behind-the-scenes used by web sites and mobile apps to manage data. This could be a single database instance or a whole technology landscape with immense complexity. It all depends on the concrete technical needs.

2. **Logical Tier** is the "brain" of the app. It is in charge of processing incoming commands from different clients (e.g. native mobile apps and websites), making logical decisions in the meantime. It is also responsible for returning an unambiguous and easy to interpret response to clients. Therefore, this layer is sometimes also referred as to the "Business Logic" one.

3. **Presentation Tier (UI)** contains the components that implement and display the user interface. This layer includes controls for gathering user input, displaying information, organizing and managing user interaction.

VERY BRIEF INTRODUCTION TO REST API

In the context of Mobile apps, the application under test will most likely communicate with the BE (backend) API through standard protocols. For example, the combination of REST over HTTP, which uses JSON or XML as data formats, is pretty common. Those APIs may be proprietary to the respective organization or provided by 3rd party vendors, as illustrated by **Figure 84.** Some prominent examples of the latter would be Google Maps, Twitter, Weather services, and many, many more.

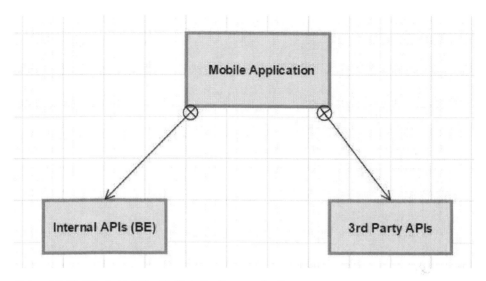

Figure 84: Mobile Apps API — Options for Communication

When referring to REST API (one that will be used in the following examples), we usually refer to the usage of the following methods over identifiable "resources":

- **POST** — Creates a new data element
- **GET** — Reads a data element
- **PUT** — Updates a data element
- **DELETE** — Deletes a data element

TOOLS TO HELP YOU AUTOMATE REST API TESTS

Now that the general concept behind the term REST API is more or less clear, one needs to pick the right tools for automation. Fortunately, there are a plethora of handy tools which turn out to be invaluable during development phases. Discussing all of them would be out of scope for the current chapter. A list of the most widely used ones that are either free or open-source could be found below.

> **1. JSON Schema Generator**[4] — used to generate an expected SCHEMA files (*.jsonschema) which will serve as the baseline for validating the structure

---

4   JSON Schema Generator — http://jsonschema.net/#/

of the body of concrete HTTP responses.

2. **XML Schema Generator**[5] — used to generate a set of expected XML SCHE-MA files (XSD) which will serve as the baseline for validating API responses.

3. **Postman**[6] — this tool is useful during development phases to learn and examine the API under test. Automation engineers need to learn the supported functionality of specific API endpoints prior to implementing the automation code that would send requests and validate the consequent responses.

4. **REST-assured**[7] — simplifies the automation of REST-Based API testing. Development is done in the Java programming language.

The code snippets in **Figure 85** demonstrate how REST-assured could help automation engineers to quickly shoot API calls and assert their responses. An example response for the input value of "5" is also provided. Going through it, one can easily deduce its basic structure. From there on, REST-assured makes it very intuitive to send the request and validate the response.

```
{
    "lotto":{
        "lottoId":5,
        "winning-numbers":[2,45,34,23,7,5,3],
        "winners":[
            {
                "winnerId":23,
                "numbers":[2,45,34,23,3,5]
            },
            {
                "winnerId":54,
                "numbers":[52,3,12,11,18,22]
            }
        ]
    }
}
```

You can easily use REST Assured to validate interesting things from response:

```
@Test public void
lotto_resource_returns_200_with_expected_id_and_winners() {
    when().
            get("/lotto/{id}", 5).
    then().
            statusCode(200).
            body("lotto.lottoId", equalTo(5),
                 "lotto.winners.winnerId", containsOnly(23, 54));
}
```

Figure 85: An Example of Using REST Assured for Testing API

---

5   XML Schema Generator — http://www.freeformatter.com/xsd-generator.html#ad-output

6   Postman — https://www.getpostman.com/docs/install_native

7   REST-ssured — http://rest-assured.io/

The provided source code clearly reads like this:

1. Execute a GET query against the "/lotto" resource and bind the value of "5" as the parameter "id."

2. Assert that the HTTP status code has the value of "200", which means that the resource identified by the "/lotto/5" relative URL exists.

3. Continue with verifying the correctness of the payload of the received HTTP response and its structure, i.e. the JSON object representing the response message.

You can get the hang of it by playing with existing REST API resources. There are many public API services out there. They can be examined, tested against, and automated for the sake of learning free of charge.

BEST PRACTICES FOR AUTOMATING MOBILE API WORKFLOWS

Service APIs can be quite complex. Unless you feel adventurous, you are better off learning from the experience and pain of others. In order to quickly provide a good testing solution, automation engineers are strongly recommended to take into consideration the best practices shared below prior to any coding activities. In many cases, this will save many hours, tears, and frustrating trial-and-error sessions.

Below, you will find a structured approach for introducing continuous API testing as a practice from scratch. Following the steps, one will be able to add automated REST API tests to continuous integration (CI) cycles.

PRODUCT REQUIREMENTS DOCUMENT (PRD)

Request and get a well-defined Product Requirement Document (PRD) from development teams. It should describe the API in terms of the points below.

Supported data formats (XML/ JSON/ both)

Each API endpoint should have its supported formats documented. Unsupported formats are expected to be handled gracefully and to generate self-explanatory error messages.

Base URL structure

A sample base URL should be provided, so that the base address for all API resources and endpoints is clear. If some endpoints are able to receive and process parameters, this should also be described as well as the supported URL formats. The following information needs to be present for each API resource:

- **Supported HTTP "Verbs"**, where an example of a combination could be:

  1. POST
  2. GET
  3. PUT
  4. DELETE
  5. HEAD

- **Example of requests** with some sample parameters (if applicable), so it will be clear what calls to the API should look like.

- **Example of responses** in the supported formats (e.g. XML, JSON), so it will be clear how responses should look like in terms of structure and values.

Request Parameters

The type and constraints applicable to every request parameter need to be described. You can find a couple of examples below.

- **Data Type** could be "Integer", "String", "Date Time", any supported date format, etc.

- **Mandatory ("Yes"/ "No")** — if a mandatory parameter is omitted as part of a request to API, an error should be raised. Empty values should be handled adequately when working with optional parameters.

HTTP Status Codes

Every API call has a response that carries a HTTP code for status with special meaning. There are many categories of status codes. Errors (4**XX**-based errors, **5XX**-based errors, etc.) and valid responses (e.g. **2XX**) should be defined and strictly governed by developers. Keep in mind that it is not uncommon for status codes to be mistaken in apps. For example, when authentication fails, a 5XX code might happen to be used instead of 4XX. You should be careful about such situations and thoroughly verify the correctness of the returned codes. If this is not done, clients may either fail to deliver a flawless user experience or adapt and start relying on bugs in order to mitigate such situations. Of course, the latter makes applications harder to support and maintain and somehow does not speak highly of the ROI of API testing.

PLAN TESTING AND TRACK COVERAGE

Now you know a lot (more) about REST API, automation development, and the necessary toolchain. You probably have sane API documentation describing all of its specifics. If you are tempted to get your hands dirty with coding, please hold on. Careful planning and proper management of stakeholders will be a key factor to success.

So, what would be the next steps then? What should be included in the scope of the planned activities? In order to find the right way, one would need to first answer the question: "What will make this test suite a success, so the organization would understand its value and invest in extending it?"

Below you will find a number of important points to include as part of a newly planned test solution.

Positive Flows

Ensure the API works as described by requirements when passing valid and expected user input and following valid use cases.

Negative Flows

Ensure API handles misuse, such as:

Missing parameters, e.g.:

1. Missing mandatory parameters — for example, password parameter in a login POST request.
2. Missing values in a request — for example, passing a parameter of type "date" with its value being blank.

Security violations, e.g.:

1. Using invalid user and password for login requests.

2. Using users with no permissions granted for accessing "sensitive" data. Imagine that you try to access and obtain some data intended for administrators by using a "less privileged" user. Such invalid requests should be handled properly by the API without disclosing any unnecessary details to clients.

3. Injecting SQL, JavaScript, and many other security attacks.

Backward Compatibility

Track newly introduced and modified APIs. Try to run the API tests in their in-use version in production against a changed API and ensure that tests still pass.

Plan Review of the Test Plan

This is a major and mandatory step. It must not be skipped as it exposes the planned coverage and the expected result definitions for assessment and approval by stakeholders before automation development is started. It is often the case that the proposed test plans bring up new use cases that have not been considered by product managers up to this moment and the scope of the product needs to change as well.

Automation Implementation

Automation projects should be treated like any other development project. Hence, delivering such a project means going through the following stages:

1. **Design** describing how:

   - Request base class should look in order to support all API verbs.

   - Data providers are used to cover the permutations within the test plan.

   - Logging and reporting for the execution of automated tests. It should be clear what needs to be logged during a test run and how the resulting report would look like. As part of the report, request-response pairs need to be shared. This makes it easier to analyze test failures.

2. **Automation code review**
   This should go without saying. It is organized and conducted in the same way that every development code review procedure is.

3. **Automation test execution**
   This is the phase in which the automation suite is being validated against

the deployed version of the API under test. It is traced, debugged, and fixed until it becomes robust and resilient against changes. This process may trigger modifications of test scripts. It may also require resolving few issues in the API.

4. **Integrate suite into nightly run (CI)**
   Once the API automation suite is stabilized and there are no more issues, it should be integrated as part of the CI workflows used by development teams. Thus, defects and regressions in API will be discovered early enough along the development process.

PRACTICAL EXAMPLES

Now that it is clear how to plan and integrate API testing solutions as part of the standard CI cycles, let us have a closer look on what makes a great automated API test. Below, you will find a couple of practical scenarios that every automation engineer will need to go through. The proposed Java implementations are based on the REST-assured framework that we discussed earlier.

START SMALL

Authentication with mobile and single-page web apps is most often delegated through REST API to a backend service which is responsible for processing the passed credentials and either approve or prohibit the authentication request. This decision is based on comparison of the passed username and password to the ones stored within the third tier of the corresponding application, e.g. a database. There are more complex ways to authenticate with apps. Once you know the basic mechanism, the rest will be a no-brainer for you, so let us get our hands dirty.

Consider a typical login screen or a web page as also sketched in **Figure 86.**

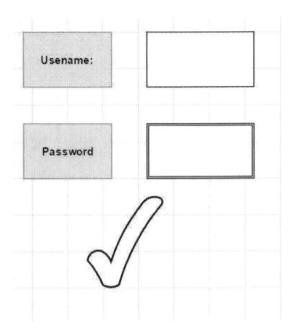

Figure 86: A Sketch of a Login Screen/ Web Page

Once the submit button is pushed, the username and password would be passed through a REST API query to the corresponding backend service. It does its fair share of complex processing and sends a response back to the client (mobile app, single page app, another API service, etc.) clearly indicating whether authentication succeeded or failed.

If an automation engineer needs to automate both positive and negative scenarios, it would make sense to be able to define and maintain a list of scenarios. Each scenario would describe the necessary user input as well as the expected response for each login attempt. From there on, the automated solution would take care to iterate through the list, call the authentication API, and verify the correctness of the input from structural and content perspectives.

This is where the concept of "DataProviders" can help a lot. A data provider is just a method which feeds your automated tests with expected user input and system output. You need to take care that your test properly maps the input parameters to the ones described by the data provider. The same applies to the expected system output. Data providers are the first step towards test configuration. You could have data providers retrieving expected input and output from a file, service, database, and so forth.

Have a look how this is done in the code snippet below. Note how easy it is to provide a brief description of the test scenario, e-mail address as a user name to match, and a password to be passed to the authentication service through the API. From there on, the response is expected to contain the corresponding HTTP status code clearly indicating if system access is allowed or not.

```
@DataProvider(name = "LoginValidationsApi")
public static Object[][] dataProviderLoginValidationsApi () throws Exception {
  return new Object[][] {
    /*{
        String description,
        String userEmail,
        String userPassword,
        HTTP_STATUS expectedResponseStatus,
        ExtensionType extensionType
    },*/
      {
        "Test positive login flow - JSON",
        A@b.com,
        123456,
        HTTP_STATUS.Success,
        ExtensionType.JSON,
      },

  {
        "Test positive login flow - XML",
        A@b.com,
        123456,
        HTTP_STATUS.Success,
        ExtensionType.XML,
      },

    {
```

```
        "Test negative login flow",
        Ab.com,
        123456,
        HTTP_STATUS.BadRequest,
        ExtensionType.JSON,
    },


    {
        "Test positive login flow",
        A@b.com,
        12345613344,
        HTTP_STATUS.Forbidden,
        ExtensionType.JSON,
    },


    };
}
```

An example of an automated test issuing an authentication request, which is fed by the aforementioned data provider, is illustrated by the code snippet below. The comments should make it self-explanatory for everyone.

```
//This test method uses in its annotations path to Data Provider class
in use and sets the test as enabled
@Test(dataProviderClass = DataProviderLoginApi.class, dataProvider
="LoginValidationsApi", enabled =true)
public void testLoginAPI(String description, String userEmail, String user-
Password, HTTP_STATUS expectedResponseStatus, ExtensionType exten-
sionType) throwsException {
    PrintToReporterAndLog("****************Starting test :" + de-
scription(;//sample log printing statement
    sendLoginRequest(userEmail, userPassword,extensionType); //in this
method you do validation against status code etc.
    }
```

Let us digest the method "sendLoginRequest", since it does the heavy lifting. In order to call the authentication API endpoint, an automation engineer would need to know how the information needs to be passed to the API. Let us assume that this is done using a POST HTTP request. The username (in our case — the e-mail address) and password are part of the "body" of this request. This means that we would need to send this request to the URL of the authentication resource (e.g. https://<server_URL>/login).

Sample URL: https://<server_URL>/login

The "body" variable basically holds the username and password mentioned above. The "url" variable holds the real value of the resource URL.

```
Response
response = RestAssured.given().contentType("application/" + extension-
Type).body(body).when().post(url); // Using string manipulation we will
build the URL to use
ValidatableResponse vresponse = response.then(); //Useful statement
in case we want to validate more than 1 element in the response like
we do here (otherwise, it can be united with the following line)
String statusCode = vresponse.extract().statusCode();
String statusLine = vresponse.extract().statusLine ();
```

The source code above would send the POST HTTP request and wait until a system response has been received. Obtaining the corresponding HTTP status code is very easy, so that its value can be asserted against the one described within the data provider.

If one needs to validate the structure of the response against a JSON or XML schema (depending on which message payload data format is supported by the API service under test), this can be easily done. The corresponding structural template can be loaded as a resource so that it is used as a baseline for assessing the structure of the actual response. A code example is found below.

```
InputStream xsd = Thread.currentThread().getContextClassLoader().get-
ResourceAsStream(xmlSchema); //xmlSchema represent the schema
file we created as our expected reference for the API
try {
    response.then().body(matchesXsd(xsd)); // If no match in XML sche-
ma, exception will be thrown
```

response.then().body(*matchesJsonSchemaInClasspath*(jsonSchema)). toString(); //**JsonSchema represent the schema file we created as our expected reference for the API – if no match in JSON schema, exception will be thrown**

} **catch** (Exception ex) {

    Assert.*fail*("Error! Exception occurred on validation XML/JSON schemas: " + ex.getMessage() + "\nFull response: " + response.asString());

}

GROW QUICKLY

Now that you know how to make the first step, let us briefly discuss the second one, namely, extending the test in order to cover an end-to-end scenario. You will see how easy it is to evolve your test solution iteratively as the functional scope for the app (and the API under the hood) evolves.

Let us assume that end users will authenticate with our app with the intention of getting to know the current weather situation in places all over the world. This kind of interaction is described by **Figure 87** below.

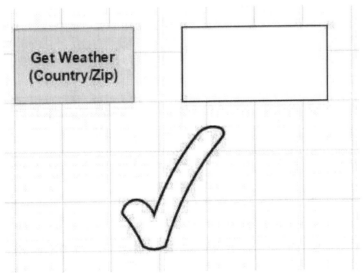

Figure 87: An Example Screen Allowing to Check Weather in a Specific Location

The first step requires the definition of a data provider, which is pretty similar to the one in the initial example above. However, this one will need to feed the consequent API call for obtaining information on the weather conditions in cities all over the world. Hence, scenario input and output need to be extended with input for a city and the expected output needs to be adjusted accordingly. Scenarios could describe both positive and negative flows. Check the enhanced data provider below.

```java
@DataProvider(name = "GetLocationAPI")
public static Object[][] dataProviderGetLocationAPI () throws Exception {
  return new Object[][] {
    /*{
        String description,
        String userEmail,
        String userPassword,
        HTTP_STATUS expectedResponseStatus,
        ExtensionType extensionType,
        String location,
        String schemaFile

    },*/
     {
        "Test positive flow - JSON",
        A@b.com,
        123456,
        HTTP_STATUS.Success,
        ExtensionType.JSON,
        "Berlin",
        "JSONSchema_fileName"
     },

{
        "Test positive flow - XML",
        A@b.com,
        123456,
        HTTP_STATUS.Success,
```

```
            ExtensionType.XML,
            "Berlin",
            "XMLSchema_fileName"
        },

        {
            "Test negative get Weather flow",
            A@b.com,
            123456,
            HTTP_STATUS.PageNotFound,
            ExtensionType.JSON,
            "NA",
            "JSONSchema_fileName"
        },
    };
}
```

The next step is to modify our test in order to extract the additional input from the data provider. Then we need to call the weather API using a GET HTTP request. You could find the structure of an example URL below.

Sample URL: **https://<server_URL>/weatherData?location=berlin**

The location will be encoded within the URL as a parameter. The extended test implementation can be found below. The method named "GetWeatherByLocationRequest" is pretty similar to the one used for logging in. It just fires a GET request instead of a POST one. As a next step, you could try out implementing it using a publicly available location-aware weather API service.

```
@Test(dataProviderClass = DataProviderWeatherApi.class, dataProvider
="WeatherByLocationValidationsApi", enabled =true)
public void testLoginAndWeatherAPI(String description, String userEmail,
String userPassword, HTTP_STATUS expectedResponseStatus, Extension-
Type extensionType, String location, String schemaFile) throws Exception {
    PrintToReporterAndLog("****************Starting test :" + descrip-
tion);
```

```
sendLoginRequest(userEmail, userPassword);//
```
Same logic as above in Login example
```
    GetWeatherByLocationRequest  getWeatherByLocationRequest = new
GetWeatherByLocationRequest (location, extensionType);
    getWeatherByLocationRequest.sendRequest(location,expectedRespons-
eStatus); //
```
Here we do validation against the returned response in terms of returned elements and values
```
    validateResponseVsSchema(getWeatherByLocationRequest,extension-
Type,schemaFile); //
```
Here we do validation on the schema -same as in Login example }

SUMMARY

This chapter only scratched the surface of the best practices for API testing. These practices are, of course, complimentary to other testing methodologies around UI, visual, user conditions, performance, and other types of testing, as described in this book. Useful tools and testing frameworks for REST API testing were demonstrated.

This chapter also aimed at increasing the awareness of test engineers with respect to how valuable API testing is. It brings the following advantages:

1. Increased test coverage — API tests can verify specific logic and architecture tiers that cannot and should not be addressed and covered by UI testing.

2. Faster testing feedback and overall TTM — API test automation is quick to develop, execute, and examine.

3. API testing and APIs in general have considerable impact on the overall stability of products. Assuring a high aquality API serves all parties — developers and test engineers.

4. API testing is more robust than UI testing since it is common across platforms, compared to UI elements that will look and behave differently across iOS and Android.

3

Integrating Digital Quality in Modern Agile/ DevOps Practices

14 Making Mobile Apps Beta Testing Painless

THIS CHAPTER WAS CONTRIBUTED BY YAIR BAR-ON, CEO AND CO-FOUNDER OF TESTFAIRY

YAIR BAR-ON is the Co-founder and CEO of TestFairy. The company helps mobile application vendors with easing the pain of beta testing their apps. Prior to Test-Fairy, Yair co-founded Macadamia apps which focused on photo apps. He had also worked as a software developer and a marketer. Yair is a Computer Science graduate and a father of 4 children. He dreams of becoming a carpenter. No doubt, one day this will happen.

INTRODUCTION

One of the most challenging tasks for mobile developers is beta testing their applications with real people. External beta testing cycles can be conducted by volunteers or paid testers. It may also be done internally by company employees. This is usually called "dogfooding". In all cases, the biggest challenge has to do with understanding what exactly happened on devices out there. It is a bit different from in-house testing activities, since devices are out there in the wild and not in the hands of skilled engineers who know how to do troubleshooting in the best possible way. What if there is a crash? How will one know what has happened before? Did anything else go wrong as well?

At TestFairy[1], for example, mobile teams are provided with video recordings which make it clear what happened with the tested app and how it was interacted with. Thus, beta testing becomes much easier and more painless. Defecting scenarios can be identified and fixed prior to going live.

Within this chapter, beta testing will be discussed. You will find a few tips that will help you initiate and run successful beta testing processes on your own.

FIND AWESOME TESTERS

You can always take a look within your own organization. Company employees make the best testers. The more, the better. This is called "dogfooding". Their only merit is not the fact that they are often considered a "free resource". They are also a devoted one. They care about your product and they want to help. If something does not work as expected, they are very likely to give you a call immediately and tell you: "Hey, something went wrong!"

This does not necessary apply only to the gang defining the product and implementing it — not at all. What about the guys from the Purchasing team? Do you happen to know the secretary of the Legal department? In this regard, do not forget about the Head of Information Security. All of these will turn out to be great beta testers. Sometimes they will even excel compared to software developers who know the product and the "happy path" scenarios too well.

What if you are running a startup company of 4 guys? You don't have hundreds of employees to rely on? Well, chances are huge that the four of you, your family, and friends might have the number of social media followers that would suffice. If you do the math, it may be the case that you would be able to count on many more people than most companies in terms of number of employees. Why don't you ask your followers to help you test your app?[2] Building a community of end users at the beta stage is a great start for each company and product.

---

1   TestFairy Web site — https://testfairy.com/

2   Beta testing site example — https://tsfr.io/cxpo6z

MAKE YOUR BETA TESTERS LOVE YOU

Your beta community is a valuable asset. You need to listen to it, pay attention, grow it, and sustain it. By agreeing and committing to test your app at an early stage they do you a favor. There are many smart ways you could go, make them happy, and boost their engagement and productivity.

Think about it. When an issue is encountered, you could give testers the courtesy of gratitude and recognition. A "Thank you, you did great" statement does not cost a dime and definitely warms hearts. Of course, this would be the bare minimum of efforts you should invest. What if you gave out small bounties and rewards? Well, this would be another great step in the right direction. Provide free chips, free coupons, and gift cards. Sending over T-shirts or movie tickets would be another great way to motivate early testers. If you would like to boost your beta testing programme to its maximum and beyond, you could apply a great many gamification techniques aiming at increased testing engagement. For example, announce a weekly contest, provide simple means of transparency (e.g. a dashboard), and award "the beta tester of the week". You do not need to stop here. Figure out a way to differentiate, rank, and award different types of contributions, such as: most critical bug found, best documented bug reports, most difficult bug to resolve.

Your beta testers do not necessarily need to be paid. In many cases, they do not have such expectations at all. However, if you figure out the right way to say "Thank you", you will end up with a more effective, efficient, and successful beta testing program.

ARRANGE FOR SUPER EASY BUG REPORTING

Getting to know about issues and defects is the main goal of every testing activity. However, you would need to think twice if you planned for your users to give you a call whenever an issue popped up. This would not work well. Most users tend to keep the bad news for themselves. If your app does not work, lots of people find it embarrassing to call you just to let you know that your product sucks.

Simple and easy bug reporting is crucial for successful beta testing. For example, at TestFairy, we allow testers to shake their phones and fill in a feed-back form that pops up. They can report visual bugs in very much the same way by just drawing simple sketches on the screen. We are convinced that the chances for a tester to shake her phone and quickly type "Not working" are way higher than having the same person send us a detailed e-mail explaining what went wrong.

NEVER STOP BETA TESTING

One of the most common mistakes that mobile developers do is to somehow dismiss their beta users once their app has been released by upgrading them to the official product version. If you plan for something serious, you should know better. Keep and grow a healthy beta testing community all the time.

Beta testing never ends. Your first release is just your first release. Your product life cycle will include hundreds, maybe thousands of versions of your app. Having a few hundred beta users test a new version before it goes live to hit millions might pretty much be the difference between failure and success. This is a matter of risk management.

This beta community could keep using your beta versions forever. They could get updates whenever you want to try something new. Do not forget to manage right the expectations of this group. This way, if you badly fail with a beta release, you will ruin the experience of 500 users instead of doing so with 5 million "spoiled" end users who accept nothing but the best. This is one of the specifics of the market today, isn't it? High quality is taken for granted. If an app constantly crashes or malfunctions, you never go back to it. After all, there are so many alternatives out there...

INTEGRATE BETA WITH YOUR ORGANIZATION

You already know how easy it is for beta testers to report bugs using TestFairy. While this is cool, you could do even more in terms of integrating beta testing within the processes of your organization. Beta users could use JIRA Connect to embed screencasts as part of every reported JIRA issue. This supports engineers and developers and could significantly reduce the number of feedback cycles necessary for an issue to be properly understood, fixed, and verified.

For example, if a bug report consisted of a plain statement "It is not working" (you would be surprised how many issues are actually described in this simplistic way), a support engineer would not approach the beta tester asking "What did you do?". Instead, she would just open and watch the video attached to the corresponding JIRA issue, as illustrated by **Figure 88.** It would be clear how exactly the beta tester had interacted with the app before it broke or even crashed.

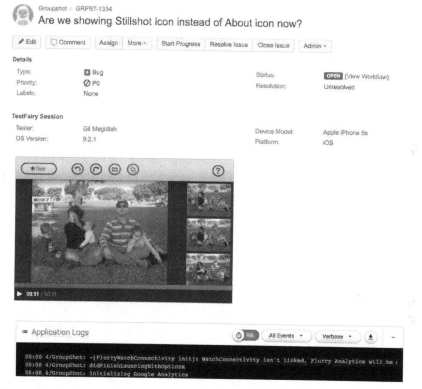

Figure 88: An Example of a Defect Discovered and Reported by a Crowdtester

There are also other benefits that need to be considered. Every JIRA issue would contain important information (e.g. name of the tester) and invaluable troubleshooting hints, such as device brand, model, version of the underlying mobile operating system. JIRA is capable of working with JQL queries that could take into consideration all of these properties. Thus, you could create convenient boards and reports facilitating further analysis on reported defects. Of course, JIRA is just an example. Trello, Bugzilla, Slack, or any other issue tracking system would fit well.

A customer of TestFairy — a Silicon Valley startup with 12,000 employees – has a program for internal testing of mobile apps named "Cat food". They use the already described bug reporting and recording procedure. Their company rolls out an official update for the respective app every 4–6 weeks. In the meantime, internal users get silent updates through the distribution channels of the Test-Fairy app almost every night. Whenever someone faces an issue, all they need to do is shake their device and add their feedback. This input is automatically submitted as an issue into the JIRA system of the company. A video with the end user interaction is also attached. This allows their mobile developers to resolve issues immediately and release bug-free apps.

If you are wondering what it would take to start with TestFairy, refer to the list of quick steps below. You can lay the foundations of a highly successful beta program in no time.

Get Started with TestFairy

1. Create an account at the TestFairy website.[3]

2. To start, Add the TestFairy SDK to your app. It is available for iOS, Android, PhoneGap/Cordova, Unity, React Native, Xamarin, Adobe Air, Appcelerator Titanium, and Ionic. You can find the SDK documentation here.[4]

3. Upload your app to your TestFairy account. Choose which testers you wish to send the app to. You could also upload a list of testers in CSV format.

4. The testers will receive an invitation to download your app via e-mail. In addition, they will be clearly instructed how to install the application.

5. Once your app has been installed and in use, you will be able to watch videos and get to know how exactly it is being interacted with.

6. From here on, testers will be able to shake their device and provide their feedback.

7. Connect your issue tracking system to TestFairy. Thus, testers' feedback will be pushed directly to the respective system feeding developers with high-quality issues containing logs, videos, contextual information, and many other details. Out-of-the-box integration with JIRA, BugZilla, Pivotal,

---

3 TestFairy — http://testfairy.com
4 TestFiary Integration instruction — https://docs.testfairy.com

YouTrack, Asana, Trello, Slack, and HipChat is already there. Open API and webhooks facilitate many other advanced integration scenarios.

8. For the sake of proper communication, you could also connect your account to your company e-mail server, so that all e-mail notifications would be sent from approved company e-mail addresses.

9. If you are working in a team, invite your teammates to join your account.

10. If you are working in a big company, connect your account to SSO such as Okta, OneLogin, Ping Identity and others, so that all user management could be done in one place.

SUMMARY

Rolling out new versions of mobile apps is getting more and more aggressive. Time to market and quality are key to business success. Organizations can hardly meet the expectations of end users if they don't employ a beta testing program of some kind. It is now clear that validating pre-release versions of apps is all about engagement, processes, and tooling. Modern beta testing is a safety net for your apps. That said, it is also a continuous effort that can be integrated within the processes and tooling of every software delivery organization.

Master Your "Shift Left" Moves

THIS CHAPTER WAS CONTRIBUTED BY MANISH MATHURIA, FOUNDER AND CHIEF TECHNOLOGY OFFICER AT INFOSTRETCH

MANISH MATHURIA has more than 14 years of professional and management experience in consulting services. With his vast knowledge and considerable experience in technology, Mr. Mathuria leads the Infostretch team in developing architecture, scalability, performance, and IT strategies for Infostretch customers. He has been a senior technology consultant in Quality, SaaS, and Mobile areas for the executive management in Fortune 500 firms and high-tech Silicon Valley startups. He speaks regularly at leading quality and software engineering conferences worldwide. Mr. Mathuria holds an Executive MBA from Santa Clara University and a Bachelor of Engineering in Computer Science degree.

INTRODUCTION

Let us examine the QA organizations of two imaginary companies — Amazing

Auto Intelligence (AAI) & Bricks 'n' Mortar Depot (BMD). They are leaders in their industries. AAI makes next generation technology for self-driving vehicles and BMD makes designer bricks. Both companies have significantly large software organizations. Both have imperatives to deliver high-quality software, as their business and competitive environment demands rapid delivery of software releases in order to remain competitive.

However, AAI and BMD write software using very different methodologies.

AAI has coordinated software releases across the company. They have divided their development teams into small scrum teams, about eight people each. As far as QA teams are concerned, AAI has no specialized QA in any scrum team. They follow the Behavior Driven Development (BDD) methodology where the scrum team develops acceptance tests as Behavior Driven Scenarios with relevant test data before they write code to implement the features.

Through the sprint, their objective is to make these tests pass. Through the sprint, their product owners and developers continuously review the scenarios and data through peer reviews and use these scenarios to discuss their progress. They develop the scenario code while they are building the feature code. Their Continuous Integration(CI) system builds the code several times a day, checks the code quality and runs the scenarios, and while initially during the sprint most scenarios fail, towards the end they begin to pass. Their sprint is not done until all scenarios pass. In addition to the BDD scenarios, developers write unit tests which also run through their CI builds.

Once the CI system successfully passes the "quality gate (the acceptable no passing tests)", it promotes the software to an integration test environment that it builds "on the fly" in the Cloud. This environment is torn down after tests are run. In the integration test environment, more tests are run which verify integration among different deliverables of the scrum teams involved. They have a small end-to-end test team which finally verifies the integration manually after integration test quality gate has passed successfully as well. After the end-to-end test phase, the software gets promoted to production.

AAI does have a QA tools team which is responsible for building frameworks, reports, and tools. This team ensures that repeatable tasks which each scrum team does are eliminated and done by the tools team.

BMD builds software very differently. Their development team is in New York. Their QA team works from Dallas. They follow an iterative development process which releases builds to QA a couple times a month. The first few days of a release to QA are frustrating because of manual installation procedures that often fail due to several setup issues. The interaction between dev and QA often turns hostile and at best is tense. There are several rejected releases to QA that cause a lot of development rework. The QA team focuses on testing the prior released iteration and they automate tests once the graphical user interface (GUI) is complete. This automation is largely used for regression testing during the release.

AAI can release software to production every sprint. BMD can barely release software once a quarter. With the same number of people AAI delivers much more featured and complex software with far more acceptance on the marketplace than BMD.

While stereotypical and extreme, these examples are not unique. We have several AAIs and BMDs among us. This chapter examines which are the traits that AAI has that BDD does not? What are the success patterns of high-performing QE function?

"SHIFT LEFT" EXPLAINED

"Shift Left" is a practice that provides an effective means to perform testing along with or in parallel to sprint and development activities.

* An entire Agile team comprising of development, test, and operations engineers works together to plan, manage, and execute automated and continuous testing to accelerate feedback, such that it can be used to optimize the development artifacts and process.

* Technology is often used to automate the software development lifecycle. Typical candidates for automation are builds, unit, integration and acceptance tests, and code quality inspection. This process of continuous integration is often staged, with each stage having a quality gate of acceptable criteria for promotion to the next one.

* An essential tenet of "shift left" is to write testable code that is unit verified

and build quality is guaranteed from component up to integration level. Essentially, this enables efficient localization of a problem. It also ensures that individual components are working before a large amount of software has been integrated.

- Testing may be performed as a part of the development process or as a service running in parallel to development activities. In either case, shifting left accelerates feedback to developers and improves the quality of code delivered for testing.

"Shift left" is an essential paradigm for Agile teams. It may be successfully leveraged by all development teams.

IS IT NEW?

No, not really. The ability to test a component and assess its validity has always been practiced at hardware level. For even basic hardware, every component is designed to self-test on power on and declare itself functioning or not. In case of an issue, you clearly know where the fault is. Before you assemble the whole solution and integration test it, you know that components themselves are working.

Shifting QA left helps achieve some of the same benefits and outcomes this component level testing has enabled in hardware assembly.

Why is it that this seemingly obvious practice that has helped hardware development has not been adopted by software teams? There could be several reasons.

a. Software is easy/easier to fix after production through releasing a patch, for example. Hosted software, such as in Software as a Service (SaaS), makes it even easier. You do not have to ship anything, you just roll out the next daily update and the case is closed.

b. Software requirements, development, and releases are more complex and volatile. This has caused software teams to test things in more of an ad-hoc way in the name of completeness and quality.

Demand for Agility is putting a different level of pressure on QA teams. Agile teams are expected to deliver working software in a sprints lifetime which typically lasts for a week or two. What used to be tested in weeks or months now needs to be performed in a matter of days, while final certification is sometimes even done in minutes. Unless teams adopt automation and component level testing, this is an impossible task.

"Shift left" is not just about automation. It is a state of mind.

KEY BENEFITS OF "SHIFT LEFT"

Enable Agile

* Enable in-sprint testing and automation with a clear definition of done (DoD).
* Release software in production incrementally with every sprint.

Find defects early

* With testing happening sooner in the life cycle, you find defects sooner. It is a well-known truth: the earlier in the life cycle you find a defect, the cheaper it is to fix it.

Improve communication and feedback

* With QA engaging earlier in the life cycle, developers and product owners get early feedback. This helps teams identify considerably faster feature ambiguities, inconsistencies among sub-systems, integration problems, and data incompatibilities.
* This early feedback increases feature velocity and reduces cost.

Reduce number of production defects

* Continuous quality maturing all the way to production.
* Dramatic quality improvements earlier in pipeline to reduce risk to production.
* Clear quality gates to migrate software closer to production reduces ambiguities and increases quality.

GETTING READY TO "SHIFT LEFT"

It is important to know how Quality organizations should evolve to the stage of being efficient and shifted-left. There are specific dimensions that an organization should look at to enhance their adoption of "shift left". This section examines the maturity of QA organizations through the lens of these dimensions.

QUALITY ENGINEERING MATURITY

"Shift left" is not a trivial change. It has far reaching impact on how QA teams are structured and skilled; also on their operating processes and best practices. The sketch in **Figure 89** classifies the maturity of QA teams according to various "shift left" dimensions in three categories "basic", "intermediate", and "expert". To conquer "shift left", QA teams need to rise to at least an "intermediate", if not an "expert" level.

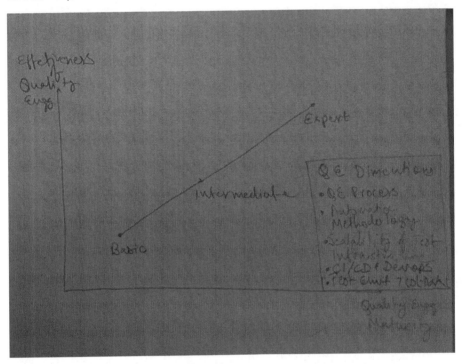

Figure 89: Maturity of QA Organizations According to "Shift Left" Dimensions

QUALITY ENGINEERING PROCESS

Quality process engrained in the overall Agile software development process is a major factor. This includes structure of teams, approach to, and integration of quality into the software process.

AUTOMATION METHODOLOGY

The ability to automate scenarios in a structured, maintainable, and usable methodology is also a significant factor.

SCALABILITY OF TEST INFRASTRUCTURE

The modern agile QA teams can fire up their automation assets on on-demand infrastructure in such an automated fashion that a large number of automated tests can be executed in a massively parallel way.

CI/CD AND DEVOPS INTEGRATION

Automation is ineffective if it is leveraged manually. The process of Continuous Integration and DevOps is the consumer of automated assets. At the end of the day, it is that process flow that actually manages and consequently automates the end-to-end test execution and the reporting based on it!

TEST ENVIRONMENT AND TEST DATA

Finally, if you have far reaching challenges with test environments and test data that prevent seamless and reliable automation runs, no matter what or how much you automate, execution will be bottlenecked and the desired goal of certifying a build automatically will remain underachieved.

Table 6 explains the tenets or characteristics of QA teams at different maturity stages. Effectively, Agile teams are between an "intermediate" and "expert" level.

In the next sections, we will learn how to achieve the "expert" level by using the "shift left" techniques.

Quality Shift Left Maturity Model

	Base	Intermediate	Expert
Quality Process	• Conventional QA methodologies • Segregated Dev and QA teams • Limited touchpoint with product teams	• Extend team collaboration • Strong Agile process • Dev & Test – One team • Processes flow across Dev / QA / Build & Operations	• Metrics based real time dashboard • Automated Quality Health Checks – Supports Go/No Go Decisions • Single owner in an integrated team – Unified view of QA between dev and QA
Automation Methodology	• Manual GUI based testing • Heavy reliance on a "few experts" • Best can certify a release in few weeks • Low degree of coverage	• Higher coverage with GUI Functional testing • Some automated tests at service layer • Final Certification is with Manual "experts" • Automated Integration Test	• Automation at different levels (unit, headless, GUI, services) • Leverage in-sprint Automation • Automated Unit level test • Comprehensive Coverage thru automation • Adopt BDD/ATDD process
Scalability of QA Infrastructure	• Leverage IT team to spin up infrastructure needs • Continuously bottle necked on unavailability of test infrastructure	• Fully virtual independent test infrastructure set up and deployment • No dependency and bottleneck on infrastructure • Potentially Leverage commercial on-demand/cloud test infrastructure	• Test infrastructure as code • Leverage containers to reliably reproduce test nodes • Leverage cloud to setup, tear-down and scale up nodes on demand
CI/CD Integration	• Effective version control & build automation for code development • Leverage a CI tool for triggering builds	• Auto triggered builds on code check-in • Build basic code quality and unit test gates in CI • Full automatic acceptance test integrated in the main CI pipeline	• Leverage containers to reliably deploy in test environments. • Integrated quality gates for code quality, unit tests, code coverage and acceptance test • Automated promotion
Test Environment and Test Data	• Automation failing frequently due to environments & test data issues • Hard-coded test data in the scripts	• Data-driven scripts but tests frequently fail due to lack of correct test data • Leverage service virtualization to achieve automation • Evolved test data strategy & tooling	• Completely automated relevant test data generation • Automated setup and tear down of test environments • Advanced tool-based service virtualization • Machine learning based automation

Table 6: Characteristics of Different "Shift Left" Maturity Stages Explained

"SHIFT LEFT" — PATTERNS AND ANTI-PATTERNS

Traditionally, in the Waterfall project management model, software is conceived of (in the form of some requirements), developed, tests are conceived of, executed and software is fixed in a cyclical order. When you try to do this cycle in a shorter (say a sprint) span, it becomes very painful for the following reasons:

- Unlike Waterfall, a sprint's time frame in agile does not give you enough time to start thinking about the tests after development is done. QA teams are forced to write tests and automate them while code is being developed.

- This cycle time also puts pressure on the entire team for effective reviews. There is no easy way to pull in the entire team to purposefully discuss test approach, test cases, and test data.

The above restrictions evolved into various test-driven patterns described below:

TEST-DRIVEN DEVELOPMENT (TDD)

This turns the aforementioned traditional software development process upside down. Instead of writing code to a spec, you first write the test, think about its data inputs and various boundary conditions under which it would fail the spec. As the code comes alive, you also try to automate these tests. Also, the emphasis is to continuously execute these tests. Clearly, before the code that implements a feature exists, the tests will fail. This is expected, but as you come close to functioning code, the tests start to pass. You perform the above process in small incremental steps.

ACCEPTANCE TEST-DRIVEN DEVELOPMENT (ATDD) AND BEHAVIOR-DRIVEN DEVELOPMENT (BDD)

These are special cases of TDD. ATDD and BDD[1] are mostly synonymous. Teams practicing ATDD would write an acceptance test describing the behavior of the user story or functionality that needs to be developed. BDD enables the team to describe the test and hence the software behavior in a Domain Specific Language (DSL) called Gherkin which reads very much like English.

The BDD scenario is made executable as a test using frameworks like Cucumber (Ruby) and behat (PHP). An executable BDD Scenario is a powerful tool to automate tests, as everyone can see exactly what the automated test does with its data by simply reading the test. It hides the automation details within its implementation. Compare this approach to the one which translates a manual test case in a programming language, such that eventually breaks the link between manual test scenarios (their intent) and the corresponding implementation. Now you can better appreciate how AAI and BMD above are different.

Following is an example of a BDD and its implementation:

---

1 Behavior-driven development — https://en.wikipedia.org/wiki/Behavior-driven_development)

Story: Hotel rooms when cancelled go back to inventory

As a hotel manager,

In order to keep track of available hotel rooms,

I want to add rooms back to inventory when they are cancelled.

Scenario 1: Cancelled hotel room should be returned to inventory

Given a customer previously booked **<no_of_rooms>** *rooms of* **<type>** *rooms,*
And I currently have **<Inventory_no>** *in inventory,*
When she cancels the rooms,
Then I should have **<upd_inventory>** *of* **<type>** *in inventory,*
And the customer gets her money back in her account.

no_of_rooms	type	inventory_no	upd_inventory
1	Queen	0	1
5	King	10	15

```
//Implementation
@Given("a customer previously booked $no_of_rooms rooms of $type rooms ")
public void theRoomBaseCondition(int no_of_rooms, String type) {

...

}
```

Figure 90: An Example of a BDD Scenario and its Implementation

SPECIFICATIONS BY EXAMPLE AND EXECUTABLE SPECIFICATIONS

This is a state reached when BDD scenarios adequately describe the acceptance criteria in Gherkin, so that the entire software test scenarios/ behavior specification is documented. These test scenarios are further annotated with the required data that describe the software behavior under certain conditions. Combined with the data and scenarios, the specification reaches a state that lends itself to be an effective test review tool, one that is crucial to bringing everyone in the team to the same page.

In the example depicted in **Figure 90,** the clarity of the intent is quite evident. This is a point to remember for test engineers.

To wrap it up, it is easy to see that TDD and its flavors help you "shift left".

Fundamentally, by forcing one to write tests before you code, you are naturally enforcing "shift left". BDD helps you automate what you see by creating executable specifications and executable test cases. Teams which embrace TDD/ BDD practices commit to early testing in their software development lifecycle. This means that they also embrace the philosophy that testing is a problem for the whole team to solve.

SOFTWARE TESTING PYRAMID AND "ICE-CREAM CONE"

The term "Software Testing Pyramid" was first conceived by Mike Cohen in his book "Succeeding with Agile"[2]. The anti-pattern "Ice-cream Cone" was introduced by Alister Scott in his blog.[3] **Figure 91** below visualizes both.

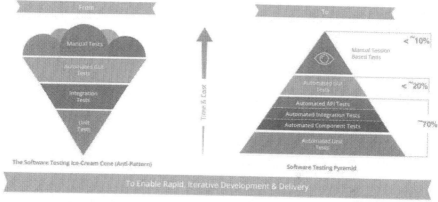

Figure 91: Software Testing Pyramid and "Ice-cream Cone" — Side by Side

Before Agile is embraced, most teams are structured like an ice-cream cone, including our friends at BMD above. They are heavy on finished product testing with an emphasis on manual testing. While that works, it does not align with the goals of Agile and "shift left". The time taken and the cost to perform testing manually is high. Note that their efforts in automation are also lopsided towards GUI automation. There is nothing wrong with the GUI automation. However, only automating the GUI is not sufficient. It is done late (GUIs get built last), it is fragile (GUIs change a lot), it is slow to execute and, at the end of the day,

2   Cohn, M. (2009), Succeeding with Agile: Software Development Using Scrum, Addison-Wesley Professional

3   Scott, Al., Ice-cream Cone, https://watirmelon.blog/2012/01/31/introducing-the-software-testing-ice-cream-cone/

it is expensive.

Overall, the ice-cream cone anti-pattern does not go well together with Agile. The "software testing pyramid" pattern, however, does. It simply states that testing should be structured in a bottom-up way with the heaviest emphasis on automating unit tests to increasingly lighter on automated API/Services/Components, automated GUI, and lightest on manual tests. The pyramid also provides recommendations on the amount of testing that is supposed to be done at each layer in %.

Note that neither model eliminates manual testing. Often, manual ad-hoc testing covers answering the question **"Are we building the right system?"** as opposed to the question that testers are typically tasked to answer, **"Are we building the system right?"** Manual testing should be used for non-automatable corner case scenarios and visual deformities. For a further discussion on visual automated testing, please refer to the respective section "Automated Visual Testing".

PRACTICAL TEST APPROACH AND TEST TOPOLOGY

Often, teams migrating into Agile and automation struggle with the right test topology. They know that they do not want an ice-cream cone, but they cannot find their way to the pyramid. Also, QA organizations cannot or do not control developers and therefore they lack a say on how much and how effective unit testing is.

Below, you will find a list of practical rules with good track record in the industry, that is, they work. The diagram in **Figure 92** maps them to the paradigm of the "Software Testing Pyramid".

1. If you do not have control on unit testing, plan your testing approach treating code as a "black box". This may not be practical all the time and you may find yourself depending on developers. Do not miss the section on "Inserting Testability in Software".

2. Assuming you have access to the service layer and it is well-defined (with the advent of micro services patterns, most modern applications are developed with a well-defined services layer), plan to test this extensively.

Services layers are typically exposed as Web services, APIs or SDKs. A huge number of functional tests with relevant data combinations and under certain boundary conditions should be done here. If done right, this could form 50–65% of the functional coverage.

3. Leverage GUI automation to facilitate the execution of more end-to-end business scenarios, so that good coverage on GUI workflows, error handling, translation, and many more can be ensured. These tests could add up to 20–30% of your functional coverage.

4. The rest can be done manually.

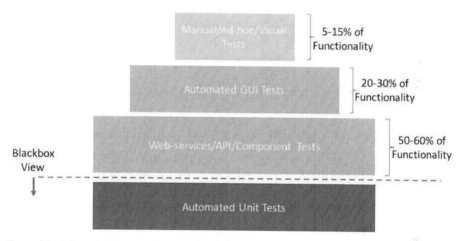

Figure 92: A Practical Proposal for Concrete Test Topology within the "Software Testing Pyramid"

INSERTING TESTABILITY IN SOFTWARE

Following are some common challenges or observations in the process of writing test automation solutions:

1. Often, testers struggle with high maintenance of testing activities and test code. Tests fail frequently and unexplainably. Upon investigation, you find that developers changed some code or some configuration parameter.

2. The only way to validate that a test fulfills its desired function is hidden inside the "black box" of the code. It is not accessible to you as a tester. Therefore, you need access to the code.

3. Your test tools require a certain level of a build instrumenting the code.

4. Your test tool is unable to access GUI widgets or the widget library used by developers.

5. Developers encode the identifiers of GUI widgets in a way that they change rapidly. You are dependent on locating and accessing the GUI widgets to run your automated test.

In all of these cases, streamlining and enhancing the code development practices, build, or release processes would significantly reduce the testing effort as well as spurious test code failures. Thus, the test code becomes more resilient. Making the code more testable or increasing the testability of the software is a real issue.

The testers should discuss such challenges openly with the developers. After all, less tested or testable code would impinge on the overall quality. The senior engineering management will often understand the impact of less testable code. Its representatives will work with the engineering team to increase testability. Following are some good practices that can help you increase testability.

1. Use configuration management, CI, and automated builds to reduce human errors in configuration and builds. This approach is often paired with a smoke test that acts as a quality gate for the build.

2. Write special functions accessible only to the tester either at the GUI or at the services layer. Exposing some validation properties, setting/resetting internal states of the application, querying state of components/objects... the examples can be many more.

3. Use consistent naming and widget identification. Developers and testers should align and agree upon a reliable GUI widget identification methodology, one that is amenable for test tools to work.

4. Do special test builds.

SPRINT TESTING TO REGRESSION TESTING PROMOTION PROCESS

QA teams have two main jobs when it comes to a typical Agile development process.

1. To ensure that the functional and non-functional testing for the features developed in the sprint has been conducted to the satisfaction of certifying the sprint.

2. To ensure that the development process progresses well with each consequent sprint, i.e. the current sprint has not broken the software developed in previous iterations.

Figure 93 describes the typical role that a QA team has in the sprint towards the objective of automating as much testing as possible during the sprint. The patterns described in this chapter help choose an automation methodology that does not get in the way of this objective.

In-sprint Activities

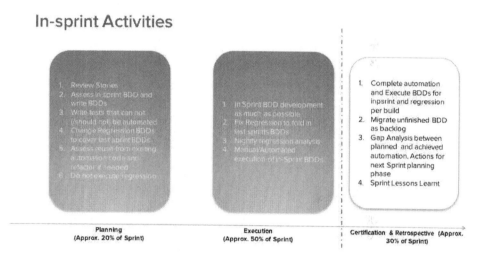

Figure 93: Migration from Sprint Testing to Regression Testing

Sprint tests are focused tests that validate and assert a specific need. For example, whether a user story was about to change the brand color from pink to purple. Imagine you wrote a test that automated this kind of validation. Such a test may find little relevance in the broad scope of regression testing. It is probably a validation point in some broader regression test rather than a standalone test scenario as it was during the sprint period.

Sprint tests often need to be reviewed, refactored, rewritten or deprecated post sprint. A retrospective period is the best time to do this or a team can set some time aside. Whenever done, it is important for teams to realize the difference between sprint and regression tests and address the migration process.

AUTOMATED VISUAL TESTING

Visual testing is the process of validating that the application is visually functional. It asserts that no part of the application has been deformed, lacks information, does not suit its purpose or is in general inadequate to appeal visually. It is usually assumed that visual testing will be done manually.

Again, in the spirit of the principle of "shifting left", it is important to find avenues that allow you to automate as much as possible.

Following are some techniques that help automate visual testing activities.

1. Every screen can be manually baselined (verified in advance) and visually inspected in real time by comparing it to the baseline screen. There are both open-source and commercial tools that make this technique possible. Sikuli, for instance, is an open-source image comparison technology. Applitools Eyes is a commercial alternative.

2. For the sake of validating HTML and CSS, there are open-source frameworks like Galen that allow you to code visual validation specs as part of the code. They are executed when the tests run, so that rendering in web browsers is verified at run-time.

Whichever technique you use, it is important to be careful with bringing in visual verifications and assertions to virtually every functional test. This will make your tests execute slower and with considerable overhead. Instead, the best practice is to identify a few end-to-end scenario tests that have been specifically written to provide broad coverage of the GUI and, hence, inspect it visually.

SUMMARY

Within this chapter, you got to know what "shift left" really means. More importantly, you are now aware of the buttons QA and development organizations can push, so that this transition can be as smooth as possible. Keep in mind that it has the potential to be a rather painful and tiresome one.

As always, the right mix of people, processes, and tools will save the day. In any case, practice makes perfect. Stick to the already discussed approaches, techniques, and industry practices and soon you will master the moves of left-shifting.

16

Advancing Quality into Dev Cycle

THIS CHAPTER WAS CONTRIBUTED BY ROY NURIEL, SR. DIRECTOR OF PRODUCT MANAGEMENT AT PERFECTO

ROY NURIEL has over 15 years of experience in the quality assurance domain, specializing in Enterprise Software. Over the course of his career, his roles have spanned across engineering, product delivery, and product management. Roy spearheaded complex projects as an innovation lead, growing ideas into market leading solutions. He is an expert in software quality, application lifecycle management (ALM), and end-to-end IT Management.

Prior to joining Perfecto, Roy held several senior positions at HP Software and Mercury. In his last reincarnation, he was responsible for building a new product line that addressed Agile processes and other modern development practices. Roy holds a B.Sc. in Computer Science from the Hebrew University in Israel.

INTRODUCTION

Smart test coverage, proper test automation, and timely go-to-market strategies are related and interdependent. In fact, defining and establishing continuous processes facilitating short release cycles of high-quality mobile apps is still a challenging task.

Many organizations are adopting Agile practices to rev up their development pace and officially release in shorter cycles. In many cases, mostly in large enterprise organizations, Quality Assurance (QA) is still performed by a centralized organization. As a consequence, testing happens very late in the development cycle, also known as Software Development Life Cycle (SDLC). This makes it much harder for both test engineers and software developers to discover and resolve issues by the end of the corresponding cycle/ sprint/ iteration. This is a problem even when significant automation testing infrastructure is in place.

Have you ever tried including specific key test scenarios as part of the SDLC? Ideally, they would be automated later on and become part of a Continuous Integration (CI) workflow. Sounds easy, right? Well, hold on, since there would be at least a couple of open questions that you would face and need to address sooner rather than later:

1. How to achieve continuous quality?
2. How to detect issues earlier in SDLC?

Within this chapter, you will go through proven ways to overcome the aforementioned difficulties. Talking about solutions, you should understand that there can be no low hanging fruit. As part of our recipe for success, different teams need to build trust, pick the right tools, and establish effective and efficient delivery processes.

"SHIFT QUALITY LEFT" IN SDLC

These challenges could not be addressed without significant changes in the processes and practices within software delivery organizations. In this regard, introducing automated testing is an absolute must-have decision for one simple reason — high quality product releases require regular regression, functional, and non-functional testing cycles to be performed. If you consider this effort as fixed overhead towards every release (daily, weekly), releasing stable versions of any given app will either be too expensive or lacking quality.

In order to get to shorter and highly innovative release schedules, automated QA cycles should be performed earlier in the SLDC, i.e. they should "shift to the left". This means that defects will be discovered earlier, often in the context of concrete development changes that are pushed to the source control system. This way, it is much more feasible for development teams to quickly find the root cause of issues and resolve them in a timely manner, so they do not disrupt the final validation QA cycle. Of course, it is a good practice to run automated tests as part of CI workflows. Now, this is what can turn a software delivery process into a continuous one.

While most teams agree upon these goals, they struggle a lot on their way of defining and implementing the right process. Keep in mind that processes are invented, enforced, and adopted by people. Thus, trust among the teams involved within is the key to getting to a rational and well-working solution. This is where many organizations stumble and fall. If you do not have a magic wand to trigger and complete the whole shift in a single spell, you better roll up your sleeves and get your hands dirty. In this case, it would be highly recommended to start small and proceed one step at a time, so that at every stage the impact would be measurable. Thus, timely corrections can be done so that the whole initiative is not compromised and held in a totally wrong direction.

In this regard, the step-by-step approach described below will help organizations catch the continuous, high quality release train with less pain and hurdles.

STEP 1 — 10 STABLE AUTOMATED TESTS AS A PREREQUISITE

Goal: Implement 10 stable automation tests

It has been already mentioned that shifting QA activities to the left in the SDLC required the availability of automated tests. If you do not have such, your first step will be implementing 5–10 automated tests covering the main end user flows of the app. These are usually referred to as "smoke" tests which provide the means for doing basic validation before new versions of an application are about to be released. Smoke tests are repeatedly run by teams and this is why it makes sense to start with them. Note that having such scenarios automated will not only save time and effort for QA teams. Later on, they will also help development teams to deliver fast increments with higher quality.

Automation engineers are strongly recommended to use open-source tools and frameworks that internally re-use the technology stack used for application development. If you are wondering why, just hold on. You will get to know why, just a bit later.

In many cases QA teams already have such tests scenarios defined and in place. Yet, these are performed by QA engineers. There is a way one can leverage "smoke" tests in order to shift quality closer to code changes, i.e. to the left in the SDLC. If you would like to know more, read on.

STEP 2 — TEST YOUR AUTOMATED TESTS

Goal: Validate that your automated tests are reliable ("dev" ready)

Duration: 2–3 weeks of stable execution

There is a huge difference in the attitude of developers and QA engineers when it comes to the way they perceive and relate to tests. QA is accustomed to executing large numbers of tests, witnessing, and struggling with many failures and false positives in results. On the other hand, developers are used to run unit tests which most of the time pass successfully. When a unit test does fail, chances are good that real issues are discovered. They are easily identified, isolated, investigated, and eventually resolved.

The ultimate goal is to execute QA automation tests as part of the development CI process. Therefore, the same testing experience needs to be ensured for the aforementioned (sometimes troublesome) automated scenarios. They should be implemented in a manner guaranteeing at least 90.0% accuracy, i.e. in most cases of failures they would indicate real issues. The rest of the failures might be due to other issues, such as application changes that require test modification and adjustments, flaws with the testing environment, etc.

Once the tests are in place, start running them a few times every day for 2–3 weeks. Integrate the test suite as part of a CI process mirroring the one used by the development teams, i.e. build a "shadow CI" process by utilizing the same CI tools and services. This needs to be done so that the stability of the tests and their resilience to application changes can be continuously assessed, validated, and improved over time. This stage is critical for "crossing the Rubicon". Before heading for the next step, QA engineers need to feel confident that the automated test suites are reliable, predictable, and behave as expected. It would be a great idea to gather execution stats. Try to measure and minimize the overhead of running the test suite. Get to any legitimate proof that the automated test solution will bring value to the development process as well.

STEP 3 — UNDER THE RADAR

Goal: Validate the stability and resilience of the test suite as part of the developers' CI process

Duration: 2 weeks of stable execution

Now, there is a stable automation suite that can be trusted. It is time to ensure buy-in from management so you can play a bit with their CI. Receiving faster quality feedback earlier in the development process makes the lives of development managers easier and more enjoyable as well. However, some of them may not be inclined to introduce instabilities to the "heartbeat" of their development processes. The CI cycles have to be stable and fast, no matter what. Management needs to be confident that there will be no side effects or negative impact on their ability to deliver increments.

Do you remember the recommendation to prove the stability, resilience, and value of the automated test solution? At this point, you went "all in", you might as well use all of the aces up your sleeves. Share the automated tests, show the statistics for continuous execution, present a brief report of the defects detected during the execution of your "shadow CI" process. Development managers need to believe in the approach, the solution, and they also need to believe in you. Are you the one who clearly knows what a stable and reliable CI solution is? Do you know how to make it work? Do you care about keeping it all up and running without any hiccups? Make them confident. You are the one.

The outcome of those meetings should be to get a "green light" to execute the automation suite on the development CI server. At this stage, developers will neither be aware nor affected by the change. Their build processes will not fail and execution results will not be reported officially. A dedicated QA engineer could be assigned to carefully monitor the execution and make sure that the tests are stable and could handle changes that occur on the development CI. This may require fixing tests, reporting issues, and collecting various execution statistics. At some point, execution needs to remain stable for at least two weeks in a row. This is the prime time for you to make the next big step.

STEP 4 — BECOME PART OF THE PROCESS

Goal: Provide fast feedback to developers during the development process

Duration: 2–3 weeks

The automated tests have already been integrated into the CI process of Development. They are stable and reliable. They are ready to be rolled out and shared with developers.

The first goal is to guarantee the sponsorship of development managers. You have already played that game, so you should know the rules pretty well. Prepare a report and share the execution results from the previous step as well as the achievements of your work. Let them know about the stability of the tests. Explain about the defects you have discovered and emphasize on the ones you would be able to detect from here on. Bring very clear focus on the efficiency gains in terms of reducing the manual testing performed by developers. Elaborate on the total time saved due to early issue discovery, resolution, and flawless final QA validation. Sell this project and sell it well.

From here on, build administrators need to expose the newly introduced test suite to the developers in the organization. The relevant CI jobs need to be configured, so that the solution is triggered few times per day. Thus, developers will be given a quick and handy tool to constantly monitor the overall quality status. Keep in mind that the test should not run for too long. Depending on the specific CI jobs being run, the full CI cycle should not take longer than 15–30 minutes.

Note that at this stage the build process will not break because of failures detected by tests. It is recommended to configure this process in a way that only a selected group of developers receive warning notifications. These would be the developers who pushed some changes in the source control system after the "last known good" state of the build. Before breaking builds officially, you need to experience the process live for some time, make certain adjustments, and fill important gaps.

Make sure that if a test scenario fails, there will be a dedicated person (being a developer or a QA engineer) who will initiate investigation and conclude whether an app issue was discovered or the test implementation was flawed. This will require technical expertise and in-depth knowledge of the automation scripts.

Define a process addressing adequately the questions below:

- Who is responsible for investigating test failures?
- Will issues/defects be reported?
- What is the Service Level Agreement (SLA) for fixing the tests?

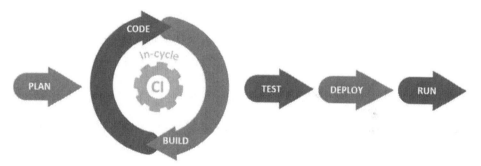

Figure 94: Continuous Release with Automated QA Early in the SDLC

If you managed to do so, you are now ready to break builds.

STEP 5 — BUILD STATUS REFLECTING BUILD QUALITY

Goal: Build status now also reflects the execution of automated tests

Duration: 4–8 weeks

The next step is to eventually change the build status. By getting to this point, it is clear that developers understand the value of the proposed change. They accept it, trust it, and support it. Changing the build status in case of test failures is important. This is a key metric for development managers. They constantly track and monitor it. It can be even more accurate, if quality indicators are brought in. By getting to this point, a major milestone is achieved.

Time for the countdown. Prepare for takeoff. Run a couple of sanity checks before it is too late.

1. Make sure that both QA engineers and developers know the new development process in detail. Double check that everyone is on the same page with regard to the status of discovered issues.

2. Solve issues with both product and tests detected by running the automated test suites in a timely manner. By doing this, they will be removed from the corresponding CI jobs sooner rather than later.

The troubleshooting action plan should be similar to the one below.

If a real issue has been detected, there is great chance that it is a critical one. Do you remember the goal of having "smoke" tests? They perform business-critical scenarios. Hence, issues breaking them need to be treated as critical ones, as well. Commits in the source control system breaking the tests should either be reverted and fixed or the issue should be hot-fixed as soon as possible, ideally before the end of the business day.

Imagine that it turns out that there is no app issue detected. Now, two additional options need to be considered:

- **Option 1:** The test needs to be updated in order to reflect disruptive changes in the application under test.

- **Option 2:** For some reason the test is not stable and reliable. It needs to be improved.

If a concrete test failed frequently, it would be better temporarily removed from the automation package. It would be returned after being fixed and proved as reliable again. Note that commenting out tests from the automation suite is considered to be an anti-pattern. In many cases such tests would never be improved and merged back in the main CI flow.

If you really want to win the race and impress everyone around, prepare and share a weekly report summarizing the outcome of several test runs. You could include information about success rates, failures, and detected issues. You could also provide visual information and basic trend analysis of critical quality indicators. This way, the management, development, and QA will be aligned. They will share one and the same view of the quality status, problems, and challenges ahead. For example, they would know, if the trend of newly discovered issues for a certain period of time would indicate increase or decrease in their number.

SUMMARY

And now what? If you effectively went through the 5 steps of success, you have made a major improvement and built a significant bridge allowing the start of quality activities earlier throughout the SDLC. You have laid the foundation necessary for achieving continuous deliveries. From here on, it should be constantly assessed, discussed, and decided upon which would be the next automated tests to enrich the QA suite integrated into the heart of the development process. It is a good idea to maintain your "innovation" environment so that the already established "shadow CI" process can be used to validate and prove the stability and resilience of new automated scenarios.

17 Enabling Mobile DevOps

THIS CHAPTER WAS CONTRIBUTED BY DONOVAN BROWN, SENIOR DEVOPS PROGRAM MANAGER AT MICROSOFT

MEET THE MAN in the Black Shirt. **Donovan Brown** is a Senior DevOps Program Manager on Microsoft's US Developer Division team. Why is DevOps one of the hottest topics? Because it hurts the most. Luckily, Donovan's unofficial tag line is #RubDevOpsOnIt and he is here to make it all better. Before joining Microsoft, Donovan spent seven years as a Process Consultant and a Certified Scrum Master. Developer Tools are his thing. Donovan has travelled the globe helping companies in the U.S., Canada, India, Germany, and the UK develop solutions using agile practices, Visual Studio, and Team Foundation Server in industries as broad as Communications, Health Care, Energy, and Financial Services. Donovan is also an avid programmer, often finding ways to integrate software into his other hobbies and activities, one of which is Professional Air Hockey where he has ranked as high as 11th in the world.

INTRODUCTION

DevOps is a union of people, process, and products to enable continuous delivery of value to our end users. This is true for every type of software development, including mobile.

The competition in the mobile world is fierce and organizations must move quickly to keep up with innovation, market competition, and to continuously deliver value to their end users. The only way to compete is to implement Mobile DevOps. Achieving Mobile DevOps requires a complete automation of the entire release cycle — development, build, testing, and releasing to production.

Mobile DevOps has a set of unique challenges, including development, device proliferation, testing, distribution, and monitoring & learning. Each of these challenges must be addressed and automated to continuously deliver value — "value" being the operative word. The goal is not to simply automate the deployment of software, but to deliver value. To prove you delivered value, you must monitor the application while it is being used in production. If you deployed a new feature, but no one is using it, you did not deliver value.

Until recently, as depicted in **Figure 95,** building a Mobile DevOps pipeline required the use of multiple vendors and products. This proved to be so complex that many companies still deploy their mobile products manually, making it nearly impossible to compete.

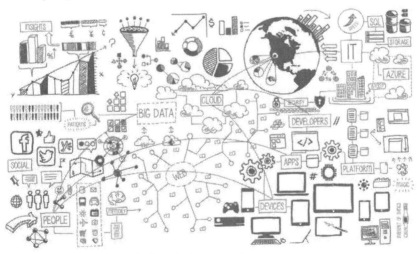

Figure 95: Mobile Transformation Has Happened

Microsoft realized that in order to sustain a working and stable Mobile DevOps workflow they needed to own the relevant tools across the various tasks that are being done, from A–Z.

THE CHALLENGE: ENABLING MOBILE DEVOPS WITH A SINGLE TOOL CHAIN

The diagram in **Figure 96** elaborates on the typical development workflow for a mobile App.

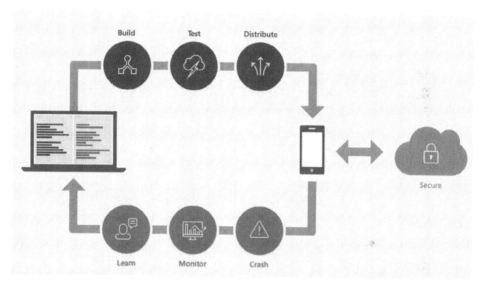

Figure 96: Typical SDLC Workflow for Mobile Apps

The typical App development workflow begins with developers writing their code for the App (whether it is Native, Web, Hybrid, Responsive, or cross-platform) within an IDE. Once coding is done, the changes are committed to a source control management system (SCM) that will trigger a continuous integration build of the newly developed source code. Unit tests should be executed during the build. The result of your build will be binaries that can be deployed to devices for exploratory and manual testing. Before the files are released to manual testers, automated UI tests should be executed. Alpha and/ or beta versions of the app will be distributed to your testers, so they can test and provide feedback. Once testing is complete, the binaries are submitted to the appropriate app stores for each platform. Finally, when an end user installs the app onto their device, the application will be constantly monitored for crashes, feedback, and custom telemetry.

With the above Mobile DevOps workflow, there is a huge level of complexity in making it work across versions, features, and ongoing mobile market changes. Microsoft is the only vendor that offers a complete Mobile DevOps solution.

Despite this fact, there are still attempts to build DevOps pipelines using as many vendors as possible.

Historically, putting all your eggs in one basket has proved to increase risk. Because systems only provided an All-or-Nothing approach, users would lose the flexibility to adopt new technology as it was released. Customers, i.e. app vendors, were forced to wait for the solution provider to offer an equivalent feature, or worse, must start over again with another solution. Hence, they started to avoid the benefits of a unified solution in exchange for flexibility.

This allowed the app vendors to adopt hot new technologies and be on the bleeding edge with their pipeline. They could evaluate each offering and select the best of breed in each area. On the surface this seemed like a great idea until they realized that the products did not play well together. By this point, vendors had convinced themselves that the cost of integration was unavoidable and just a cost of doing business.

This change in customer mindset had vendors focusing on having the best CI or source control system instead of an integrated system. With vendors only focusing on a part of the pipeline, there were great achievements in each area. However, the integration effort continued to increase at an alarming rate. Eventually, the cost of maintaining the pipeline became too great and started to have a noticeable impact on developers' productivity.

Even when all the products play nicely with each other, it can be difficult to enable good traceability from a code change all the way to production. This is the reason why more and more vendors are starting to expand their offerings to reduce the cost and risk of integration.

CALCULATE TRUE COST OF OWNERSHIP

When building your DevOps pipeline, you must consider the true cost of ownership. The cost is much more than what you paid for the products. It includes the amount of time and effort to integrate and maintain these products. Time spent on integration and maintenance is time not spent on software innovation that makes money. With each new tool and vendor you incur a cost of integration. Someone on your team is now responsible for maintaining that pipeline by making sure all products are upgraded and that the integration is still intact. This is time much better spent delivering value to end users.

Adding vendors also complicates your billing, as you are paying multiple vendors instead of one. The opportunity for bundle or volume discounts is also reduced.

IS BEST-OF-BREED THE BEST FOR YOU

We have met many customers that claimed they wanted the best-of-breed products. However, when asked what made one product better than another, we often found out that they did not even use that feature. They were complicating their pipeline out of vanity. "Everyone else said this was the best, so we wanted to be on the best." You need to find the best product for you, which might not be the best of breed for that area. Just because Product A does not have all the bells and whistles of Product B does not mean that Product B is the right one for you.

RECOMMENDED SOLUTION: MOBILE DEVOPS WITHIN MICROSOFT TOOL CHAIN

Microsoft offers developers everything they need to turn an idea into a working piece of software. Visual Studio — an IDE with Xamarin built in — enables cross-platform mobile app development with C#. This allows developers to target all three mobile platforms with a single language and an enormous amount of code reuse. Once the app is ready for testing, the IPA and APK files can be uploaded to the Xamarin Test Cloud, so that automated UI tests could be run on thousands of physical devices.

At this point, the fear of vendor lock in definitely needs to be addressed. Although we provide our own test Cloud, we also allow integrations with other systems at any point in your pipeline. For example, if you already have experience with the Perfecto Cloud, you could use it instead of the Xamarin Test Cloud. In addition, each portion of Visual Studio Team Services, Agile Planning, Source Control, Continuous Integration, Continuous Deployment, Release Management, and Package Management could be replaced with tools of your choice.

When you combine Team Services, HockeyApp, and Xamarin, you are able to automate the entire process of Mobile DevOps. The screenshots in **Figure 97** illustrate how the corresponding processes could be automated in a way that releases are monitored and tracked.

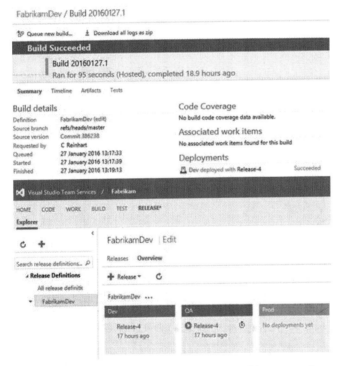

Figure 97: Visual Studio Team Services Release Management

By using Release Management from Team Services, you can automate the deployment of your mobile application directly to each app store.

To accomplish the last and most important Mobile DevOps activity of monitoring and learning, Microsoft provides app vendors with its HockeyApp[1] tool suite, as presented in **Figure 98,** which is fully integrated in the Microsoft toolchain and closes the DevOps loop. After the acquisition of Xamarin by Microsoft the monitoring Insights solution was integrated with HockeyApp and, as mentioned in the workflow, allows full feedback loop from production back to the Application developers.

The Latest on HockeySDK for UWP

Since the first Preseason release of our HockeySDK for UWP we've received great feedback and we're happy to announce that HockeySDK for UWP apps on Windows 10 is available to all customers.

Distribution
Build and upload your apps to HockeyApp. Testers can now download and install them. You have full control of who can access which app. Think of it as your personal App Store for testing.
Learn more about Distribution

Crash Reports
Nobody wants their app to crash. But when it happens HockeyApp provides you with the right information at your fingertips, like symbolicated stack traces and environment details.
Learn more about Crash Reports

Feedback
Testing your app is way more than preventing crashes. With HockeyApp, your testers can provide valuable feedback and suggest new features or improvements right from the app.
Learn more about Feedback

User Metrics
HockeyApp provides you with insight of how users are using your app. Take advantage of User Metrics, improve your apps and measure success.
Learn more about User Metrics

Teams
Sophisticated team-management features make distributing applications to different sets of test users quick and easy. Full access control included.
Learn more about Teams

Enterprise
Well-suited for large companies developing many different apps. HockeyApp integrates with your environment and scales with your needs to achieve the best Mobile DevOps experience.
Learn more about Enterprise

Figure 98: HockeyApp Product Capabilities

The three steps that follow the build process are the app distribution, the production monitoring, and learning, in which the development team learns how their end users engage with the app, what are the pitfalls, and if there are any issues within the app.

---

1   Microsoft HockeyApp — https://www.hockeyapp.net/

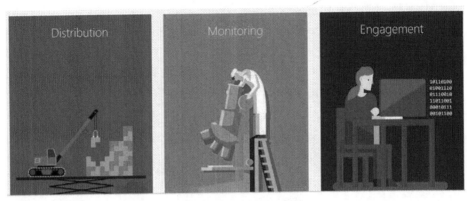

Figure 99: Deployment Workflow as Part of the Mobile DevOps

Having a fully automated Mobile DevOps pipeline allows your team to respond quickly to the information they learn from the data captured during production usage. This is key to enabling your teams to continuously deliver value to your end users.

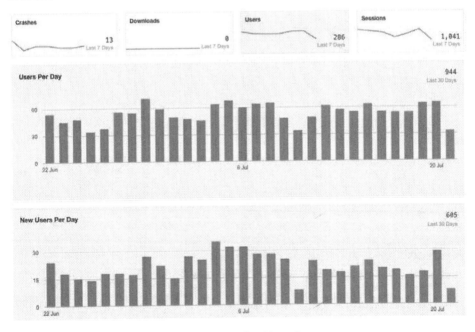

Figure 100: HockeyApp Sample App Monitoring Dashboard

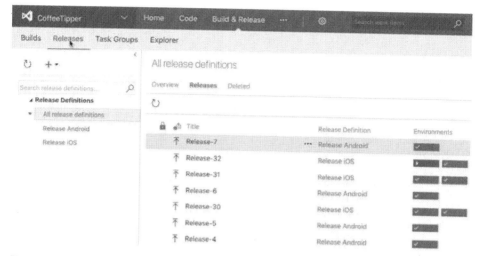

Figure 101: Release Management Automated Workflow Using HockeyApp

SUMMARY

This chapter described a working end-to-end Mobile DevOps workflow which you can build yourself or simply use the offering from Microsoft. Although mobile has unique challenges, the goal of DevOps is the same: to continuously deliver value.

To learn more about Mobile DevOps and get hands-on experience, follow Donovan through the below references.[2] [3] [4]

---

2   Donovan Brown online sessions — https://channel9.msdn.com/niners/donovan#usersessions

3   Donovan Brown DevOps Blog — http://donovanbrown.com/

4   Microsoft Ignite New Zealand 2016 Live Session — https://channel9.msdn.com/Events/Ignite/New-Zealand-2016/M309

Actualizing Quality While Practicing Agile

THIS CHAPTER WAS CONTRIBUTED BY ANGIE JONES, CONSULTING AUTOMATION ENGINEER

ANGIE JONES is a Consulting Automation Engineer who advises several scrum teams on their automation strategies. She has developed testing solutions for countless software products. As a Master Inventor, Angie is known for her innovative and out-of-the-box style of thinking which has resulted in more than 20 patented inventions in the US and China.

Ms. Jones shares her wealth of knowledge internationally by speaking and teaching at software conferences, serving as an Adjunct College Professor of Computer Programming, and leading tech workshops for young girls through TechGirlz and Black Girls Code.

INTRODUCTION

Testing mobile applications is difficult. In addition to the features being delivered, there is a vast array of other testing considerations that teams need to take into account, such as the diversity of devices, versions of OS, latency, interruptions, network switching, offline capability, user experience, and many, many more. With so much to test, mobile development teams struggle to do an adequate job of covering all their bases. As teams consider adopting an Agile software development methodology, a common fear is the possibility of falling even further behind on their testing efforts. With the pressure of delivering a release to the market and ensuring that the release's quality has been verified, many mobile development teams question if going Agile is the right move for them.

Within this chapter, it will become clear that Agile is the only way organizations could basically survive while competing for better engagement, exposure, and revenues and pushing up for aggressive release schedules. Thus, many techniques which will ease up the pain of transition as well as industry trends will be discussed.

WHY GO AGILE?

The Agile software methodology is a set of methods and practices that encourage communication, collaboration, and cross-functional teamwork to enable short development iterations that allow for the flexibility to respond quickly to changing demands. By developing and releasing within short cycles, which are typically timeboxed as two week sprints, teams can obtain fast feedback and adjust their future deliveries accordingly.

Agile practices lend themselves very well to mobile app development. Frequent releases can help to keep your audience engaged and improve user retention — an area that many mobile apps struggle with. Mobile app users are also very vocal in regards to their experiences with apps and are not shy about recommending features that they would like to have in addition. Incorporating this feedback into the planning of future releases is a great way to improve customer satisfaction.

The software industry is competitive, especially on the mobile applications market. The faster you can get a minimum viable product to market, the sooner you can grow your user base, credibility, and revenue. These are some of the key indicators that potential users and investors are looking for.

Everpix, a photo organization mobile app startup, is a great case study of what can go wrong when adopting a more traditional approach to software development when creating a mobile application. They released a beta version of their app which is a good thing. However, the company spent the next nine months working to perfect the app. Once released, the app included several new features and its quality was undoubtedly a focus for the company, as the work they produced was top-notch.

However, the development pace was not ideal for a company that needed to be focused on growing a user base. During the time of developing the app, Everpix spent all their investments on paying their employees and other costs associated with maintaining the app. By the time they released, they were breaking. Without generating enough revenue to cover their expenses, the company eventually folded.

What Everpix did do right was focus on developing a quality mobile application. However, it was not done rapidly enough to survive in the fast-paced mobile industry. In this chapter, we will explore how to accomplish this while subscribing to the Agile methodology, so that you can release high-quality features in a timely fashion.

QUALITY AT SPEED IS A MUST

Fully embracing the Agile software development methodology can be a challenge for any team. In particular, it could be especially challenging for a team that is developing mobile applications. Within an Agile sprint, the team must not only develop new app features, but also ensure that the app is of high quality.

Unfortunately, testing for the quality of mobile applications involves many different facets. It is unrealistic to expect traditional testing techniques alone to be as effective to testing a mobile application within an Agile sprint.

Many teams have come to this conclusion the hard way. With what seems like not enough time to do adequate testing, they forego a lot of it and release anyway. The issue here is that the bugs will be found one way or another — either by your testers or by your users. The bad news is that your users are not nearly as forgiving as your testers. The app stores are littered with negative reviews from users complaining about quality issues. Unlike traditional web applications, the user ratings and reviews are in plain sight at the point of purchase of mobile apps and these factors play a significant role when users are about to make up their minds whether having this or that app might be worth it.

Given the limited amount of time in an Agile sprint and the abundance of testing that needs to be done to deliver a high-quality app, you may easily find yourself wondering "How do we get this done?"

Here are three techniques to help you achieve your quality initiatives while working in an Agile process.

SHIFT TESTING LEFT

The term "shift left" means to move testing efforts from the end of the development cycle to much earlier stages. A common misconception is that this only applies to the test engineers as part of concrete teams. "Shift left" does not just mean that testers get more technical; it also means that developers are needed to focus more on quality.

Below you will find some practical ways developers can contribute to shift testing left.

UNIT TESTS

No matter what software methodology you subscribe to, unit testing should be the norm for software developers. Unit tests individually validate the smallest units of an application and every testable unit should have one. Furthermore, these tests should be automated and executed as part of your code integration strategy. Also, because they are automated, they can be run easier against your lab of devices to provide a sanity check. For this reason, unit tests are key to the successful testing strategy for mobile apps. These tests should make up the most of the automated test suite.

ALLOW TESTERS TO DRIVE DEVELOPMENT

Another approach towards improving quality even further is to use Test-Driven Development (TDD) as a means of specification. TDD is the process of developing your tests before writing the production code. It encourages developers to ponder the problems that they are trying to solve and only write enough code to solve them. This prevents developers from overdesigning a solution and adding more code than necessary. While it may seem that this process would lengthen the development phase, in most cases it shortens it because significantly less production code is written and less debugging is required. Thus, TDD contributes a lot to higher quality and more frequent releases, reduced support efforts, and better potential for further evolution of any app.

EXECUTING HAPPY PATHS

Another technique that developers can use to shift testing left is to execute the non-automated "happy path" flows against the set of environments that is supported by the application. A happy path is a basic straightforward scenario that does not anticipate any abnormal behavior or actions by the end user or the device. Ensuring that these works across all the environments is a requirement that development can satisfy.

As Agile is an all-hands-on-deck sport, these are just a few ways that developers can pitch in to help shift testing left. In doing so, this frees up the testers to focus on other critical areas that need their attention.

EXPLORE MOBILITY WHILE TESTING FEATURES

Besides what is executed by development, there are a lot of other scenarios that still need to be tested. These include the less common, but still probable paths that many end users will follow, the ones that exercise the mobility of the application. There are so many of these to cover. To hit two birds with one stone, you could throw them right into your feature testing.

For instance, if testing an in-app purchase feature is in the middle of a transaction while an incoming phone call or a text message is received, how does the app behave? Is the purchase compromised and therefore revenue lost?

Another example would be testing an upload or download feature. Try switching the network from cellular to Wi-Fi in the middle of the process. How does the app behave? Does the process continue after the network switch or is it discontinued?

If you are testing an app where your changes must be reflected on a server, try starting a scenario online, continuing the process while offline, and then going back online again. Is all data synched up as expected?

When dealing with mobile environments, these are the types of occurrences that are bound to happen, yet end users are oblivious to their impact and still expect apps to operate properly. Anything short of that will be a perceived as lack of quality.

AUTOMATE THE REGRESSION TESTS

As your team develops new features, there will be plenty to test without worrying about retesting existing features. Simply put, time is never enough to perform regression testing and verify the quality of new features at the same time without significant compromises in either direction. Therefore, you need a pragmatic approach towards automation activities. You need to strive to automate important tests providing lots of value and build a stable and reliable regression test suite step-by-step. This will offload you and your team when it comes to repetitive testing of vital scenarios.

This automated suite can be run unattendedly, so no human intervention will be necessary. Hence, it will detect and warn for regressions as often as desired. Of course, executions will be done against the diverse set of device types and operating systems needed for full coverage.

Adding test automation may seem like yet another activity that will consume a lot of development time, but if you implement it strategically, it does not have to. Adopting practices such as Behavior-Driven Development (BDD) — which is a collaborative process that promotes specification of the desired behavior of the potential feature — can not only ensure that the business analyst, developer, and tester are all on the same page before development begins, but can also serve as an executable document to drive automation efforts. Using this approach can greatly increase the quality of the application, since everyone agrees on what should be built and how it should behave. As a bonus, automated steps can be written to validate the scenarios.

Another approach to speeding up your automation efforts is by using the app's web services for as much of the scenario as possible. For example, let us assume that we are testing an e-commerce mobile app and we would like to automate the "Increase Quantity" feature of the shopping cart. Every step before an item actually gets inside the cart is necessary, yet irrelevant to the testing of this specific feature. These types of steps should be done in the most cost-efficient way possible — and most times that is via web services.

To best accomplish this Agile-friendly approach towards automation development, a sophisticated framework is needed that will support the implementation of BDD with interface and web services testing.

Figure 102 depicts an example scenario written in a business readable format suitable for BDD.

```
1 Feature: Manage Cart
2 As a user, I want to manage my cart so that I can make final adjustments before purchasing
3
4    Scenario: Increase quantity
5       Given product with SKU CM01-R is in the cart
6       When I update its quantity to 3
7       Then its price should be $80.00
8       And its total should be $240.00
```

Figure 102: An Example of a BDD Scenario Automating "Increase Quantity" in e-Commerce App

The intent of this scenario is to test the "Increase Quantity" functionality of the shopping cart, so we will use web services to add the product to the cart since that is not the functionality under test, as illustrated by the code snippet in **Figure 103.**

```
28 public class CartStepDefs {
29    BaseStepDefs stepData;
30    CartPage cartPage;
31
32    public CartStepDefs(BaseStepDefs stepData) {
33       this.stepData = stepData;
34    }
35
36    @Given("^product with SKU (.*) is in the cart$")
37    public void addProductToCartViaService(String sku){
38       stepData.sku = sku;
39       CartServices.addProductToCart(sku);
40       Assert.assertTrue(sku + " added to cart", cartPage.isProductInCart(sku));
41
42       cartPage = stepData.currentPage.clickCart();
43    }
```

Figure 103: Line 39 Calls a Web Service to Add a Product to the Cart

Now that once the product is already in the cart, we can automate against the app's user interface to test the aforementioned functionality. Go through the test code in **Figure 104** and get to know how UI testing could be elegantly plugged into such "hybrid" BDD scenarios.

```
45   @When("^I update its quantity to (\\d+)$")
46   public void updateQuantity(int quantity){
47       cartPage = cartPage.updateQuantity(stepData.sku, quantity);
48   }
49
50   @Then("^its price should be (.*)$")
51   public void verifyPrice(String price){
52       Assert.assertEquals(stepData.sku + "'s price", price, cartPage.getPrice(stepData.sku));
53   }
54
55   @Then("^its total should be (.*)$")
56   public void verifyTotal(String total){
57       Assert.assertEquals(stepData.sku + "'s total", total, cartPage.getTotal(stepData.sku));
58   }
59
60   @Then("^the product should be in the cart$")
61   public void verifyProductInCart(){
62       CartPage cartPage = new CartPage();
63       Assert.assertTrue(stepData.sku + " is in cart", cartPage.isProductInCart(stepData.sku));
64       Assert.assertEquals("Number of items in cart", 1, cartPage.getNumberOfProducts());
65   }
66 }
```

Figure 104: An Example of UI Testing as Part of a "Hybrid" BDD Scenario Relying Also on API Calls

SUMMARY

There is a lot of ground to cover when testing mobile applications. While it may seem daunting to achieve this while practicing Agile, the collaboration and cross-functional aspects of this methodology are perfect for bringing in and evolving sustainably quality applications within short periods.

Keep in mind that aggressive release schedules require constant focus on continuous improvement, so ideally your Agile practices will evolve, mature, and then mutate again with the same fast pace.

4

Mobile App Quality — Non-functional Practices

19

The Benefits of Crowdsourced Testing for Mobile Apps

THIS CHAPTER WAS CONTRIBUTED BY DORON REUVENI, CEO AT APPLAUSE

DORON REUVENI — the CEO and co-founder of Applause — is the driving force behind one of the fastest growing tech companies in New England. He has grown the company exponentially in just few years. In 2007 his evolutionary vision for "In-The-Wild" software testing through a crowdsourcing model disrupted the industry.

With more than 25 years of experience, Doron has become an internationally recognized expert in software development and testing as well as startup formation and entrepreneurship. Prior to Applause, he was the CEO and Owner of Re.D Consulting, where he advised enterprise firms on their go-to-market strategies, company direction, and product roadmaps. Earlier, he helped startups in raising capital and also held important management positions leading global teams working on multi-million software implementations.

Doron is a husband and father of three active children. He helps coach his children's soccer teams and is an avid skier, cyclist, and runner. In fact, he has run the Boston Marathon ten times. He also regularly competes in triathlons.

INTRODUCTION

Maintaining a strong digital presence is becoming increasingly important for businesses across every industry. Digital experiences can now be thought of as the front door for brands, and between websites, mobile apps, and connected devices, and there are many ways for brands to establish a lasting impression. The emergence of mobile technology has triggered a major shift in the way businesses connect with their target audiences. Brands have powerful new approaches to reach people on an individual level but they also need to account for a whole new level of complexity.

While tens of millions of people can download the same mobile app, the experience that each of them has with it will be completely unique. This is not a philosophical assertion or a statement about the individuality of the human mind. This is simply a result of how fragmented the digital world has become.

Between the broad variety of devices that people can use to access mobile apps, the increasing number of different operating systems that those devices can be running, and all the different mobile service providers that are connecting those devices to the Internet, there are thousands of permutations of mobile devices that are in existence today.

In addition, mobile apps are being used in an increasing number of scenarios. Whether at home and connected to Wi-Fi, on the subway while using mobile data or on the side of a mountain in offline mode, it appears there is an endless list of contexts and situations in which they can be used.

Mobile apps are also expected to work in all locations across the globe and this fact introduces the need to have interfaces available in different languages and adapted to a variety of cultural norms.

Taking into consideration all of this, there is a seemingly infinite number of unique digital experiences that one build can create. While this is a step forward, it also presents a new challenge. The increasing number of ways that brands can interact with their target audience is also simultaneously creating more ways to potentially deliver a poor and costly experience to users.

Amazon is a great example of a brand that recognizes this challenge. With no brick-and-mortar locations, Amazon relies heavily on digital channels for its revenue. If Amazon's retail apps fail to accommodate the newest versions of devices and operating systems, it would be the equivalent to Walmart or Target turning people away at the door because of the phones they own.

It is easy to understand why brands like Amazon have a thorough QA process in place that covers as many different devices and use cases as possible. However, a lab-based effort is ultimately restricted in what it can test and there are issues that only manifest themselves in the hands of its customers as they are using digital channels in the conditions of the real world.

CROWDTESTING

Simply put, crowdsourcing is the process of leveraging the distributed power of different people across the globe through the Internet. It has probably been made the most popular by companies like Uber, Kickstarter, and Waze. However, when you combine crowdsourcing with the world of digital experiences, you get the concept of crowdtesting.

Crowdtesting is the process of putting digital properties into the hands of the people they have been designed for and creating a completely objective picture of how they stand up to the authentic scenarios and environments where they will eventually be used. It is the testing solution that most closely represents the way that digital properties will work on every device, in every location, and in the conditions of the real world.

Companies like Applause have assembled communities of crowd-testers that can be leveraged for what is called "In-The-Wild" testing. In general, there are two different approaches to this type of testing. Crowdtesting can be done with communities of QA professionals or communities of everyday people that have no background in QA. Both approaches have the power to provide unmatched levels of insight, but it is important to understand where would each one of them be applicable.

The crowdtesting industry provides brands with the opportunity to flourish with either of these approaches through a variety of different community types. Some communities have rigorous vetting processes and a merit-based rating system to ensure that only the most qualified and talented testers are assigned to client projects. Within these communities, brands can view profiles for all of the crowdtesters that are assigned to their projects and reach out to them directly if they need to. There are also communities that have minimal vetting and simply act as a middleman between a brand and a handful of people that can try out their digital property while providing some immediate feedback on how well it is currently working.

THE BENEFITS OF CROWDTESTING

When done properly, there are numerous benefits gained from adding crowd-testing to an existing QA effort.

DIVERSITY

The first of all benefits is diversity. Let us use Applause as an example. Its community contains 250,000 testers located in over 200 different countries and territories. Within it, clients have access to 2,500 unique device models on 600 mobile carriers as well as fluent speakers of more than 50 different languages. Crowdtesting enables brands to filter through these diverse pools and put together test teams representing each of their target markets.

Let us consider the example of a quick service restaurant that has an international presence to see how this type of testing can be beneficial. With a customer base that transcends cultures, these types of brands need to deliver a mobile ordering app experience that is tailored and targeted to each of the unique markets in which it does business. Checkout issues — related to things like currencies and tax rates — could lead to customers not completing orders or experiencing poor brand journeys. By crowdtesting, they can set up teams of testers that are local to each of the different markets that they are operating on. Thus, true coverage of the devices, use cases, and mobile ordering preferences can be ensured. Now, if you think about it, they will reflect the ones mostly relevant to the people for whom the product has been designed.

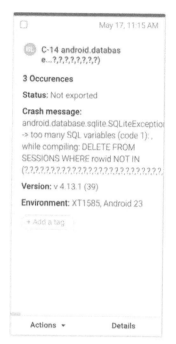

May 17, 11:15 AM

C-14 android.databas
e...?,?,?,?,?,?,?,?)

3 Occurences

Status: Not exported

Crash message:
android.database.sqlite.SQLiteExceptio
-> too many SQL variables (code 1): ,
while compiling: DELETE FROM
SESSIONS WHERE rowid NOT IN
(?,

Version: v 4.13.1 (39)

Environment: XT1585, Android 23

+ Add a tag

Actions ▾   Details

Figure 105: An Example of a Crash Message Detected by Crowdtesting in a Real Mobile App

There is also another type of diversity that crowdtesting offers: a diversity of the perspective. When internal teams inevitably become familiar with a digital product they create, it becomes difficult to assess it objectively. Crowdtesting brings in new sets of eyes to take an unbiased look.

FLEXIBILITY

Another benefit of crowdtesting is flexibility. Brands that crowdtest can scale up their testing efforts to get lots of eyes on a build when they have a fast approaching deadline to meet while scaling down the number of testers involved in projects just as easily during slower periods. Also, when testing with a crowdtesting community, there are no restrictions on when a test cycle can be run. For companies that need as much time as possible to focus on developing and improving the design of their apps and websites, it may seem like there are not enough hours in a day to perform testing. However, by crowdtesting, brands can ship out a build for its crowdtesting team to look at outside of business hours or over weekends. By the time they are back at the office on the following business day, all of the crowdtesting defects found can be exported into their internal workflow.

OVERALL IMPROVEMENT IN DIGITAL QUALITY

A third benefit of crowdtesting is an overall improvement in digital quality while avoiding the traditional overhead that comes with adding QA headcount. By extending the reach of internal testing, brands can find more defects that would have otherwise reached their user base without committing time, energy, and resources into adding more full-time employees. There is no intention of devaluing the QA employees at companies. The intention here is to highlight crowdtesting as a force multiplier that can enable the teams that companies have in place to accomplish a much more thorough level of testing.

No matter what the business model of a brand is, crowdtesting uncovers additional defects and allows for fixing them before releasing the respective apps or websites into production. If a defect does make it to production, crowdtesting could also be a catalyst for identifying the root cause, so that a timely hotfix may be released shortly.

CROWDTESTING AND UX ASSURANCE

Crowdtesting has been effective in scenarios like the hypothetical one about Amazon described earlier, where it is important to make sure a digital product is working as it has been designed to. However, there are also other ways to harness the power of a crowd while trying to build a better digital experience. Usability testing is one of those ways.

There are few things more valuable to a brand than being able to know exactly what its target audience thinks about the digital experience it is delivering. Testing with a crowd enables brands to accomplish this mission. The diversity that a large, well-established crowd has goes beyond enabling access to a variety of devices and locations — it enables brands to target demographics and psychographics.

DEMOGRAPHIC AND PSYCHOGRAPHIC FILTERING IN PRACTICE

If a manufacturer of connected baby monitoring systems utilizing web cameras wanted feedback on the prototype it had just finished putting together, crowdtesting would be a simple way for them to get access to the opinions and feedback of mothers of newborns who are currently living in the exact context and circumstance that this product has been designed for.

The manufacturer may have put years of market research into formulating its design and then executed the development plan perfectly, but without crowdtesting it would lack real world feedback on how its product would be rated once it reached the shelves of stores. While it may be designed to cover all the needs of the mothers of newborns, that design may not be intuitive or easy enough for them to use every time they put down their infant for a nap. If it took the same amount of time to set up as it does for their baby to take a nap, it would hardly be something that they will end up using. Furthermore, it will not

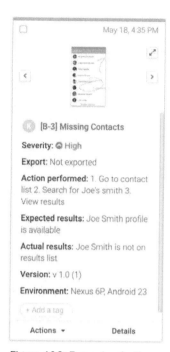

May 18, 4:35 PM

[B-3] Missing Contacts

Severity: High

Export: Not exported

Action performed: 1. Go to contact list 2. Search for Joe's smith 3. View results

Expected results: Joe Smith profile is available

Actual results: Joe Smith is not on results list

Version: v 1.0 (1)

Environment: Nexus 6P, Android 23

+ Add a tag

Actions ▾   Details

Figure 106: Example of a Defect Detected by Crowdtesting Found on a Real Mobile App

be something that they would recommend to their friends. This kind of user behavior usually causes long-term negative impact on brands.

Tapping into the thoughts of its exact target audience by crowdtesting is a critical step in the design process.

While crowdtesting for usability within very specific demographic requirements is useful in scenarios like the one described, sometimes having something broader, such as a "person-off-the-street" perspective, will provide the most valuable feedback. This type of feedback is also something that crowdtesting is effective at providing and big-box retailers are a good example of companies that benefit from it.

With a major shift toward omni-channel shopping experiences taking place, customers are now able to shop with a single retailer in lots of different ways. They can browse online and show up at the store later that day to pick up an item. They can also order something online and then end up returning it in a store. They can walk the aisles of stores while reading product descriptions on the mobile app. They can even receive personalized offers from beacons upon entering a store. This variety of channels adds convenience for customers, but also creates an entirely new dimension of digital experience that needs to be accounted for by these retailers.

Crowdtesting is a solution that enables these brands to get teams of "people-off-the-street" exploring their mobile apps and in their stores providing feedback on each step of the process. A possible lesson learnt could be that customers receive too many push notifications immediately upon entering a store. Or it may be the case that they do not receive enough push notifications. It is also possible that they simply cannot find what they are looking for. Regardless, by gaining this level of insight, brands can view a complete picture of how intuitive and simple the process of spending money with them is. This way, they get candid feedback on whether they are ahead, inline with, or behind competitors.

THE PROPER ROLE OF CROWDTESTING

Crowdtesting offers capabilities that no other type of internal testing does, but an important emphasis would be that it is most effective when positioned as complementary to lab-based testing.

The brands that position crowdtesting as an extension of an internal process are the brands that end up maximizing the value of their investment in it. When they put their mobile apps through basic tests in a lab first, they can ensure that when those products reach the hands of crowdtesters, they can put them through complex use cases that are more challenging and sometimes impossible to cover in a lab.

While working with third-party vendors usually comes with disjointedness, this does not necessarily need to be the case with crowdtesting. Once a test team is in place, crowdtesting companies can make it simple to set up a continuous feedback loop between crowdtesting teams and in-house development teams. Most crowdtesting companies make the bugs reported by teams of crowdtesters available for clients to view in real time. Crowdtesting team leaders typically review and triage bugs before clients even see them. In some cases, bugs can even be exported directly into a client's internal bug tracking system.

The whole idea behind this approach is to integrate the crowdtesting teams and their feedback directly into the client's internal testing and development teams. In some cases, clients will prefer to have the same crowdtesters participating in every test cycle and take advantage of the familiarity they establish with their product. Other clients like and prefer the ability to cycle through lots of different crowdtesters to ensure that they are constantly bringing a fresh perspective into their testing and development process.

Applause offers clients freedom to choose how involved in the crowdtesting process they would like to be. There are crowdtesting companies that specialize in offering self-service platforms and tools, others that are geared toward customers looking for a white glove service, and everything else that is in between. The bottom line is that crowdtesting works best when it is positioned as a way

Figure 107: Example of a Defect Detected by Crowdtesting Found on Real Mobile App

to augment existing QA efforts.

IN-THE-WILD BUGS

There are lots of ways companies could potentially account for every device on the market. However, even after a company accomplishes this, it is still unable to fully replicate the coverage that crowdtesting provides. The reason for this is that there are certain types of defects — sometimes called "In-The-Wild" defects — that only show up when digital properties are taken outside of QA labs, into the "wild," and are in the hands of the people that they are designed for. Whether someone is walking the streets of New York City, switching from a Wi-Fi connection in their office to a cellular data connection in their car or jogging through the back roads of a remote town, there are going to be use cases that simply cannot be replicated in the confines of a QA lab.

These types of defects can be found everywhere. It does not matter what the purpose of the digital property is or which industry it serves. While they are rarely noticeable when they are in a testing lab, they can be the costliest of all bugs.

REAL WORLD EXAMPLES ACROSS VERTICALS

There are countless examples that can illustrate the merits of crowdtesting. Below, you will find true stories about the armageddon in a world without crowds readily exploring mobile apps. They capture the experience of app vendors across different verticals. Yes, crowdtesting suits them all well.

Retail

One major multinational retailer had gone through the process of merging all its English language eCommerce websites into one unified site. Once they completed the integration, they ran a large amount of in-house testing using their standard testing procedures and found very few problems. As a final step in the process, they turned the website over to the crowdtesting community to perform exploratory testing. At that point, a critical defect was noticed; once real users, in real locations, using real devices started entering orders, they discovered a systemwide bug that automatically appended a string of text to the description and item number of every item ordered. Because of this bug, the retailer's back-end fulfillment system was unable to recognize any of the items that customers were buying and no orders could have been processed.

The retailer managed to fix the issue in a matter of hours before taking the integrated site live. It was estimated that if this bug had reached production, it would have cost them at least several million dollars in unfulfilled orders, not taking into account the damage to loyal customers.

Media

In media, "In-The-Wild" defects have proven to have the potential to wreak the same type of havoc.

A Fortune 500 media brand that primarily interacts with customers through videos prioritizes video streaming quality and advertising issues as the most critical types of bugs. These two categories of defects result in less viewer engagement, less willingness from advertisers to purchase ad slots, and, ultimately, less revenue. In fact, these are the types of defects that are the most thoroughly tested and covered in this media brand's QA process. However, no matter how thorough its internal QA process may be, there is still no way for it to the replicate the real world conditions of a production environment. This is exemplified by what was uncovered when this brand extended its QA effort with crowdtesting.

Once the content was brought into the homes and hands of crowdtesters using its mobile app, some critical issues that had escaped lab testing started showing up. Crashes during launch, crashes during ads, videos stalling after pre-roll, and missing advertisements are examples of some of the issues that crowdtesters were finding. There was no rhyme or reason explaining how they were showing up. Some of them were only showing up on devices with Android operating systems, some were exclusive to devices that were using Safari as a browser, and some only existed on Samsung devices. Even the most intricate and thorough internal process could not have isolated these types of defects as efficiently in order to supply all of the necessary information for a quick fix. This was all done while enabling the development team to maintain its release cadence.

Since this brand started crowdtesting, it has seen a reduction in its two most critical levels of defects by nearly 50%.

Finance

In the finance vertical, brands that are responsible for personal checking and bank accounts have no margin for error. While a trustworthy reputation takes a long time to establish, it may disappear in no time because of something as small as one escaped defect. Within this vertical, "In-The-Wild" defects can disrupt the business of more brands than the one whose mobile app they are discovered in. Here is the story of a popular digital wallet which stands out as a great example.

As part of a monthly release, this digital wallet was migrating to a newer platform. After putting the updated platform through its typical QA process, it was prepared for release. However, it also lined up teams of crowdtesters to participate in guided testing immediately after the updated platform went live.

This additional layer of testing proved to be a very valuable decision as its crowdtesting teams discovered several defects that were preventing customers from making purchases on merchants' sites that offered it as a payment option. In the mobile wallet's production environment, crowdtesters were being prevented from signing into their accounts and were also unable to reset their passwords if they attempted to change their credentials as a possible remedy for being blocked from signing in. Customers trying to move forward with their transactions were stuck and had to find another way to pay.

This digital wallet quickly reached out to the crowdtesters reporting the afore-mentioned defects for more details, identified root causes, and released quick fixes before it had any impact with real customers. However, the consequences of this type of "In-The-Wild" issue might have been steep to overcome. Not only does this type of defect trigger customers to start searching for a new digital wallet, but it also gets merchants looking for other digital wallets that they can rely on to facilitate their business.

These stories demonstrate the value of crowdtesting and justify that any brand across any vertical has a lot to lose by leaving it out of its QA process.

THE FUTURE OF CROWDTESTING

When Roy Solomon and the author of this chapter originally had the idea that turned into Applause, the smartphone had not yet been invented. Back then, they had the concept of crowdtesting desktop and web applications in mind.

After Apple released the iPhone and the smartphone began its meteoric rise into the forefront of the lives of people across the globe, it became clear that the crowdtesting concept would adapt magnificently to mobile apps.

Now, in the age of the Internet of Things, companies are designing mobile apps to accompany connected devices. As more devices are connected to the Internet, it becomes clear that crowdtesting is an incredibly effective way for brands to ensure that these devices are performing in tandem with their companion apps. The manufacturers of traditionally "offline" products, such as refrigerators, coffee makers, and even door locks, are now being tasked with delivering their own version of the digital experience. Crowdtesting is perfectly positioned to help them cope with that.

The pattern of crowdtesting playing an increasingly important role in delivering digital experiences as technology advances will continue. The reason behind this statement of belief is simple and follows the same underlying message that has been carried throughout this entire chapter. As the number of ways that people can experience a brand increases, so does the complexity of ensuring that all those experiences are good ones. With all the digital progress that has taken place over the past decade, the process of consistently delivering great customer experiences is as complex as it has ever been. And it is only going to get worse.

Quick service restaurants are a good example as digital experiences have made the quality of food just a small piece of generating loyal customers. Beyond the core requirements of keeping restaurants clean and great places to eat, there is now an entire realm of digital experience for brands like McDonalds,

Starbucks, and Chipotle to make sure they are getting it all right. Their responsibilities now include ensuring that:

* Their digital properties are working on any type of device that customers could be using them with (including smartwatches and other wearables) at any location.

* All that technology is working in tandem with their restaurants, so that the food that is ordered is prepared on time and in the correct locations.

* Their mobile payment processes are fully functional and that they are offering the most relevant mobile payment options in each of their unique target markets.

* Their digital properties are intuitive and enjoyable to use.

The consequences of failing to deliver a high quality digital experience are only getting more and more serious. Crashes and failed conversions can directly cost brands lots of money, but they are also indirectly impacting businesses in the long run. We live in a world of infinite choice. It is not difficult for customers to start using competitive apps if they have poor experience with yours. Quick service restaurants are no longer earning business based purely off the food that they prepare. Rather, the battleground for where business is being won has shifted to the digital experience leading up to food. Because of this, there are not only more and more things that brands must get right, but there is also an increasing pressure on them to get them right all the time.

A lot of trends support the notion of companies prioritizing their digital experience. Brands are now working as hard as ever to deliver a consistently great customer experience and they are still fighting just to keep up. Chief Digital Officers are hired to build teams that are completely focused on managing digital experience and its assets. It is now as if managing all the different ways that customers are interacting with a brand, in the digital space alone, has become equally as important as the commonly known fixtures of successful companies, such as high quality products and great customer service.

The emergence of new technologies such as virtual/augmented reality is going to add another layer of required digital experience testing and will only make things more complicated for brands. There is an undeniable shift happening towards digital becoming involved in every interaction brands have with their target audiences. Brands need to understand the experiences which people undergo through their digital channels. Crowdtesting will remain the best approach for brands to ensure the experience they hope to deliver is in line with what they are actually delivering.

SUMMARY

Within this chapter, the ideas behind crowdtesting were discussed. The merits of using services such as Applause should be clear. It is essential for companies to understand the impact of "In-The-Wild" defects in production. They can quickly ruin the digital experience and damage brands behind mobile apps when reaching customers. Crowdtesting reduces the risk of slapping end users hard in their faces by releasing apps with proven quality over different demographics and psychographics.

This is only the beginning for crowdtesting. The digital transformation has already reached the point of no return. With the advance of technology and ever growing device coverage, more and more crucial defects will slip through the lab-based QA test cycle just to be discovered by crowdtesters "off-the-street". Digital will prevail.

20

Including Non-functional Testing in Build and Continuous Integration Cycles

THIS CHAPTER WAS CONTRIBUTED BY AMIR ROZENBERG, SR. DIRECTOR OF PRODUCT MANAGEMENT AT PERFECTO

AMIR ROZENBERG is a Senior Director of Product Management at Perfecto — the leading digital, Cloud, and automation company. As such, he is responsible for the core product strategy of Perfecto. Amir has pioneered many practices in order to extend the company's offering across the whole application life cycle. He has vast experience in the digital industry with expertise in areas such as infrastructure, applications, application delivery, and monitoring. Amir has led many successful synergies with technology partners to optimize the value delivered to Perfecto's customers. Prior to working at Perfecto, Mr. Rozenberg was heading the mobile monitoring practice at Compuware. Prior to Compuware, co-founded Adva Mobile, a direct-to-fan mobile marketing startup, and held various leadership positions at Groove Mobile, Nextcode Corp., and others.

INTRODUCTION

Verifying compliance with a number of non-functional requirements has been studied the hard way by most software vendors. While this is a fundamental challenge for every software delivery organization, reality whispers about consistent failures to do so.

Within this chapter, more details on this highly important topic will be revealed. You will have a walk through the trends and biggest challenges in performance testing today. You will also find good practices easing it all up a bit. Real-world examples and case studies will back up this thesis in order to make you fully realize the crucial relation of performance and user experience, as well as the corresponding impact in terms of money. Last but not least, valuable insights on the huge pain of guaranteeing great user experience and high-end user engagement for mobile apps will be provided.

MODERN TESTING OF NON-FUNCTIONAL REQUIREMENTS

The traditional approach towards non-functional testing mandates a focus on such activities at the end of the software delivery process, sometimes even extending beyond. The net effect? Well, perhaps these critical tests never really run in time to fully guarantee the delivery readiness of upcoming releases.

We can definitely do better. There are ways for improving non-functional coverage emerging every day. Modern testing frameworks and Cloud Labs allow the execution of some of these tests earlier in the SDLC, thus smoothing the transitions from development to functional and to non-functional testing. Yes, technology provides the means for early identification and resolution of non-functional defects that have the potential to become showstoppers for the release, thus reducing costs, unnecessary efforts, and risk. Technology is just a tool, though. On the road to success you will need to learn to stick to agile principles. Furthermore, you need to constantly monitor, fine-tune, and promote them in such a way that they are aligned, well-perceived, and trusted by all of the development and testing teams involved.

EVOLUTION OF PERFORMANCE TESTING

The world of performance testing has changed dramatically in the last few years. It is no longer about testing the service API layer or stressing a single server with a bit of load. Distributed Cloud architectures, increased integration and consumption of 3rd party services, and different types of content (static, dynamic, streaming, large, extra large in volume) means just one thing — modern applications operate in fragmented, siloed, and latency-rich environments. These artifacts often cause serious flaws in terms of user experience (UX) which is crucial for client facing applications. That said, in many cases, UX shall also be taken into account and measured during load testing. Easy to say, but difficult to achieve.

TRADITIONAL APPROACHES AND THEIR SHORTCOMINGS

In order to ensure the right test coverage, one would need to run massive tests with thousands or millions of virtual users which can theoretically only happen in a staging environment (just before production). Isn't such an approach a good recipe for release showstoppers? There are several challenges related to this traditional approach:

1. Maintaining different environments (such as test, staging, etc.) is expensive.
2. The time it takes to create and update such environments to the latest build is simply not available anymore.
3. As mentioned many times in this book, finding issues just before an upcoming release is very expensive.

Therefore, we need to be able to scale up and down our performance testing architecture in terms of test scope and required target environment. It would be highly appreciated to execute such tests as part of nightly continuous integration builds. This way, any major performance regressions introduced the day before can easily be detected and resolved on the day after, before it is too late.

ON THE ROAD TO SCALABLE ARCHITECTURE FOR PERFORMANCE TESTS

You do not need to test the application under heavy load. Sometimes, it might collapse due to a severe, brand new bug causing excessively increased memory usage (or leak). And, talking about memory, you could measure and track the memory usage on daily basis. You would not be interested in absolute values, but in trends of consumption — on daily, weekly, and release bases. This knowledge could be used to define and align clear thresholds of what is acceptable and what is not. Those could be propagated to the backlog for software development teams as done criteria for each developed feature/user story, thus effectively avoiding serious performance regressions as the developed software evolves. In addition, such an approach could come in handy with pinpointing potential memory leaks or inefficient implementations that could turn into bottlenecks later on. The same applies to measuring, tracking, and analyzing other important performance metrics, such as CPU load. Resolving these kinds of issues today guarantees that they will not cost a sack of money for the organization tomorrow.

What if you need to run this same test suite in your pre-production environment, taking into consideration real-world constraints and workloads? This leads us to the conclusion that the target test architecture needs to be highly configurable by design in order to scale well.

Then, what about user experience? Can we also measure and track the impact of development changes over UX while putting different "loads" on the tested application? Depending on our use cases and the nature of the tested application, we can achieve this if we have an orchestration layer that is able to generate "load" while also running carefully selected UI tests against the tested application in parallel.

OPEN SOURCE WILL SAVE THE DAY — JMETER AND TAURUS

You can harness the real power of existing tools and frameworks and scale according to your needs by introducing complex (from testers' perspective) scenarios, such as using a technology backbone to run both functional and non-functional tests in parallel so you can correlate results from performance and UI tests, for instance. The scalability and configuration capabilities of a similar testing architecture can be ensured by a framework like Taurus.[1] Since it plays nicely with JMeter[2] and Selenium WebDriver, we are able to execute complex, highly configurable, and context-dependent test scenarios by mixing different types of tests and providing timely and valuable insights at any point of the SDLC.

When the build matures, the number of virtual users applied to the infrastructure can easily grow using scalable solutions from vendors like Blazemeter (now CA). The solution can scale up the number of virtual users thanks to global Clouds and multiple scripts, thus allowing testers to observe the true scalability of the application under test. By plugging in and triggering Selenium WebDriver scripts while the application is effectively being "loaded up", one could also measure, quantize, track, and analyze the way UX is affected by any change within the source control management system.

USER EXPERIENCE TESTING: WIND TUNNEL AND USER CONDITION TESTING

As digital applications proliferate and their functionality expands, the expectations of end users towards reliable, consistent, and responsive behavior grow higher and higher. There are numerous articles discussing the penalties vendors incur over poor user experience, independent of whether it is their fault or due to 3rd parties. End users cannot make the difference and they do not need to. Mature software delivery organizations understand that. They also understand that UX can be severely affected by circumstances outside the control of software developers.

MAJOR PITFALLS FOR GREAT MOBILE USER EXPERIENCE

The sole nature of mobile apps mandate that they are extremely vulnerable to a whole bunch of flaws caused by the underlying carrier and network infrastructure. In terms of remote connectivity, some of these could be poor network quality, roaming artifacts derived by the local carrier network, server downtime, and many more. There might be a whole lot happening while users explore an

---

1   Taurus web page — http://gettaurus.org

2   Jmeter open-source web page — http://jmeter.apache.org

app, as also evident in **Figure 108.**

If you put mobile devices into the equation, you might draw the conclusion that mobile apps sometimes function only due to some kind of dark magic that could lose its effect at any point in time. There are a plethora of possible application failures related to improper usage of shared system resources (memory, storage, CPU, camera, geo-location, sensors, etc.), application conflicts on the device, improper interaction, unpredictable behavior of a (defective) sensor, to name just a few. Would you care to imagine how the different versions of mobile OS and their peculiar constraints might make you stumble and fall?

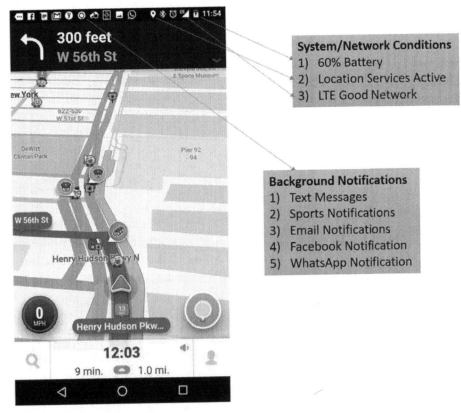

Figure 108: Real User Journey Example — Multiple Notifications and Background Services

THE THREE STEPS TO SUCCESS

The road to superior user experience is steep and hard to walk. There is hope, though. In order to tackle some of the aforementioned challenges, organizations can choose to follow the staged solution below. It consists of three steps.

1. Identify the scenarios that may harm the UX of the tested app

You may not know everything in advance, but you can safely start by analyzing the behavior of the app under poor network conditions. What would you discover if you started a number of background applications running concurrently on devices? Will they somehow affect the UX of the app under test? Load tests are another technique that you can employ at any time in order to identify low performing and less scalable application functionalities. But hey — if your application really underperforms, why don't you source some input from your end users? Ideally, you will find some evidence about such issues in your application log, in user contributed reviews published in the corresponding app store and/or in social networks. The most important thing that you should not forget: defining potentially harmful scenarios is not a one-time activity. You need to iterate on it. Gradually, you will ensure that all important performance indicators will be taken into account while the app evolves.

2. Define thresholds and enforce Key Performance Indicators (KPI) for UX.

Incorporate them into every test script, so that time for launching and logging in with the app, for example, can be measured and compared with previous test runs. Take your time to define sane timeouts for notable events and interactions with the app as part of your test suite. Perhaps, if an application is launched after 20 seconds, while you are chasing 3–5 seconds, you would appreciate the notification of a suddenly failing test. This is also one way to drive the alignment of software and testing teams along the SDLC.

3. Ensure that your testing activities are in line with the needs and behavioral patterns of end users.

As illustrated in Figure 109, you could pick 2–3 personas that resemble your users and parametrize your testing strategies with their needs in mind. Repetitive testing using personas as part of your test suites — integrated and measured along the SDLC — allows detecting and resolving issues early. It also introduces a continuous and objective indication for the quality of the application throughout the sprint. No doubt, this will turn out to be invaluable information for project leads, stakeholders, and decision makers in general.

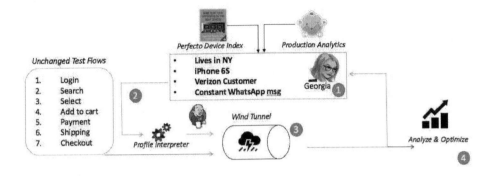

Figure 109: Connecting a Test Scenario to a Possible Target Persona

PERSONAS GO THROUGH WIND TUNNEL

Perfecto offers a type of testing called "Wind Tunnel". It is a unique offering in terms of tooling and test execution support. You could use "Wind Tunnel" for defining environmental profiles named "personas". Essentially, a persona summarizes the characteristics of a distinct group of end users. This solution gives you the opportunity to manage alternate workflows based on the config-uration of different personas. This way, you can emulate and verify the quality of core scenarios and interaction patterns relevant to a given group of users of your app. There is also a catalog of typical ready-made personas available with "Wind Tunnel." They would serve well many types of mobile apps and will ease the whole personification exercise at your end. Feel free to re-use them as appropriate.

TROUBLESHOOTING LATENT AND INCORRECTLY RENDERED CONTENT

There is a unique challenge for native, and sometimes hybrid, mobile apps, namely, the detection and troubleshooting of incorrect content rendered by mobile applications. This is difficult due to the network traffic usually being encrypted. From a technical perspective, the typical website network traffic does not have the potential to bring so much sorrow. One can easily detect/ see that a large image was incorrectly downloaded to a smartphone with a small screen. With native mobile apps, this is often close to impossible. The ability to examine the network traffic between the app and its backend(s) is key to many roles within a software delivery organization. Mobile developers, functional, performance and security testers rely on it in order to:

1. Assess, optimize and validate the efficiency of downloading and rendering the correct media objects necessary to fit the device screen — not too small and not too large. In many cases, it may be reasonable to download such objects only once and cache them for some time. We may also need to download these objects according to a predefined order.

2. Ensure user content is sent in an encrypted manner and to the correct backend server.

3. Guarantee efficient interaction with 3rd party service APIs.

A traditional approach to addressing this challenge has been the provisioning of team access to tools similar to the Charles proxy. The challenge with this approach is that many organizations would object to incorporate a Charles proxy, or man-in-the-middle facility, in their own corporate network.

Solutions like Perfecto recently added the ability to produce a HAR file out of every script execution in the Cloud. This practice could also be employed or inherited by others. The HAR file[3] is a layer 7 (HTTP) decrypted network traffic log containing device or page interaction with the various backend system(s). Every piece of downloaded content can be easily examined, as demonstrated in **Figure 110.** The timestamp and duration of each download phase (DNS time, connect time, download time, etc.), as well as requests and response message body and headers are just some of the interesting insights bundled with HAR files. Since the solution is deployed in the Cloud, it is very easy for mobile developers and testers to use this feature extensively.

---

3   Har File — https://en.wikipedia.org/wiki/.har

GET pipeline0.html	200 OK	configuration.appli	213 B	46ms		
GET pipeline1.html	200 OK	configuration.appli	213 B	+3.5s	Started	
GET pipeline2.html	200 OK	configuration.appli	213 B			
GET pipeline3.html	200 OK	configuration.appli	213 B	NaNm	12ms	Connecting

Headers Response HTML

Response Headers

NaNm	1ms	Sending
NaNm	28ms	Waiting
NaNm	5ms	Receiving

Last-Modified Thu, 17 Mar 2016 04:47:24 GMT
ETag "d5-52e3753966f00"
Server Apache
Content-Type text/html

Figure 110: An Example of a HAR File

TESTING BATTERY DRAIN AS PART OF NON-FUNCTIONAL TESTING

Teams will often focus on the usability, functionality, performance, and security of an app. If this same app does what it was designed to do, it will often get pushed to production as is.

Figure 111: Battery Drain as Part of App Quality

RESOURCE CONSUMPTION AS AN APP QUALITY PRIORITY

Let us review one of **most popular mobile native apps for 2016,** namely, Pokemon Go. This mobile app alone requires constant GPS location services while active. It keeps the screen fully lit (when in the foreground), operates the camera, plays sounds, and renders 3D graphics content.

Research shows that this kind of resource consumption will drain the battery of a fully charged Android device in **2 hours and 40 minutes** in average; that is, this is the time required for your battery indicator to **drop from 100% to 0%.**

The thing is, of course, that end users will typically have at least ten other apps running in the background, hence it would happen way faster than estimated above.

From recent research done by AVAST[4] in Q3 2016, two groups of "greedy" apps could be distinguished. They are rated in **Figure 112** and **Figure 113.**

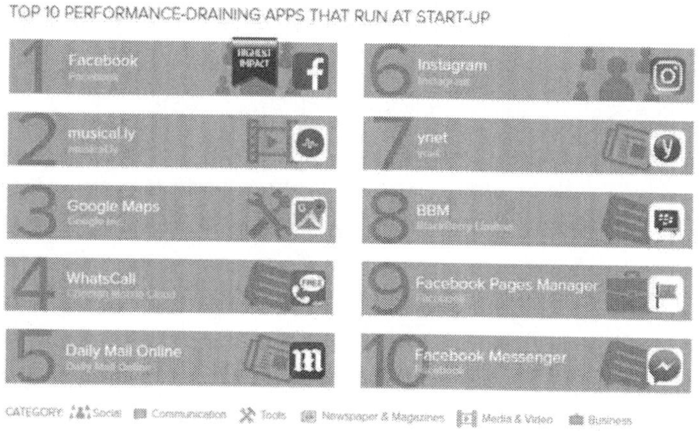

Figure 112: Top 10 Performance-Draining Apps That Run at Startup

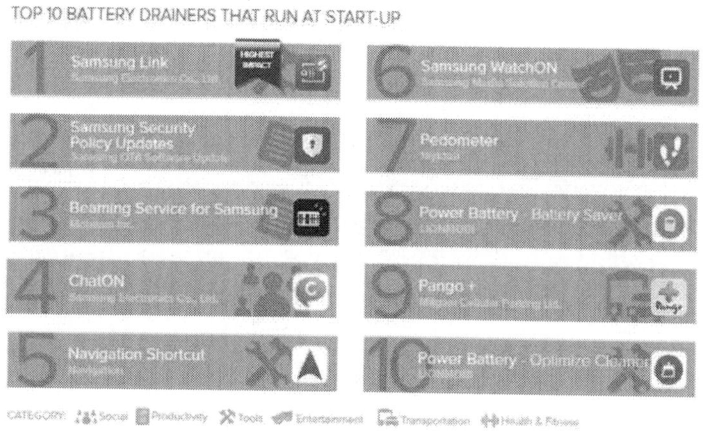

Figure 113: Top 10 Battery-Draining Apps That Run at Startup

---

4   AVAST Research — https://blog.avast.com/these-top-10-most-performance-draining-android-apps-might-shock-you

General awareness of this pitfall for all of the mobile apps out there seems to be the first step in the right direction. Let us now take the second step and ask the question that is going to be discussed till the end of this chapter: how can we detect deviations in terms of reduced battery life? Furthermore, how could we be sure that these will have been caused by your app under test?

HOW TO TEST AN APP FOR BATTERY DRAIN

Teams need to know as much as possible about their end users. This is a clear requirement of the market today. From a battery drain testing perspective, the test environment needs to mimic the one being used by target end users. This often implies careful selection of devices (with different battery states and health) and versions of mobile OS, as well as a typical mix of popular apps being installed and run in the background. In addition, testing is conducted under real network conditions (2G, 3G, LTE, Wi-Fi, Roaming, etc.).

Test Against Multiple Devices

Device hardware is different across manufacturers. Each battery will obviously have a different capacity compared to others. After a while, devices will experience degraded battery chemistry, which has certain negative impacts on its performance, the duration it can last without recharging, and more. This is why a variety of new, legacy, and different battery capacities needs to be available and taken into consideration in any mobile device lab. This is a general requirement for mobile app quality and a very specific one in the context of battery testing.

Listen to the Market and End Users

Since the market is constantly changing, the "known state" and quality of your app – including the consumption of battery and other system resources — may degrade as well. This could happen due to lack of experience of running your app on "unknown" devices or because of a new version of the underlying OS that was just recently released. We have witnessed plenty of examples, including the recent iOS 10.2[5] release.

There are free native apps leveraged by mobile teams to obtain valuable battery

---

5   iOS 10.2 battery drain reports — http://www.forbes.com/sites/gordonkelly/2016/12/21/apple-ios-10-2-iphone-battery-problems/#5e2a4f1d4f2c

stats in real time, such as Carat.[6] You can make good use of some of these.

If you happen to detect battery consumption performance degradation due to a major release of the underlying OS once it has already been released, you may risk losing some clients due to unacceptable behavior of your app. A better approach would be to take your time and plan for running manual and automated tests against the beta versions of the OS (vendors often provide such). Thus, you will have the chance to detect any major functional and non-functional discrepancy rather early, prior to the Global Availability (GA) of the corresponding version of an OS. Another feedback channel for mobile teams would be the users' reviews in app stores and social networks. Yes, it works. The only issue with this approach is that feedback gets to you a little bit too late and may also have certain negative impacts on converting new users and retaining existing ones, as presented in **Figure 114.** Continuously enriching your automated test suites on a refreshed device lab will reduce the risks and will help you identify issues earlier in the SDLC, prior to production releases. Make sure to incorporate such tests (or a subset of them) as part of your CI cycle, thus enhancing test coverage and reducing risks.

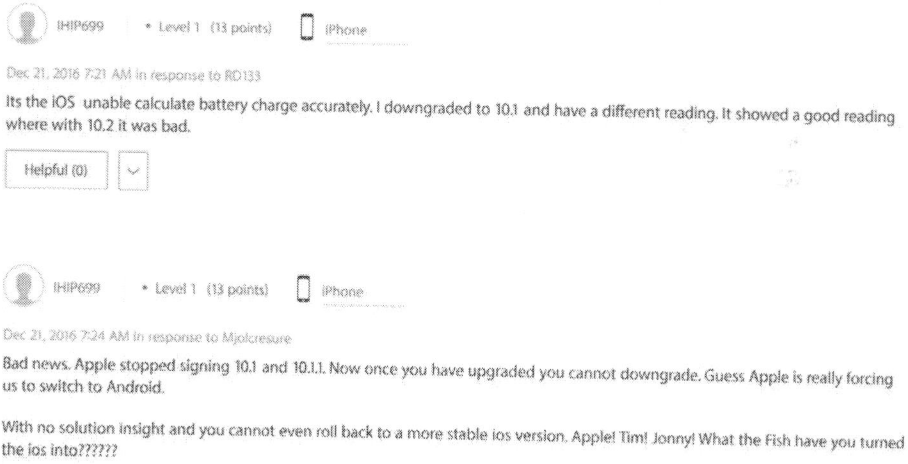

IHIP699   • Level 1 (13 points)   iPhone

Dec 21, 2016 7:21 AM in response to RD133

Its the iOS unable calculate battery charge accurately. I downgraded to 10.1 and have a different reading. It showed a good reading where with 10.2 it was bad.

Helpful (0)   ⌄

IHIP699   • Level 1 (13 points)   iPhone

Dec 21, 2016 7:24 AM in response to Mjolciresure

Bad news. Apple stopped signing 10.1 and 10.1.1. Now once you have upgraded you cannot downgrade. Guess Apple is really forcing us to switch to Android.

With no solution insight and you cannot even roll back to a more stable ios version. Apple! Tim! Jonny! What the Fish have you turned the ios into??????

Figure 114: The Power of User Reviews

---

6   Carat battery drain app — http://lifehacker.com/5918671/carat-tells-your-which-apps-suck-up-your-battery-power

SUMMARY

Modern performance testing is quite difficult, but extremely important. Bad performance and scalability have quite a negative impact on user experience and profits. Fortunately, technology wise, these challenges can be tackled. Oh, yes, this requires also organizational support, strong discipline and culture. Do not forget about personas. They can contribute a lot to amazing UX.

As for testing app battery drain, there are not really any good automation methods facilitating it. Therefore, the general recommendation would be to bring a plethora of devices in various conditions (as already explained above) to your lab and measure the battery drain through native apps installed on these devices. At first, the tests should be run against the app on a clean device and then you will usually go for the same exercise on a real end user device.

21

Keep It Going "On the Go"— Integrating Mobile App Performance Testing into the Continuous Integration Cycle

THIS CHAPTER WAS CONTRIBUTED BY CA TECHNOLOGIES — BLAZEMETER, JACOB SHARIR & NOGA COHEN

JACOB SHARIR is the Principal Support Engineer at CA Technologies — BlazeMeter. Jacob has more than 3 years of experience in the world of performance testing, technical customer support, and computer networking. He has vast knowledge in open-source testing and continuous integration tools, such as JMeter, Selenium, Jenkins and Taurus, as well as in Java.

Noga Cohen is the Senior Product Marketing Manager and Content Manager at CA Technologies — BlazeMeter. Noga has 4 years of experience in writing, marketing, and analyzing data, including work with software developers, DevOps, and QA engineers on technology content.

INTRODUCTION

Quickly gaining the lion's share of digital activity, mobile apps are a growing market for load and performance testing. Websites need a mobile app version, while many products are only available through mobile apps. Today mobile is at a point of no return.

Take a look at some Black Friday statistics in **Figure 115. In 2015 mobile traffic was 57.2% of all online traffic,** growing from 49.6% the year before and 39.7% the year before that. The percentage of sales coming from mobile is growing as well.

This is the general trend. According to comScore, **between 2010 and 2014 the use of the digital media time on smartphones grew by almost 400% and on tablets by more than 1,700%!** In comparison, the digital time on desktops grew by just 37%. Impressive, isn't it?

The conclusion is clear: once you go for the first release of a mobile app, you commit to its perpetual evolution. It is really a never ending story. You cannot fire and forget a native app into the wild just like that, as it is so much intertwined with the core product offering. In many cases, it *is* the product minimizing the relevance of other entry points for end users, such as flavors for desktops and websites.

A crashing app might be a deal breaker, no matter how heavy the load that an alternative website entry point can handle would be. Therefore, the SDLC for mobile apps is often significantly shorter and more demanding than what we are used to for the desktop. Fast, accurate, and reliable feedback cycles among

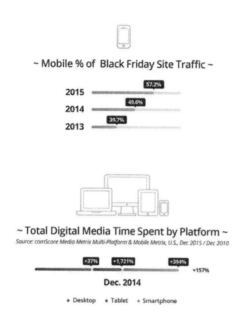

business, development, and test teams is a must-have. Essentially, the techniques that help us manage the increased complexity would be smart testing and automation. Yes, it is all about quickly verifying compliance against key functional and non-functional requirements in order to meet aggressive release schedules as part of the Go-to-market strategy. This means positioning unit testing, UI testing, API testing, and, of course, performance and load testing — as pillars of SDLC. Detect and fix issues early, release in time.

Figure 115: A Notable Trend of Increasing the Share of Mobile Digital Time

WHAT ARE PERFORMANCE AND LOAD TESTING?[1]

Performance testing is the general name for a testing practice performed to determine how the system behaves and performs in regards to different workloads. It examines a number of important quality attributes, such as responsiveness, stability, scalability, reliability, speed, and resource usage of software and infrastructure.

Load testing is a flavor of performance testing that checks how systems function when a high number of concurrent virtual users perform interactions over a certain period of time. In other words, it reveals how systems handle load in different volumes. Poor performance, which results in app crashes or slow loading times, has an immediate and long-term business impact, diverting customers to competitors and damaging the brand.

---

1   Performance Testing vs. Load Testing vs. Stress Testing https://www.blazemeter.com/blog/performance-testing-vs-load-testing-vs-stress-testing

HOW TO IMPLEMENT PERFORMANCE AND LOAD TESTING FOR MOBILE APPS?[2]

First, you need to choose a tool. There are many open-source load testing tools out there, with JMeter being the most popular one. Open source and Java-based, JMeter sends requests to application servers for different loads scenarios and concurrencies. JMeter is also able to receive and parse the corresponding responses, as depicted on the screenshot in **Figure 116.**

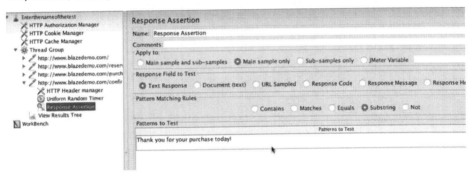

Figure 116: Apache JMeter Test Configuration

Figure 117: Apache JMeter Test Configuration

On your local machine, you can scale up to approximately 100 virtual users, but you can go up to more than 1,000,000 VUs with CA BlazeMeter (blazemeter.com), which is kind of a JMeter in the Cloud. CA BlazeMeter also adds multiple geo-locations to JMeter and and runs tests in parallel.[3]

After downloading JMeter to your desktop from the apache.jmeter.org site, you need to create a script, or, in other words, determine which endpoints on your app you want to load test. The easiest way to do that is to

---

2   Getting started with JMeter in 60 minutes (webinar) http://info.blazemeter.com/get-started-jmeter-60-minutes-webinar

3   How CA BlazeMeter enhances JMeter https://www.blazemeter.com/jmeter-load-testing

"record" the scenario you want to test.

The two options are either the JMeter or CA BlazeMeter Recorders. Both are free to use, but the CA BlazeMeter recorder, visualized in **Figure 117,** is more user-friendly.

After recording a test, you can either open it up in CA BlazeMeter or in JMeter. There you can configure parameters like the number of users, ramp-up time, duration, and many more. A sample test configuration is presented on the screenshot in **Figure 118.**

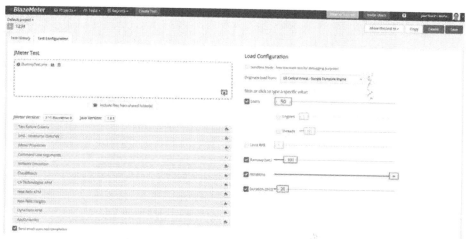

Figure 118: CA BlazeMeter Test Configuration

Finally, you will run the newly created and configured test and analyze the results. By looking at the key performance indicators (KPI) and researching the correlation in between, you can analyze trends and statistics, find bottlenecks in your app or server, determine the health of your system, and decide how you would like to keep developing your product.[4]

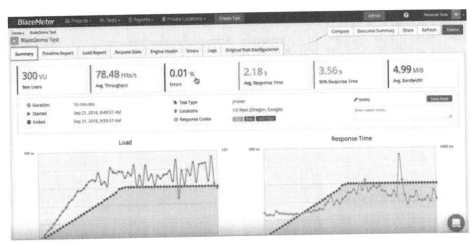

Figure 119: CA BlazeMeter Reports Dashboard

When configuring the number of virtual users, we recommend to run the test for a small number of users (threads) at first. This will ensure that your test runs properly. Afterwards you could increase this number to the desired values.

What is the magic number? That depends on your business goals. In general, we recommend that in addition to testing with the expected number of users, you should also push the limits of the system under test (SUT). This lets you figure out and characterize its strengths and weaknesses, enabling you to plan better and react in real-time to unexpected bottlenecks and errors.

IS THERE A REAL WORLD SHOWCASE?

Sure! Upic Solutions[5], a technology provider for United Way's, hosts various business apps for non-profit organizations, including a donor pledge app, facilitating companies with raising funds for local causes. During the campaign season in 2015 the performance of this key app was poor. Slow pages meant that donors could not pledge.

Before the start of the 2016 campaign season the Upic team decided to look for a tool to test and get to know why the donation system was so slow. Using JMeter, CA BlazeMeter, and an application monitoring tool, they built a test plan, executed the tests, and analyzed the results.

5   Upic Solution case study https://www.blazemeter.com/case-study/upic

Over two weeks, they ran 150 tests for up to 100 concurrent users. Each test scenario had up to 2,400 page loads, with an average of 600 databases calls on each page load. CA BlazeMeter allowed them to prove that the app was not scaling well enough. The team quickly identified that excessive SQL queries were to blame and reported those results to the application developer. While waiting for the developer to fix the root cause, the team also identified other areas for potential improvement. By rapidly iterating on changes and testing those changes with CA BlazeMeter, they identified and did certain configuration changes with immediate positive results.

After the testing and fixing process the average page load time for the app dropped from 5.33 seconds to 2.84 seconds, meaning an improvement of 46.74%. Furthermore, donation conversion rates improved by 9.17%.

Upic Solutions still uses CA BlazeMeter to constantly evaluate the performance of their app. This is crucial in regards to vendor changes in development phases, all the way up to the busy campaign season.

CONTINUOUSLY TESTING PERFORMANCE

Not so long ago, load testing immediately before releases was enough. Now testing practices are changing — load tests are moving to an earlier point of development, often being implemented and run by software developers. Instead of testing before releases, which is on the right side of the waterfall, developers are leaving the waterfall, "shifting left", and testing automatically each time they commit a new change in the source control system. The essence of this trend is explained by the diagram in **Figure 120.**

The advantages of ongoing earlier load testing are, in short, making developers' lives easier and the product better. To be specific, testing earlier on in SDLC reduces the risk of performance degradations whenever adding a new feature or fixing a bug in the product. By identifying errors, issues, and bottlenecks earlier development teams and product managers could plan enough time and resources to resolve them "before the flood", i.e. before such defects reach end users. This also saves the avoidable effort of deploying with problems and makes debugging easier.

Shift Left [And Right]

Test Performance

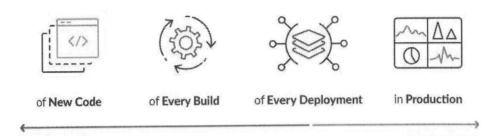

of **New Code**   of **Every Build**   of **Every Deployment**   in **Production**

Shift Left   **Shift Right**

Figure 120: Shift Left of the Waterfall

Shifting left also lets us integrate performance and load testing into the continuous integration (CI) cycle through open source tools like Jenkins. CI systems monitor source code repositories, trigger builds whenever code changes are detected, run tests against compiled software (unit, acceptance, automated, performance, integration, etc.), and generate artifacts (binaries, documentation, installation packages, etc.).

A CI cycle is the automated process of building, optimizing, testing, and packaging source code and other content as a software unit that could either be executed as a program or integrated as a component of larger systems. CI platforms play nicely with testing tools like JMeter and Selenium, making the software build, test, and deployment process automated and efficient.

MOBILE APP PERFORMANCE TESTING INTO THE CONTINUOUS INTEGRATION CYCLE[6]

To integrate mobile app testing into the complete cycle, you need to add your load tests to the build jobs of CI tools, such as Jenkins, Travis, CircleCI, and many more.

If you use Jenkins, which is open source, one way to do that is to export your mobile app recording to Taurus instead of to JMeter or CA BlazeMeter. Taurus

---

6 Automated Performance Tests in Jenkins Continuous Integration environments (webinar) http://info. blazemeter.com/automated-performance-tests-in-jenkins-ci-environments

(gettaurus.org) is an open source test automation framework. When exporting to Taurus, a YAML file will be downloaded to your computer, which you can open up in Jenkins.

On Jenkins, install Taurus, create a build job, add the Taurus command to run the script (in the Execute Shell section, as depicted in **Figure 121**), and run the test. It is always a great idea to manage Taurus scripts together with the source code of the tested app in a designated source control management system (e.g a git repository in Github) and view and analyze the reports by using CA BlazeMeter. The options for analysis of the execution results are visualized in **Figure 122** and **Figure 123**.

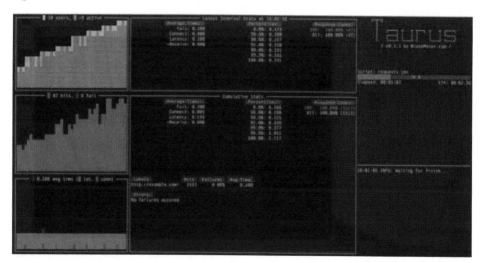

Figure 121: Jenkins Execute Shell Section

Figure 122: Taurus Reports Dashboard

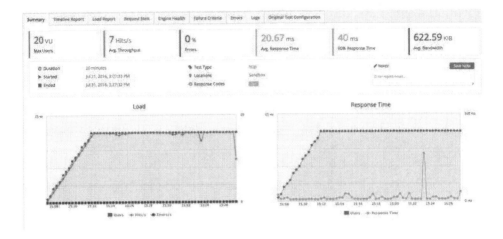

Figure 123: CA BlazeMeter Reports Dashboard

That's it, enjoy and load test forever!

SUMMARY

In this chapter, we covered:

- The growing importance of mobile apps and the necessity to incorporate testing deep in SDLC
- Performance testing and load testing as a crucial part of app and website development
- How to do performance and load testing of mobile apps with the open source tool JMeter and the possibilities CA BlazeMeter offers
- The importance of "shifting left" and continuous integration as a means to save time, effort, and ensure high quality product release
- Integrating mobile app load and performance testing into the CI cycle with the open source tools Taurus and Jenkins

22 Performance Testing of Mobile Apps

THIS CHAPTER WAS CONTRIBUTED BY LEE BARNES, CTO AND CO-FOUNDER OF UTOPIA SOLUTIONS

LEE BARNES has over 20 years of experience in assuring software quality with a focus on performance testing and test automation. As founder and CTO of Utopia Solutions, he is responsible for the firm's delivery of software quality solutions which include process improvement, test automation, performance management, and mobile quality. He is a recognized thought leader in his field and speaks frequently on software testing related topics.

INTRODUCTION

There is no doubt that performance matters. For e-commerce systems, a one-second increase in response time can decrease conversion rates by up to 7%.[1] As users rely on their mobile devices, their expectations for performance

---

1   Work, Sean, "How Loading Time Affects Your Bottom Line", Kissmetrics Blog, https://blog.kissmetrics. com/loading-time/.

only increase. The good news is that performance testing of mobile applications is not that different in comparison with testing traditional desktop systems. With a few important exceptions, though.

This chapter highlights the important factors to consider when conducting performance testing of mobile applications. For the purposes of this writing, the term "performance testing" is used as a generalization for various types of testing (both single- and multi-user) that are executed to obtain information about how an application "performs" in response to test input.

UNDERSTANDING YOUR USERS

Understanding the profile of your users — who they are, what they do, and how they access the system — is an important aspect to successful mobile app development. Furthermore, it is absolutely essential to designing and performing successful performance tests of apps.[2]

The first step in investigating the user profile is understanding that users have options. Many mobile apps are just one of multiple channels to a backend system. Chances are high that other means of access to functionality would be provided for web (i.e. full browser over broadband connection) and back office users, for example. Typically, performance engineers look at the following factors to determine user profiles:

* Activity — the processes and paths that users take through the app
* Client type — the browser, the mobile platform, or the devices they use to access the app
* Network — the type and condition of the network between the user and the system
* Location — the physical location within the network (or the world) of users with respect to the system
* Volume — the quantity of users accessing the system
* Throughput — the frequency of users performing activities and interacting

---

2   A successful performance test doesn't necessarily mean the app meets performance objectives. It does mean that a good test was designed and executed, and the team learned something about the performance of the app.

with the system

A whole book could be dedicated to the task of properly determining the appropriate user and load profile. However, from a mobile perspective, there are three factors that hold extra importance: client type, network, and location.

CLIENT TYPE

If all users access the system under test (SUT) from the same client type, this will likely lead to suspect results. Understanding how users access the system ensures that you are creating realistic input to the SUT. Depending on the system architecture and technology, the SUT may respond to varying client types in the following ways:

* Execute different server code

* Return different content (both size and volume)

* Enforce different connection limits, keep-alive limits, etc.

NETWORK

The days of executing a performance test over a LAN connection are over. Systems and their users are not just distributed in a building or campus, but all over the world. Just as important, the state of the network they use to access the system could vary dramatically. Two users executing the same activity, but over very different networks (e.g. high-speed broadband vs. poor 3G mobile network), may cause very different impact on system resources.

LOCATION

Mobile apps, by definition, imply that users are in distributed locations. Location has extra importance for apps because network latency severely undermines performance independent of the available bandwidth.

Users performing activities across long distances and/ or over a poor mobile network(s) will keep open connections longer, effectively utilizing more system resources than the same number of users performing similar activities over a high-speed broadband connection. Naturally, the negative impact grows with the increase of the volume of active users. This is also reflected by the example results on the chart in **Figure 124.**

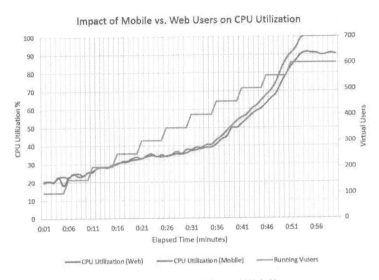

Figure 124: Typical CPU Utilization of Mobile and Web Users

In this example, CPU utilization was high (90%) at the maximum load for web users accessing the system over a broadband connection. However, the same test — configured to simulate mobile network conditions — resulted in higher CPU utilization, as the user volume was increased to the point where CPU was maxed out. Thus, the system could not accept additional load.

The user load profile for a single performance test is just a snapshot in time. User behavior and technology will change over time and so will user profiles. It is important for organizations to constantly collect feedback from system monitoring data and application logs to ensure that the assumptions behind each performance test correctly reflect the needs of target users.

SIMULATING NETWORK VARIABILITY

Simulating the network variability of a single user is a relatively simple task. Mobile operating system development kits include fairly capable solutions (e.g. Apple iOS Network Link Conditioner and Android Emulator). However, simulating the same variability as part of a load or performance test with high number of virtual users requires specialized solutions. Fortunately, such solutions — commonly referred to as network virtualization tools — exist. They allow performance test engineers to simulate various network conditions for the virtual users accessing SUT.

A list of commercial and open-source network virtualization solutions is available in **Table 7.**

Solution	Supports Multi-user Tests	Comments
Android Emulator	N	Android Studio feature
Apple Network Link Conditioner	N	Apple Xcode feature
BlazeMeter	Y	Load test tool with built-in network condition simulation capabilities
Charles Proxy	Y	Open-source web debugging proxy application
HPE Network Virtualization	Y	Dedicated network virtualization solution
Neotys NeoLoad	Y	Load test tool with built-in network condition simulation capabilities
SOASTA CloudTest	Y	Load test tool with built-in network condition simulation capabilities

Table 7: List of Network Virtualization Tools — Open Source and Commercial

EVALUATING NETWORK IMPACT

Before executing a large-scale load or performance test, it is recommended to assess the performance for a single user over varying network conditions. A baseline for each required network condition should be captured. Thus, you will have common ground to better understand the impact of load on system performance. This is ideally accomplished using a real device behind a network virtualization tool.

Mobile test automation solutions provide an effective way to capture baseline response times on real devices. It is optimal to use a solution that integrates with your load test tool. For example, Perfecto integrates effectively with both

BlazeMeter and NeoLoad, thus allowing real device measurements to be captured — both for baseline measurements and while the system is under load.

Once a single user baseline has been captured, a full volume performance test can be executed. To get an apples-to-apples comparison to baseline results, the same mobile devices that were used to capture the baseline numbers should be included in the test. This allows end user response times to be measured while the system is under load.

CONFIGURING USER GROUPS

Most load test tools allow virtual users to be categorized in groups, as indicated in

Figure 125. Each group should represent a set of users in the user profile (e.g. mobile users over Wi-Fi, mobile users over poor 3G network, etc.). This allows for capturing and analyzing results separately across the varying network conditions.

Figure 125: Categorization
of Virtual Users in Groups

INCORPORATING USER LOCATION AND VOLUME

The user profile of mobile apps very often includes a high volume of distributed users. Network virtualization tools can simulate the network conditions associated with the various locations. However, it is often beneficial to test from outside the firewall in order to ensure that all system components are included in the test. Also, it is often prohibitive to simulate a large volume of users in a lab. To address both issues, Cloud-based load test tools could be utilized to simulate very large user loads — accessing the system from a variety of global locations — in a cost-efficient manner.

Available solutions include Cloud-based offerings from legacy load test tool vendors, as well as companies that are focused solely on Cloud-based load testing.

Cloud-based testing capabilities vary across solutions, but most offer the following features which should be considered the minimum to meet the requirements for testing of large scale mobile/ web systems:

* Generate adequate load — ability to support current and future load generation requirements

* Integrate with multiple Cloud providers — seamless provisioning and control over load generation servers across various cloud vendors and global locations

* Execute realistic user traffic — ability to simulate realistic user diversity including user agents, network conditions, and contemporary technologies (e.g. AJAX, etc.)

* Efficient analysis and reporting — provide real-time monitoring of end-user and system metrics along with analysis and reporting tools for effectively communicating results

Some Cloud-based testing solutions satisfying these requirements are briefly described in **Table 8.**

Tool	Vendor	Strengths
BlazeMeter	BlazeMeter	Import and execute existing JMeter scripts
CloudTest	SOASTA	Real-time analytics, large number of Cloud provider integrations
NeoLoad	Neotys	Simultaneously generate load from the Cloud and local area network
StormRunner	Hewlett Packard Enterprise	Execute existing LoadRunner scripts in the Cloud

Table 8: Cloud-based Performance and Load Testing Tools

TEST CREATION DIFFERENCES

The process of creating a mobile performance test — specifically test scripts and scenarios — is similar to creating such for traditional web applications. However, there are few key differences when it comes to:

* Capturing client/ server (i.e. mobile device/ server) communication

* Specifying user agents

* Emulating network conditions

CAPTURING CLIENT/ SERVER COMMUNICATION

The most common way to capture mobile traffic for the purpose of creating test scripts is to route mobile traffic through a proxy that allows the test tool to capture the communication in the same way it does for desktop applications, as reflected by the diagram in **Figure 126.**

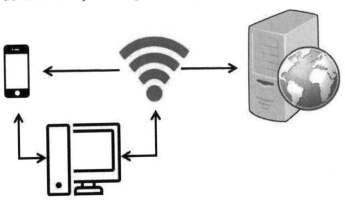

Figure 126: Routing Mobile Traffic through a Common Proxy

For most test tools, this involves configuring the device proxy to point to the machine where tool's script development component is running, as illustrated by the figure below. In addition, some tools also have an app or an agent that runs on the mobile device and captures traffic that can then be transferred to a desktop machine where it is used to generate a test script by the tool.

SPECIFYING USER AGENT AND NETWORK CONDITIONS

The importance of understanding how users access the system (i.e. client type and network conditions) was discussed previously. However, it is equally important that those factors are incorporated appropriately in test scenarios within your test tools. In general, the following practices should be considered when setting up test scenarios.

- Map user agent and simulated network conditions to virtual user groups in test scenarios in order to promote efficient results analysis.
- Use predefined test tool or network virtualization settings to keep setup and results analysis as straightforward as possible. For example, most load test

tools will have a preset list of user agents (i.e. device and/or browser) and network conditions (e.g. 3G — Poor, LTE — Good, Wifi, etc.).

A screenshot of a real-world example of incorporating these practices could be found in **Figure 127.**

In this LoadRunner scenario, four scripts that emulate the activity of e-commerce users have been run with 10 different virtual user groups — each representing different locations and/ or network conditions.

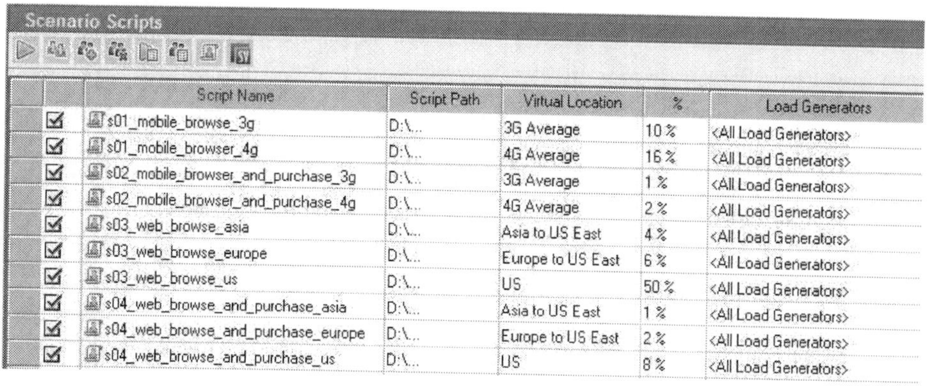

		Script Name	Script Path	Virtual Location	%	Load Generators
☑		s01_mobile_browse_3g	D:\..	3G Average	10 %	<All Load Generators>
☑		s01_mobile_browser_4g	D:\..	4G Average	16 %	<All Load Generators>
☑		s02_mobile_browser_and_purchase_3g	D:\..	3G Average	1 %	<All Load Generators>
☑		s02_mobile_browser_and_purchase_4g	D:\..	4G Average	2 %	<All Load Generators>
☑		s03_web_browse_asia	D:\..	Asia to US East	4 %	<All Load Generators>
☑		s03_web_browse_europe	D:\..	Europe to US East	6 %	<All Load Generators>
☑		s03_web_browse_us	D:\..	US	50 %	<All Load Generators>
☑		s04_web_browse_and_purchase_asia	D:\..	Asia to US East	1 %	<All Load Generators>
☑		s04_web_browse_and_purchase_europe	D:\..	Europe to US East	2 %	<All Load Generators>
☑		s04_web_browse_and_purchase_us	D:\..	US	8 %	<All Load Generators>

Figure 127: A Screenshot of a LoadRunner Scenario Using Simulated Network and User Conditions

MEASURING DEVICE PERFORMANCE

Performance testers have become accustomed to assessing the performance of the backend system and network, while ignoring the performance of end users' client machines. With relatively thin clients and an abundance of resources in terms of power, processor, and memory that is not a terrible practice. However, mobile devices certainly have limits on resources and these limits affect the performance of apps. It is important to understand that apps also affect the performance of devices. For example, an app that significantly accelerates battery drain impacts the usefulness of other apps and the device itself.

For these reasons it is essential to know how your app affects key performance metrics on the device. These include:

* Processor

- Memory

- Battery

As performance characteristics and base configuration (apps and processes run during device startup) vary across devices and carriers, it is important to assess these metrics across key devices in your user profile as well.

The following process presents a holistic approach towards assessing the impact of an app over device performance. In many cases, just measuring the impact of an application under test (AUT) activity is adequate to understand the app's impact on device performance.

1. Measure Baseline Device Performance
    a. Fully charge and reboot device to ensure it is in a baseline state (only startup apps and processes running).

    b. Ensure device is not charging, if battery drain testing is in scope.

    c. Monitor and log device metrics over a period of time in order to gather adequate data (30 minutes to several hours, depending on your needs). This can be done using 3rd party tools or a functional test automation solution that supports monitoring and logging of device performance metrics. Do not interact with the device as this is a baseline test.

2. Measure Baseline Impact of AUT on Device Performance
    a. Repeat steps 1a and 1b.

    b. Open the AUT on the device.

    c. Monitor and log device metrics over a period of time to gather adequate data (30 minutes to several hours, depending on your needs). Do not interact with the device or AUT as this is a baseline test.

3. Measure Impact of AUT activity on Device Performance
    a. Repeat steps 2a and 2b.

    b. While executing user activity on AUT, monitor and log device metrics over a period of time to gather adequate data (30 minutes to several hours, depending on needs). Note that it is a good idea to use automated test scripts and execute the activity in order to ensure consistent input to the AUT from one test run to another.

Results for each test run should be tracked to identify trends and anomalies as early as possible.

Memory leaks are the most common issues found using this technique. An important lesson learnt is to perform device performance testing as early as possible, effectively minimizing the effort and cost to address any issues detected.

SUMMARY

Testing and verifying the performance of mobile apps is not an easy task. It requires vast technical knowledge and experience. This chapter explained why the performance of mobile apps is vulnerable to so many external factors by design. It outlined the crucial points that need to be kept into consideration, as well as valuable practices and techniques that will help you to reach, break, and go beyond the limits of virtue with performance testing.

23

User Experience for Mobile Apps — Vital Approach to Mobile Testing

THIS CHAPTER WAS CONTRIBUTED BY JEANANN HARRISON, MOBILE SOFTWARE TEST & QA CONSULTANT

JEAN ANN has been in the Software Testing and Quality Assurance field for over 16 years, including 5 years working within a Regulatory Environment and 10 years performing mobile software testing. Her mobile software testing experience is vast. She did work on ensuring the quality of various hardware and software solutions, such as police ticket generator device, heart monitor device, mobile gaming, social mobile media, mobile weather, mobile finance, mobile meeting planner.

Jean is a speaker at many software testing conferences. She conducted webinars on mobile testing and wrote dozens of articles. She is a former columnist for Software Magazine and a Weekend Testing Americas facilitator. Jean Ann has been a technical resource reviewer

for a couple of mobile testing books and also submitted content for published books. Jean is an active participant in the software testing community on a global scale.

INTRODUCTION

The topic of user experience (UX) is hot throughout the whole software industry. It is even more so when it comes to consumer facing products, such as mobile apps. Many things in life are easy. However, Testing UX is not one of them for the simple reason that outstanding UX is quite hard. While different UX needs to target different personas, a common and structured approach towards ensuring excellence could be figured out and shared with mobile testers.

Within this chapter, you will find lots of useful insights related to ensuring great user experience in mobile apps. It all starts with proper and aligned understanding of what UX really means.

DEFINITION OF UX TESTING

UX or user experience testing is a necessary testing approach to mobile apps. UX is often misunderstood and test coverage becomes a factor as it is incomplete. To better understand UX testing, a more inclusive definition needs to be uncovered. UX is often mistaken for "usability" testing. However, this is only a partial approach to UX testing. Think of UX an umbrella term for the characteristics outlined in **Figure 128:**

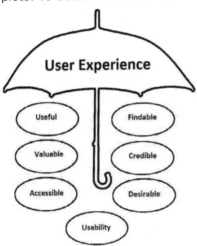

Figure 128: A Visual Definition of User Experience (UX)

These attributes cover appropriate tests for mobile software. They are a guideline to help narrow down the types of tests to include for mobile software testing. Not all of the attributes need to be covered as testing scenarios guaranteeing for more productive user experience. They just give solid test coverage for a mobile app. Some UX tests can be automated with some limitation. Automation for UX tests will be discussed later in this chapter along with being efficient in the approach to mobile testing.

ATTRIBUTE DEFINITIONS

Let us break down the meaning of each attribute and then apply to some mobile example test ideas.

The characteristics **"useful"** and **"usability"** can be misunderstood and often combined. However, these terms have different meanings when considering tests. Evaluating whether a function, object, and/ or wording provides users with a purpose that could be taken advantage of relates to usefulness. Usability testing aims at answering the question HOW do users take advantage of that function, object or wording.

Usefulness

Testing **"usefulness"** does have a dependency on the type of user/ customer using the app. An example might be to assess the location of the objects within an app. This is a judgement evaluation which can be difficult to automate because testers must set up criteria to determine usefulness. Therefore, evaluating usefulness manually could be more efficient. If criteria can be determined and added to an automated script, the maintenance of that script could become costly and ineffective. Testers need to evaluate efficiency of automated tests and consider the maintenance of that same script based on how often criteria will change throughout the evolution of the app.

Examples of criteria to determine usefulness can include:
1. Location of objects or text make sense for using the app.
2. Assessment of functions, objects or text needed to use the app.
3. Type of representation or appearance of objects or text displayed in the app.
4. Evaluation of how often repetition of a function, object or wording may be required.
5. Does the function, object or wording satisfy the user's purpose?
6. Is the size of the object or wording helpful to the user?

Note: The provided examples are guidelines to consider for various UX attributes.

They should not be applied blindly against all tested apps. Each app does have its own context considerations and may only be relevant for a particular domain industry, company, and/ or country, culture. The examples are provided in a way that could inspire and help testers determine what works best for their apps, their customer market, their company, and their overall culture.

Usability

Evaluating **"usability"** requires proper understanding of how different users will take advantage of functions, objects, and/ or wording. The assessment is facilitated by concluding how easy, effective, efficient, and satisfying its usage is. Defining the criteria necessary for determining the "usability" of the app in regards to each type of user can be a major task. Testers should work with their mobile app project team members in order to get to aligned understanding of this attribute before setting up the acceptable criteria to measure usability factors. Some of them could be: the look, the feel, the orientation of the screen, languages required, how the installation is done, how users can recover from errors, and many more. Some of them could be automated, while others would require manual assessment. Taking advantage of project team members to assist in determining acceptance criteria will make the process efficient.

Examples of criteria to determine usability can include:
1. Is the function or object easy for the purposes of end users?
2. Can the user achieve a task efficiently?
3. Does the function, object or wording provide the user with a purposeful task to achieve?
4. Is the location of the function, objects, wording most effective for use?
5. Do the icons, labels and/ or text provide users with a clear direction of what to do in the app?
6. Is the app available to be used with different languages?
7. Is the installation easy for the customer/ user?
8. Does the app gracefully recover from erroneous situations and place the user where the error occurred? Are the error messages good enough?

Findability

Users expect to be able to use the app with ease. This means that functions, objects and/ or text need to be easily and quickly **"findable"**. For example, if the app navigating functions, objects and/ or texts can be located easily, the corresponding functionality should be clear to end users.

Can users train themselves to use the app without calling for assistance? It is time for another practical example. Some apps have menu icons to allow users to navigate to a specific function within the app. However, it turns out that users need to be familiar with the standards and semantics of menu icons used. As a consequence, certain functions can hardly be found – which leads to frustration. This is where the mobile app testing team needs to understand their customer base, i.e. what kinds of users would use their technology. If your app is about to introduce a "hamburger" menu, hold on for a second and ask yourself a few simple questions, such as "Does my primary user base understands what a 'hamburger' menu is?" or "Do they know how to reach it and utilize its capabilities in order to use the app?"

Persona testing can help testers plan for different types of tests which will take into account separate user types. However, this type of testing could be very time-consuming. Alternatively, test teams can take advantage of the insights and knowledge of sales and marketing teams to better understand the types of users or expected users of the mobile app and create tests to address the gaps.

Examples of criteria for testing and verifying "findability" include:

1. Can users find out within the "help" of the app how a certain function works?
2. Are app icons easy for the user to figure out what to do?
3. Do users understand what to do next when an error occurs?
4. Does the app guide users through recovering in erroneous situations?
5. Can users find within app-related tutorials how to use the app?

Value

The best app teams are used to constantly evaluate whether the functions, objects and/ or texts are **"valuable"** to their users. Testers should work with their project team members to learn what the most valuable user experience for their app is. Understanding what users value is the key to success. A lot needs be considered about the way an app is being used. Many factors could be important, such as hardware and operating system conditions as well as software functionality.

Teams need to figure out a list of priorities based on the value users find in using their app. Furthermore, once identified, they need to be well communicated and governed within the team. Customer reviews are a useful resource to learn about what users value when using the app. In order to gain further knowledge, testers can rely on the marketing and sales teams. Testers should be proactive in learning more about what this important user experience attribute means in the context of the app under test. They are highly recommended to engage with team members who have direct access to users and ask them to try out this or that function of the app. Ask them to share their opinion on the potential value these cool features would bring to the customer base. The more testers learn what is valuable, the better testers can communicate and justify these expectations with product managers and development teams. Generally speaking, end users highly value apps that work according to their own expectations. The ultimate goal of testers is to ensure that upcoming releases make more and more users happier, meaning also to detect any deficiencies in value before the release hits millions of users. Therefore, test engineers need to plan for and perform tests which verify the value in terms of UX.

Below you will find few examples for questions determining the value of the UX of apps:

1. While using the app, does the battery drain faster than with other mobile apps?

2. Does the app perform fast enough, so that users would like to keep on using it?

3. While using the app, does the user care about how much space is required to use the app?

4. Does the app take advantage of device capabilities such as the device clock or the geographic location? If so, did users confirm that they found value in doing so?

5. Do the users value the text included in the app? Is the text necessary to

enhance the user experience? Alternatively, is the text a nuisance? Does it take too much space on the display?

Credibility

The **"credibility"** (as an UX attribute) of an app to great extent depends on its "value" in the sense that building high credibility requires acknowledging what users value high. Everyone wants to trust that an app will fulfil their functional needs when installing it. If it fails to deliver the expected value, it will quickly get uninstalled. Users rarely give discredited apps a second chance.

Credibility could be assessed and tested in terms of customer reach. The presentation in the app store will be important to increase reach to all existing and potential users. If testers monitor customer reviews, they could address issues with customer usage as well. Product managers are also interested in such insights, so they could either bring valuable features in the product roadmap or just get back to customers and communicate their needs further. In doing so, companies establish high credibility by empowering users to express concerns or perhaps convey new features that they wish to be added. Testers can evaluate customer loyalty with each release of the app. By exploring customer reviews, test engineers could figure it out that a specific functionality is decreasing the trust in this particular app. Team members could plan for and conduct researches to understand if users take advantage of specific functions, objects, and/or text. Proper usage of the app under test could also be assessed. This could be done in many ways, including user acceptance testing, interviews with end users, surveys, polls, and what not.

Examples of credibility tests:
1. Do users feel they can accomplish their purpose in using the app?
2. Do users feel loyal to using the app?
3. Are users able to communicate their satisfaction or dissatisfaction directly with the app development and delivery team?
4. Are users convinced that the access to their data is well-secured?
5. Are there any permissions required for downloading and installing the app? Are there any that could be avoided at this point or rather requested later when a functionality would need it? In general, the less the number of the

permissions required, the higher trust of end users would be.

Accessibility

"Accessibility" is another key UX attribute to test. This way, you will guarantee that an app could be used by people with varying degrees of disabilities. In order to ensure fluent usage of a mobile app, one needs to answer a number of tough questions, such as "Do users take advantage of reader devices to use the app?", "Does the mobile app require special version to display on devices assisting users to increase their visual experience?", "Does the app have a feature which translates the functionalities to audio?", "Can users have all or most functionalities available using voice commands and audio interaction patterns?", "Is the app usable by someone constrained in terms of vision and hearing?" By working closely with product managers, marketing, and sales teams, testers could understand what kinds of accessibility support is needed to make a pleasurable and useful app for all of its users.

Examples of accessibility tests:
1. Can the app be used on different devices other than a phone in order to improve visual experience?
2. Can the visual experience be adjusted by the user?
3. Can one take advantage of audio features throughout the app, so it could be used by visually impaired people?
4. Can features be adjusted to provide more pleasant and useful experience for those with disabilities?
5. Can the app recognize voice commands in order to make use of the device camera or keyboard? This should be tested throughout the app or where giving voice commands might be valuable.

Desirability

Last but not least, **"desirability"** needs to be discussed. The goal would be to verify that the app, its functionality, objects, and text drive customers to use it more and more. Testers should understand why customers or potential customers would like to use the corresponding app under test. One way for testers to learn more about users' incent would be to constantly monitor and go through customer reviews. Essentially, they need to understand why end users would like to use their app. In addition, it is very important to understand why some people abandoned or uninstalled the app. Colleagues in direct contact with end users could turn out to be invaluable sources of such insights as well. This exercise should be a consistent activity of the testing team monitoring the direct communication that end users provide. Testers can then communicate their findings with development teams, so that the app could be improved if necessary. If such researches are also established as pre-release procedures, end users feel empowered to communicate their requirements in an open and honest way. Such practices have also positive impact on customer reviews and mouth-to-mouth recommendations. Last but not least, improving desirability will have very positive impact on the brand and the presence of the app in app stores.

Examples of testing whether the app, its functions, objects, and/ or text are desirable to the user:

1. Does the app contain functions that are intensively used?

2. Do customers leave more positive or negative reviews regarding the app, its functionality, any of the objects, and/or text?

3. Do end users give out proposals for new functionalities as the current one does not satisfy their requirements?

4. Are functions within the app monitored by testing, marketing, and sales teams?

5. Are there more than one team members monitoring customer reviews? The recommended setup would constitute to one tester and someone from the product management team, marketing or a sales team, so that critical input from end users could be communicated immediately to the persons in charge.

Exploring, researching, and validating the attributes of UX reveals a lot. In order to get to quality insights, test engineers are recommended to work closely with all functions within an organization. Testers should be thinking about: who, what, where, how, and why would their customers use the app under test.

MOBILE APPS ACCORDING TO THEIR ARCHITECTURE

Not all apps have been created equal. There are 3 distinct architecture patterns followed by mobile apps and each one of them imposes specific tests to be planned and performed. Let us break down each pattern and discuss the most efficient tests from the perspective of end users. Some mobile apps take advantage of device specific features like cameras, clock, device storage, microphone, bluetooth, notifications, LED or audio indications. These may have strong positive impact on user experience. Understanding which tests are appropriate to apply is critical for maintaining efficient app releases.

As depicted in **Table 9,** there are three architecture patterns for mobile apps:

- Native

- Hybrid

- Web apps

ARCHITECTURE FEATURE DIFFERENCES #1		
NATIVE APP	**HYBRID APP**	**MOBILE WEB APP**
Code written device specific.	Code written with a WebView & Native code wrapper.	Runs directly from the browser and no code is downloaded to the device
Code: for iOS (Objective C), Android (Java, C++, .Net or combo).	WebView code: HTML5, CSS, Javascript or a combo wrapped with Native code for device O.S.	Mobile web app connects to the web server from the browser where all processeing is done on the webserver. Mobile web apps are written primarily in HTML5.
Code is written to take advantage of device features like camera, audio, notificaitons, swipes.	Code is written to interact with the internet and still take advantage of device features like camera, audio, notifications, swipes.	HTML5 is not capable to interact with device features like camera, audio, notifications, swipes.
No direct internet interaction & no real time interaction.	Immediate connection to the internet & real time interaction.	Immediate connection to the internet & real time interaction.
Consistent "look & feel" with other native apps making trainability easier to users = ease of use.	Combination of "look & feel" specific to device and standards used for WebView.	"Look & Feel" depends on the user's knowledge of how to take advantage of browser and web app functionality.
Installation and updates are not automatic as specific device needs to be connected to location where the software can be downloaded onto the device.	Installation occurs when user connects with the Store (either AppleStore or GooglePlay). Once downloaded & installed, udates can be automated.	Mobile Web Apps are not installed but used only through the browser. Updates are done to the webserver directly.
		Jean Ann Harrison Copyright 2016

Table 9: Architecture Patterns for Mobile Apps as well as Their Specifics in a Nutshell

Their strengths and limitations are often misunderstood by app teams and management. Testing apps is not one and the same and each pattern implies a different subset of supported system scenarios. Therefore, specific knowledge and solid understanding of the whole system (specific device, version of operating system, and app) and the interdependencies. Apps may often cause effects beyond the ones displayed on the screen. These need to be carefully explored and verified to work flawlessly. This is precisely where the complexity of designing tests for mobile apps becomes evident. Mapping all of the UX attributes with the capabilities of the aforementioned architecture patterns turns out to be a troublesome exercise.

Let us make a deeper dive and briefly discuss some of the most notable specifics for each pattern.

MOBILE WEB APPS

They are the least complex to test because the architecture only makes use of web browsers. Web apps are not dependent on the underlying hardware and operating system. Submission to app stores is not required since they are not available for download and system installation. Thus, end users are not being asked for any specific permissions. This pattern brings very limited possibility for accessing device and OS capabilities from within web apps. Hence, testing efforts could be more focused on verifying the functional side of apps themselves. **Table 10** shares seven "good" and the same number of "bad" practices for planning UX tests for mobile web.

Good/Solid UX Tests for Mobile Web	UX Type	Bad/Poor UX Tests for Mobile Web	Reason test is poor
Can user utilize app with device browser?	Useful, Usability	Does device have internet connection?	Don't test something existing functionality
Can users figure out how data can be retrieved?	Findable, Usability	Data exists on the page	Why test if the data isn't relevant to user's purpose in using the app?
Does the app have an option to select other languages?	Useful, Usability, Valuable	Text appears on each page	Text needs to be readable. Ability for user to choose a language.
Can users see they can accomplish a goal using the app?	Credibility, Valuable	Users can enter data in fields.	Why would the user want to enter their data in the fields? Is there a clear purpose?
Does the app have an option to select other languages?	Findable, Usability	Test only for English text	Assuming your audience can only read English is very limiting. User frustration.
Do the menu options make sense for the user to accomplish their goal(s)?	Desirable	Are the colors for the items on the page pleasing?	Need to define what is pleasing to user and write a more specific test case.
Can the user access the browser voice technology to give commands?	Accessibility	Can a blind person use their reader on the mobile Web app?	Readers cannot be used on Mobile Web apps so this test isn't necessary.

Jean Ann Harrison Copyright 2016

Table 10: Seven "Good" and "Bad" Approaches to Great UX of Mobile Web Apps

Plan for performing test scenarios based on the good side of the table. Knowing some anti-patterns will help you avoid wasting time and resources in meaningless tasks.

Tests can also validate proper visualization on device screens with different sizes, browser compatibility, comparisons phone and tablet, etc. This should be fairly straightforward. Mobile web apps require internet connection to function. They are usually coded once to work on any device. Hence, their performance is lower compared to native and hybrid mobile apps.

Testers should design tests around the expectations of end users regarding how the mobile web app should work. This does include performance measurements verifying the speed of rendering images (+ icons filling out the viewport), whether this is done in synchronous or asynchronous manner, etc. Users do not like waiting for apps to respond while retrieving data. It is reasonable to combine load testing of the web server with retrieving data from a mobile app. Thus, test engineers could verify that the app is still usable under heavy loads. It is also a good idea to define benchmark values and key performance indicators (KPI) for various user-related activities.

If customers are known to use various types of devices, make sure that the already explained testing approach has been applied using as many of these devices as possible.

There are many other tests that could be relevant and performed as also illustrated by the mind map in **Figure 129.**

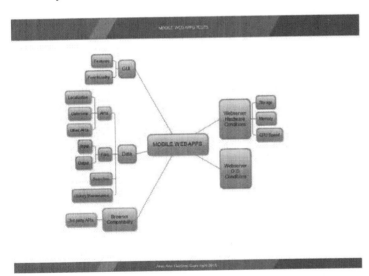

Figure 129: A Mind Map of the Testing Activities Relevant to Mobile Web Apps

It is the responsibility of the testing team to assess and define which of them would be relevant to the concrete mobile web app under tests, so that they could be planned for and performed accordingly.

Examples of mobile web apps include news magazines which ask the user to fill out subscription forms, calendar apps creating meetings and appointments, sales lead apps, and many, many more. The idea behind such apps is to facilitate end users with sharing data without downloading and installing the app.

MOBILE NATIVE APPS

Native apps take full advantage of device-specific features, such as notifications, camera, microphone, bluetooth, physical memory, storages, gestures, etc. All data processing is done by the device CPU/ GPU, i.e. these apps are downloaded (generally speaking from app stores), installed, and run on devices. They are usually implemented in languages supported by the different operating systems. iOS native apps are mostly written in Swift and Objective-C. Android apps are written in Java, .Net, C++, and others. They do not make use of the WebView.

Native apps are the fastest to respond to instructions, thus they are tuned to provide outstanding user experience. In most cases, they have been developed specifically for a single operating system. This way, consumers could benefit from using all of the device specific capabilities. In some cases, proprietary hardware and operating systems are used for native apps to serve a function or series of functions needed by customers. Testing this kind of apps requires thorough knowledge of the entire system including the inter-dependencies between hardware, operating system, and conditions affecting software behavior. Therefore, testing is particularly complex. In addition, users expect native apps to play nicely with each other by providing seamless integration experience. This should be also taken into consideration and testing activities need to be planned for accordingly.

Figure 130 illustrates the attributes of software behavior (the ones on the left) having strong impact on UX under certain system conditions (on the right). This means test engineers need to organize their strategy smart by defining test scenarios which explore and verify the installation experience, performance, communication, integration, and all of the respective attributes listed below.

This should be done under various system conditions, such as low battery, many apps working simultaneously, poor connectivity (2G, 3G, LTE, Wi-Fi), etc.

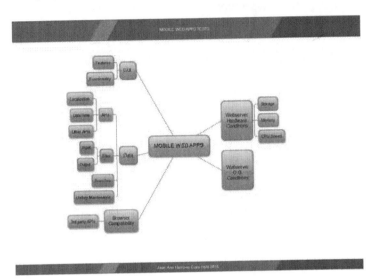

Figure 130: Software Behavior Affecting User Experience (Left) under System Conditions (Right)

Each element on the right has specifics of its own that could be broken down in very specific conditions. Thus, test scenarios could be performed systematically taking into account conditions that make sense in the current context.

Good/Solid UX Tests for Mobile Native	UX Type	Bad/Poor UX Tests for Mobile Native	Reason test is poor
When the App is performing a search, does app drain the battery too fast before the user can finish the search?	Usability, Credibility	How fast the app drains the battery while in sleep mode.	This test doesn't really give the tester or project team much useful information unless the battery drain is noticeable by a user.
App responds to audio instruction to perform functions. Verify a blind person can activate the app to perform a purposeful function.	Accessibility, Useful	Does app respond to audio commands?	Add specifics in testing whether someone who can't read the screen can still perform a function by audio commands
App saves data before device storage reaches limit. App gives warning message before stopping to save data.	Useful, Valuable	App gives a popup message for the user to dismiss everytime data is saved to storage.	User would find messages to be tedious and frustrating to dismiss. User wants to be informed but not to do any action.
App responds to touch to perform a function.	Accessibility, Usability	How fast the app respond when the user presses the button to use the camera?	One singular action for a text. This test can be combined with other instructions to ensure app responds to user.
App records the time once a function is complete and data is saved with that timestamp.	Desirable, Useful	Can the user see the device time while using the app?	Doesn't serve a purpose from the user's perspective of needing to see if app recognizes time & links to data.
App displays picture icons to direct user in what to do.	Usability, Valuable	Tapping each icon to see if the app responds.	Test is too general and doesn't really test on the user's needs in testing the user's purpose in selecting the icon.
App displays instruction on how to incorporate the use of the camera to perform a function.	Findable, Useful	Does the camera work within the app?	This test is too general and can be included with another test to verify the camera works within the app.

Table 11: Seven "Good" and "Bad" Approaches to Great UX of Mobile Native Apps

Assessing which test scenarios make sense to be run under specific specific conditions is kind of tricky. It turns out that performing certain scenarios may look reason reasonable, while bringing zero value to the process of drawing reliable conclusions about the current state of UX. **Table 11** aims at assisting practitioners by describing good practices and their impact on UX. Alternatively, there is the same number of anti-patterns included. They make it clear why testing under certain conditions would only be waste of time and efforts.

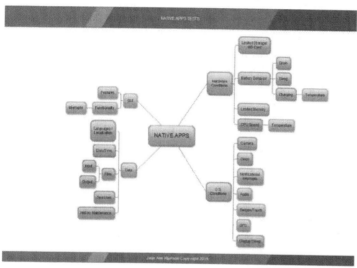

Figure 131: Tests That Need to be Considered When Testing Native Mobile Apps Under System Conditions

Testing Mobile Native apps can get convoluted. Refer to **Figure 131** and find more detailed lists of tests applicable to native apps and system conditions. Imagine the ever growing diversity of devices, versions of operating systems, and the respective subsets of system conditions. It is not about smartphones and tablets anymore. Today, there are tons of proprietary medical devices, restaurant ordering devices increasing the efficiency of service. Car rental companies provide mobile ordering and reconciling of car rentals for customers. Traffic police officers issue traffic tickets by using specialized devices. These are just some prominent examples of mobile native apps satisfying different needs on a plethora of devices. Mapping out and planning which tests would have high impact from the perspective of users is crucial to the success of every native app out there.

MOBILE HYBRID APPS

You should already have a pretty good idea what native and web apps are. Well, hybrid mobile apps are just what their name states. These are native apps which are able to incorporate HTML content, much in the way this is done by browsers. In fact, the common approach to render HTML in native apps is to use an UI component which is named "WebView". It is a lightweight web browser. End users could benefit from certain system capabilities which are not available for web apps, while also reusing and interacting with existing web apps and websites. Such features would include using the camera, audio, notifications, device storage, and many more. Naturally, hybrid mobile apps require connection to the Internet, at least for the screens where "WebView" components are used.

Theoretically speaking, hybrid apps aim at bringing the best of two worlds. However, this makes their testing even more challenging compared to native applications.

Social media and e-commerce apps are the usual suspects when examples for mobile hybrid apps are needed. Users are able to take photos and share them through the app, allowing others to view the photos as well. Recording an audio or shooting videos within an app for the sake of posting it is another way of leveraging system capabilities.

Like native apps, hybrid ones have inter-dependencies with hardware and operating system conditions. It is often the case that users will not be aware of these conditions. They would not become evident unless the behavior of the app would be affected. It is critical for mobile test engineers to understand the full picture, so that sane system conditions could be integrated as part of test scenarios exploring and verifying user experience. Figure 132 contributes to more effective test planning exercise. Different attributes of UX could be tested for excellence in different contexts, such as bad internet connection, battery drained, various screen sizes and orientations, etc.

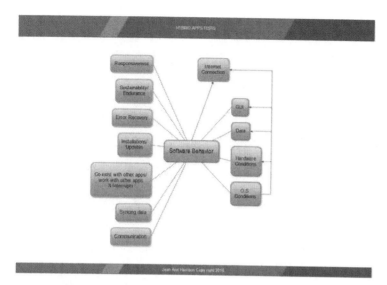

Figure 132: Software Behavior of Hybrid Mobile Apps Affecting User Experience Under System Conditions

One should always think how to adjust UX testing in the context of any given hybrid app. Imagine that it takes for an app unusually long time to receive a notification. In such situations, end users quickly get annoyed. Timely app notifications are already a commodity. They are expected to be received in the timeframe of seconds after something important happened. Receiving timely and adequate notifications is one of the most neglected conditions when it comes to releasing official app versions. Do you remember that in a sense a hybrid app has all of the power of native apps, plus even more? They could also emit signals to devices using audio, visual, LED, and on-screen notifications. Analyze the requirements towards hybrid apps and plan for thoroughly testing their means for interaction with end users.

Which of the test scenarios would make sense in the context of hybrid mobile apps? Which ones among them would explore and validate the vital attributes for achieving breathtaking user experience in the right way? Table 12: "Good" and "Bad" Approaches to Great UX of Mobile Hybrid Apps **Table 12** sums up a number of good and bad practices/ anti-patterns that mobile testers could use in order to address these questions.

Good/Solid UX Tests for Hybrid Native	UX Type	Bad/Poor UX Tests for Hybrid Native	Reason test is poor
When downloading and installing the App, does installation drain the battery too fast?	Useful, Desirable	How fast the app drains the battery while installing?	This test doesn't really give the tester or project team much useful information unless the battery drain is noticeable by a user.
Does the app respond when device changes rotation based user action to view the data?	Accessibility, Useful	Does the app display data horizontally or landscape mode because data displayed doesn't fit?	Unless the user rotates the device, the app should not display data in landscape mode because this would be frstrating to read.
Does the app signal to the user a notification is received when the app is nnot in use?	Useful, Valuable	Does the app signal a notification received but only when the app is in use?	Users might be using another app and won't be informed a notification is received. Not useful.
App responds to touch to perform a function.	Accessibility, Usability	How fast the app respond when the user presses the button to use the camera?	One singular action for a test. This test can be combined with other instructions to ensure app responds to user.
Once the user loses internet connection, can the user still access the app and use with limitations?	Desirable, Useful		
App loses connection to internet but saves data from last function completed.	Usability, Valuable	If app loses connection, the app is restarted but loses data from the last function being used.	User should receive a warning before any data is lost despite the connection is lost.
App displays instruction on how to incorporate the use of the amera to perform a function.	Findable, Useful	Does the camera work within the app?	This test is too general and can be included with another test to verify the camera works within the app.

Jean Ann Harrison Copyright 2016

Good/Solid UX Tests for Hybrid Native	UX Test Type	Bad/Poor UX Tests for Hybrid Native	Reason test is poor
While app is in use, viewing a items within a catalog of items available to purchase, searching several pages does drain the battery too fast?	Useful	Using the app drains the battery	Not a very specific test to assists the developers to utilize power more efficiently. Create a test which monitors battery drain for obvious needs of more power like
Is the app available to users who are blind or visually impaired and can listen to selected content offered as compared to users with no visual disability?	Accessibility, Usability		
A game app allows the user to continue to play the game and save achievements if connection to the internet is lost. The game gives user indication their data is being saved and can be synced up to the game once connection is restored.	Valuable	While using the app, the user can get notifications only.	Users might be using another app and won't be informed a notification is received. Not useful.
The app gives indications of what the user can do to save data after a loss to the internet and then a way for the user to retain data after reconnection.	Findable, Usability	Game displays usable when internet connection is restored.	This test doesn't give the user an indication if their achievements while playing the game was saved or what happens once a reconnection occurs. Is the game playable while offline?
Retail App loses connection to internet but saves shopping cart data from last function completed. The app is still usable after connection loss. Once reconnected, app asks user if ishes to add saved items to cart that were saved while offline or use data when last connected?	Usability, Valuable, Desirable	Error message appears when loss of connection to the internet occurs.	This test is not too helpful from a user perpective. The user wants an indication of what data has been saved to the shopping cart once reconnected.
Using a health app, the user wants to learn what kinds of exercises help increase the metabolism.	Credibility	App provide a single one exercise but doesn't indicate what that exercise purpose is.	Users want to have some sort of information regarding content that is relevant to what they are searching.

Jean Ann Harrison Copyright 2016

Table 12: "Good" and "Bad" Approaches to Great UX of Mobile Hybrid Apps

Again, there is a whole lot to be considered when testing, as illustrated by **Figure 133.** For example, with hybrid apps the loss of Internet connection might be really tricky. It is not only important what happens when the connection is lost. Proper reconnection is equally important. Think of someone playing a game when a connectivity issue occurs. Is the game still usable? Could users add their achievements to the game and continue from there, once reconnected? Have users been informed of the loss of connection and the consequent reconnection?

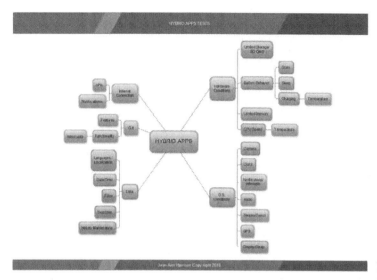

Figure 133: Map for Testing Hybrid Apps Under Various System Conditions

Understanding the differences of native and hybrid apps will make it possible for test engineers to approach test design and planning in a more efficient and informed way. Deciding on the right tests with wide UX coverage and accompanying conditions is crucial for the success of hybrid mobile apps.

Let us finish the quick tour through the architecture patterns followed by mobile apps with illustrating few more points to keep in mind in **Table 13.**

ARCHITECTURE FEATURE DIFFERENCES #2		
NATIVE APP	**HYBRID APP**	**MOBILE WEB APP**
Best noticable performance, user experience, security.	Performance & UX are dependent on user's connectivity to a webserver, familiarity with their device & device settings along with the webserver's performance rate & interaction with the device.	Performance & UX dependent on the type of browser used as well as the webserver's optimization for high performance.
Highest security as the interaction with the internet is more controlled and singular access point.	Access to the device by outside sources is less secure than Native apps but although access to device specific features is limited as permissions need to be granted and known.	Security is the lowest for the mobile architectures due to the reuse of web application coding. Hacking from unknown sources can be more easily accessible than other architectures.
Most expensive to develop & maintain but slowest to release & market.	Code used to create the WebView can be copied, reused and less expensive to develop & maintain but because contains Native code, the cost to release & market to the WebView code.	Code used for web apps are easily copied and reused for fast delivery of apps to market. These apps are least expensive to develop.
App is utilized without internect connection.	App can be utilized with or without internet access.	App cannot be utilized without having internet access.

Table 13: Differences Among Native, Web, and Hybrid Mobile Apps (Part 2)

Did you get it already? The reality, from testing perspective, is harsh. The only thing that different applications — following each distinct architecture pattern — share in common would be the loosely-defined term "mobile".

TEST DESIGN BASED ON ARCHITECTURE/ CONTEXT/ USAGE

Test engineers can plan for and develop their testing approaches by combining the knowledge of the app architecture, its context, and the incentives of customers to use it.

One of the hurdles in mobile app testing is the overall number of the unknowns, though. Users are rarely aware that a certain feature is on their personal wish lists until they need it and try to find it. "We don't know what we don't know", customer-facing team members often conclude as well. Therefore, test engineers need to develop a "What if I do this and this... under such and such conditions?" attitude. They need to stretch the limits of their vivid imagination and bright minds in order to come up with smart plans about ensuring the right test coverage from the perspective of the most typical end users. This might be a pitfall for many inexperienced testers. One needs to follow a pragmatic approach. Identify what serves well 85% of the user base and make sure that the most common scenarios for them will be tested end to end. Later, corner cases could be explored and assessed further in terms of value and potential impact, as part of an exploratory testing phase, for example. Do not overengineer your test plans and maintain strong focus on the end user.

Contextual understanding does not end here. Since it is the key to successful testing cycles and great app releases, it should be gathered and shaped from as many sources as possible. Ideally, it should be promoted and supported within organizations by all teams and members, respectively. From testing perspective, having full contextual understanding at any point of time helps test engineers to define, perform, automate, and continuously run sane and valuable user-centric scenarios.

Test engineers would like to know how the respective app is utilized, why a given feature is adored/ used/ hated. Any direct and indirect feedback on performance would be highly appreciated as well.

It is essential for teams to distribute and share insights, information, and knowledge about:

1. Who are the end users of an app.

2. What are their incentives to use it.

3. Expectations towards the app from the perspectives of distinct groups of end users.

Keep in mind that defining distinct groups of end users according to their incentive to use the app is crucial to testing complex mobile apps. For example, a music streaming app will be used by many for the sake of listening to music. On the other hand, music artists, producers, and executives will presumably use it as well. Every distinct group of users will do this for reasons of their own. Expectations among the groups towards functionality and UX may not be quite the same as well.

The question "Why does this app exist?" needs to be asked by mobile testers. Knowing about the issues and pain of end users in this long forgotten pre-app world helps us generate more ideas about increasing the test coverage in sane, structured, and user-oriented ways.

GAMES AS A CASE STUDY FOR MOBILE APP TEST PLANNING

In order to to feel confident about test coverage of mobile apps, teams need to combine and perform their tests in smart ways rather than rely on functional checklists. For example, when testing a game, test engineers would like to assess, explore, and verify whether and how an objective could be achieved. However, they need to also measure and track how the app performs over a period of time. Saving and loading a single and many game sessions are also very important user interactions. They are often automated further in a way that players would return to the point they left, once users start the app again. Achievements need to be preserved during restarts. Response time of user interactions is very important. Of course, "lagging" is a deal breaker and cannot be tolerated. This is valid for both the gameplay and the administrative functions, such as loading a game session. Progressing through the game scenario should not end up with session loading times constantly getting higher and higher. These details could only be cleared out with playing the game. In the context of games, this would mean different types of testers with different gaming skills, since in most games the individual players are not equally developed and positioned all the time. They usually have different "levels".

Let us think of certain conditions that could be encountered meanwhile. For example, a notification could be received while playing. This scenario raises few questions. Does the game allow for interruptions? What kind of interruptions does the game acknowledge? Does the game transmit audio notifications and alerts? Are there any notifications displayed while the game app is in use? Some games do not display notifications, but the device might indicate its existence through the audio system or the LED indicators. Mobile apps have different ways of handling notifications which is why it is vital for testers to understand both the features of their apps and the ways other apps would use to interact with the device in the meantime.

Notification testing — as outlined by **Figure 134** — is one test concepts that could be applied by test engineers contemplating other tests while the app under test is in use. Teams are highly recommended to draw such a map for each one of the key conditions which make it clear what is accepted by users and what cannot be tolerated. Thus, acceptable response times, expected app and device load, levels of pick stress, and duration before app/ operating system crash could be documented and available for everyone to explore and question. Of course, potential issues with critical impact on UX need to be identified in advance, so that everyone takes care not to let such defects pass through and hit end users hard.

Where should one start when defining the map for the system condition "XYZ"? Asking questions from the perspective of an user often turns out to be a good start. If you do not like mind maps or their concept is not applicable to the purposes of your organization, you do not need to stick to them. The same exercise could be done using spreadsheets, for example. You could use any format that would work well for you and your teammates. Test engineers will constantly need to work with their colleagues from product management, sales, and marketing departments in order to prioritize and re-prioritize test cases from the perspective of end users. They will need to plan testing each app release under specific user, hardware, operating system, and software conditions. When it makes sense, different test strategies could be combined, so that more conditions could be tested in a single cycle.

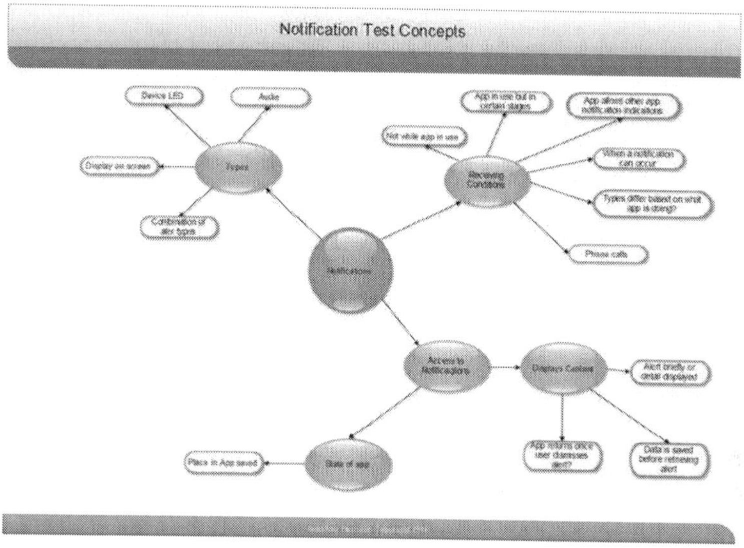

Figure 134: The Concept of Testing Notifications Explained

If we get back to the game testing example above, in reality lots of conditions could be triggered almost simultaneously while the game is being played. Internet connection could be lost, storage could reach its limit, battery could be drained to critical levels. The ability of the game to recover and bring back the player to the point the game was left without any data loss is vital. How could a test engineer help?

Well, initiating regular discussions with the development teams would for sure bring benefits for both sides. Test engineers would get to know how the app works under the hood, while also verify what is supported and what – not. Developers would get to know better what works well and why. They would need to think how the game integrates with other apps. Concrete issues, as well as their resolution, could be communicated efficiently. Talking to development has always boosted healthy and successful releases.

PERSONA TESTING AND TEST PRIORITIZATION

Persona Testing is the exercise of creating a list of distinct types of expected users according to their incentives to use the mobile app. Each group is mapped to exactly one persona — a fictional character describing the "ideal" representative of the group. In order to motivate empathy and thorough understanding of a "real" persona and its ways to engage with the app, these characters are described in quite some details. They are named after real persons. A mini-world could be created around their daily routines and work duties. Depending on the needs, personas feature appearance, physical condition, emotional intelligence, professional skills, general demographics, and what not. Anything that could help the involved teams to create vivid and aligned understanding of the character, its needs, motivation to use the app, and expectations would do good. Empathy is the key to defining good personas, so put some effort to build up interesting characters that would also engage the rest of your teammates in adopting the concept. Using personas is a very convenient way for conducting fruitful sales, marketing, testing, and technical discussions. If everyone knows the character, even representatives from different organizations have common ground for effective and more efficient communication.

Developing personas of expected customers or users gives test engineers the means to focus on how the app will be used, thus avoiding disastrous reviews damaging the brand. Personas are developed based on user tendencies and trends. Therefore, it is essential to regularly update personas, i.e. their development is continuous and rolls on hand in hand with the product itself. The more information about the users, the better the user experience of the app will be. The behavior of end users gets anticipated and understood by app vendors at scale. Poor UX decisions have been stopped before they cause critical damages to masses. It is important for testers to ask the Five "W" questions: "Who?", "What?", "Where?", "When?", and, of course, "Why?". Once personas are created, testers can develop a more comprehensive full system approach covering UX. If properly maintained and updated according to the user trends, personas could be a handy tool facilitating communication about customers and their needs across all levels of an organization.

Figure 135 draws an expressive map of the key attributes that could be attached to personas. It is specifically tuned to describe users of mobile apps.

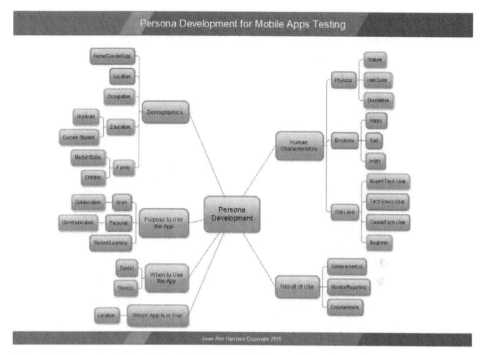

Figure 135: Important Aspects to Consider During Persona Development

Context Type of App	Demographics	Human characteristics	Skills	Why use app	Uses app When/Where
	Emily, Female, 32, NYC, Elementary teacher, single	Medium height, long Blonde hair, no disabilities, quiet	fairly tech savvy, comfortable with tech, uses mobile device	Uses app for teaching strategic thinking in her students. Shows students progress.	App is used only during school days & hours in classroom
	James, Male, 15, St Louis, high school student	Lanky, curly brown hair, no disabilities, angry, competitive	Expert tech knnowledge, uses various gadgets frequently	Entertainment, Displays achievements while playing with friends.	At school, at home, in car, at mall, everywhere. Morning, Noon, Evenings, At night.
	Henry, Male, 68, Boca Raton, Retired Engineer, Married, children, grandchildren	Medium height, white hair, left hand partial paralyzed, happy	Grandchildren helps teach him about his mobile device but he's willing to learn.	Help to keep his mind busy in quiet times. Loves the challenge to gain new levels.	App is used late afternoons & evenings at home. Not used daily.
Puzzle Game App	Olivia, Female, 21, San Diego, personal trainer, single	Shorter, short bright blonde, no disabilities, energetic, happy	fairly tech savvy, comfortable uses mobile device, tablet & laptop	Teaches her clients to keep track of their health, keeps track of own health	App is used at gym, out & about the city, maybe used in traveling, day hours. Everyday.
	Luke, Make, 39, Gary Indiana, security guard, military veteran, married 1 young child	Medium, Husky build, bald, no disabilities, quiet, contemplative	Novice using technology, only uses his mobile device but has limited knowledge	doctor prescribed to keep track of vitals and send report of daily records.	Works at night so app is in use evenings & night hours. No use during day hours. No used weekends.
Health app, tracking heart rate, blood pressure # of steps	Janice, 77, Scottsdale AZ, widowed, children, grandchildren	Short, Silver curly hair, partially blind, lonely	Never uses her phone for apps, very unskilled	Health care worker set up this app to record vitals and needs Jancie to send reports manually	Daily, used once per day at home and used at noon.

Jean Ann Harrison, Copyright 2016

Table 14: Sample Personas Defined for a Game App

Defining personas at the right level of detail is tricky and requires practice. **Table 14** helps newbies with providing a real world example of the list of sample personas developed for a game app. You could use it as a reference when doing the same exercise on your own.

Personas are usually defined in terms of real human characteristics. Testers should be interested in knowing more about how various end users would use the app. On the other hand, colleagues from the sales department would be much more intrigued with making them pay. This is why personas are a great tool – their features could be analyzed for the sake of answering many questions asked from different perspectives.

Smarter and more effective testing is boosted by the usage of personas. They contribute to a more complex understanding of the needs of end users. This way, test engineers could go beyond the basic functional and GUI testing by mixing up important measurements on a number of conditions that were identified as critical for user experience. It is already clear that user needs are not always evident until it is too late. By creating personas, testers can efficiently increase test coverage to prevent glitches in UX.

In order to develop the right persona, insights from marketing and sales departments may turn out invaluable. In this regards, test engineers are highly recommended to communicate their questions with any customer facing members of the organization. These are the ones knowing your personas firsthand. An alternative valuable source of information would be the customer reviews on app stores. App monitoring in production is another huge topic to explore and build hypothesis on UX upon. It does provide lots of food for thought, since this is the way to track user activities within apps for the sake of improving engagement, anyway. As much as possible needs to be known about customer and user base. One way or another, the Five "W" questions need to be answered. Test engineers will communicate further with development teams the expectations of end users and their incentives for using or not using the app or some of its functionalities. Thus, UX of apps could be improved and governed by teams, while bringing more and more value and recognition of the corresponding brand.

AUTOMATION OF UX TESTS

Automation is a necessity for software testing today. It needs to be done in a conscious and structured way, though. Knowing about user experience, the architecture patterns for mobile apps, as well as your end users, you need to go through the list of questions below.

Mobile App Automation Questionnaire
1. Are tests repeatable?
2. Are there any unknowns for some situations?
3. Are there any imitations and benchmarks known for all UX situations?
4. How likely would it be for new features to affect the existing tests?
5. Do the automation tests apply to all types of supported devices?
6. How long will it take to create automated scripts exploring and verifying all of the conditions and combinations of conditions to test the UX of the app?

The combination of the answers will draw a clear picture of whether you need automation for the purposes of testing UX or not. Imagine, if you need to change your test scripts for one and the same scenarios on different devices in a fast-paced delivery cycle where new features pop out for each device and operating system every day. Even different versions of one and the same operating systems may cause flakiness of tests being run against different versions. Sometimes, revealing the unknowns means manually exploring situations or combinations of conditions a user might face. They may turn out to be low in priority, but high in severity if not known. Thus, creating automated UX tests might turn out to be inefficient.

SUMMARY

Proper test planning for testing UX is vital. In order to do that, test engineers need to understand the basic concepts of user experience as well as many specifics about their own end users and their incentives. Of course, the right prioritization of the tests within the plan need to be defined according to the number of end users affected, the frequency of impact, specific user conditions for any supported device.

Planning UX tests based on profiles of typical users, outling users, and conditions will factor into test strategy. Test automation is also an option, unless assessed as inefficient for the particular use case at hand. Test engineers must not blindly accept dogmatic approaches for testing mobile apps. Use intelligent and informed approaches to build the right test scenarios under the necessary conditions as needed by your target user groups/ personas.

Keep in mind that some of the topics discussed within this chapter deserve books of their own. It is certainly so. Yet, there is a "secret sauce" that most entrepreneurs know about. A successful venture is not about knowing all in advance, but about starting it in time and intelligently ramping up with real tasks. The first steps are the most important ones, because they give you a direction to follow and momentum to benefit from. Now, you know enough to define your personas and start with conscious UX testing of mobile apps under sane system conditions. This is already a pretty good start, isn't it?

24 Extending Mobile Testing to Gain Insights in Production

THIS CHAPTER WAS CONTRIBUTED BY AMIR ROZENBERG, SR. DIRECTOR OF PRODUCT MANAGEMENT AT PERFECTO

AMIR ROZENBERG is a Senior Director of Product Management at Perfecto, the leading digital, Cloud, and automation company. He is responsible for the core product strategy of Perfecto. Amir has pioneered many practices in order to extend the company's offering across the whole application life cycle. Amir has extensive experience in the digital industry with expertise in areas including infrastructure, applications, application delivery, and monitoring. Mr. Rozenberg has led many successful synergies with  technology partners to optimize value delivery to Perfecto's customers. Prior to working at Perfecto, Amir was heading the mobile monitoring practice at Compuware. Prior to Compuware, he co-founded Adva Mobile, a direct-to-fan mobile marketing startup, and held various leadership positions at Groove Mobile, Nextcode Corp., and others.

INTRODUCTION

In recent years, strong, game changing forces have been driving radically new Go-to-market strategies for digital applications, effectively disrupting the general understanding of user experiences and customer journeys. Nowadays, the digital competition is stronger than ever. Shortening time to market does not necessarily mean iterative delivery of "saner" functional and non-functional scope. No, not at all. Dealing with shorter timeframes, organizations are racing to bring in as many highly innovative and disruptive features as possible.

In order to cope with the aforementioned dynamics, more and more tools for automatic code generation and almighty frameworks for rapid application development have been utilized by software developers. Test engineers harness the power of other fancy code-generation solutions for the sake of ensuring proper test coverage. They learnt to maintain, parametrize, and scale their test suites early in the Software Development Lifecycle (SDLC). Well-organized continuous integration (CI) workflows have become pillars of product quality. They are pretty much a commodity for modern and highly efficient software delivery organizations.

However, having a packaged mobile app ready to be (certified and) uploaded to an app store is just the beginning. Earlier in this book, performance testing (which is often conducted as a post-development or staging activity) was discussed as well as its serious impact on User Experience (UX). Thus, we arrived at viable ways for organizations to measure the correlation. We talked about engaging end users and how crucial it is from a business perspective. Go through this chapter in order to discover what comes next.

MONITORING OF DIGITAL APPLICATIONS IN PRODUCTION ENVIRONMENTS

This is how organizations usually get to know about major operational flaws and outages causing severe negative impact on UX and, consequently, loss of profitability. It is also done in order to provide data for further analysis and enhancements of UX. Today this kind of monitoring activity is a prerequisite for attracting new (and retaining existing) customers/end-users.

Historically, the responsibility and accountability for production monitoring has been handed out to dedicated Ops or central IT teams. Lately, monitoring and operations have been gradually shifting more and more to the application/feature development teams. It is all about empowerment, autonomy, and domain expertise, i.e. a timely reaction in the most appropriate way.

Within this chapter, some of the aforementioned trends will be discussed in detail and will be backed up with relevant real life examples.

OPERATIONAL + BUSINESS METRICS = INCREASED AWARENESS AND SUCCESS

There are multiple ways of examining, diagnosing, and validating application behavior in production environments. The major trends that more or less rule the industry are:

- **Synthetic Monitoring** — scheduled repetitive testing of key user flows using dedicated equipment with the aim of detecting and fixing flaws and outages, ideally before the work of many end users is affected.

- **Real User Monitoring** — a monitoring technique relying on collecting UX-related data — while users work with the monitored app — for the sake of bringing back valuable insights used for consecutive trend and business analysis.

Being the result of a scheduled and repetitive effort, Synthetic Monitoring gives us a chance to increase operational awareness. Depending on its scope and timing, it may reveal performance degradations (or even outages) that could dramatically decrease UX and customer satisfaction. Typically, this kind of monitoring goes toward exercising the frontend layer of apps, sometimes being extended toward the service API as well. The performance of middleware or backend systems would less likely be the subject of Synthetic Monitoring.

Real User Monitoring, on the other hand, does not imply any restrictions in terms of infrastructure coverage. It could be spanned through and exercised over all of the architecture layers of tested apps. Any combinations of software components and services — building up client, middle, and backend tiers —

could contribute to the insights gathered during real use of software deployed in production environments. Therefore, this kind of monitoring is a powerful tool facilitating data-driven business decisions. If a group of Product Owners/ Managers has continuous and measurable insights related to the way their product is used, then they could figure it out what works well and what does not. From there on, it is a matter of drawing the right conclusions in order to improve the product definition and roadmap. They could make up their mind on easing the pain with existing features by enhancing them. Alternatively, they may go for new ones that are assessed as "badly wanted" by the ecosystem. Of course, this monitoring technique shall not be perceived as the one and only driving force behind similar decisions.

The results of comparing the above approaches are summarized in **Table 15.**

Criteria	Synthetic Monitoring	Real User Monitoring
Common use	Operational monitoring	Trend analysis and business impact
Outcomes	Alerts, reports about outages, and performance-related issues	Trends in behavior of end users and application issues with projected business impact
Equipment required	Dedicated equipment	Relying on real users
Additional Details	▪ No end user privacy concerns ▪ Outage avoidance ▪ Ease of deployment ▪ No instrumentation needed	▪ Gains insights on business impact ▪ Assists to understand UX at scale ▪ May require the consent of end-users ▪ Requires masking of sensitive data, if such has been gathered

Table 15: Synthetic vs. Real User Monitoring — Comparison

Reality made modern organizations realize that they actually needed both. Nowadays, businesses strive for compliance with very strict Service Level Agreements (SLA) directly translated into operational excellence, thus retaining and attracting new customers and partners. At the same time, the ability to identify and act upon trends and application weaknesses — affecting your own users — is not a competitive advantage anymore. It is just one of many prerequisites for staying relevant on the ever-changing software market, let alone the mobile one.

PRODUCTION MONITORING IN THE HANDS OF APP AND FEATURE TEAMS

Perhaps one of the most notable trends observed with shifting towards Continuous Delivery (CD) is related to shifting responsibilities and ownership, hence accountability. Quality in production is more and more taken care of by the application and feature development teams themselves. Time is slipping like sand through the hands of dedicated Ops and central IT teams trying to operate and support complex software solutions in "black box" mode.

This huge change is also facilitated by the business transformation that the world is currently undergoing, i.e. the wide adoption of more rational/convenient business models such as the flavors of Software as a Service (SaaS). From a business perspective, this means a shift from capital expenditures (CAPEX) towards operating expenses (OPEX), which might be a topic for another book, but in short: organizations will not acquire expensive software licences anymore, they would rather "rent" software solutions for as long as they need them.

Organizations would happily give away software deployment, IT operations and application maintenance to their respective software vendors. Public, private, and hybrid hosted deployment models (a.k.a. Cloud) are taking over, thus opening up a whole lot of opportunities to redefine the general understanding of the term "IT Operations". In addition, the increased expectations towards best-of-breed Digital User Experience, the popularity of Agile/DevOps software development and delivery practices, as well as the wide diversity of data sources utilized by modern distributed applications, resonate with the "old ways", effectively leading to the renaissance of "almighty" application/feature teams taking care of everything, end-to-end.

Let us iterate over the challenges of keeping up with "classic", i.e. centralized, IT Operations, while delivering and supporting software solutions in an innovative, highly disruptive, and demanding reality.

Throughout this book, we have had a lengthy discussion on the topic of Digital User Experience. We all know that it is utterly important for application/feature teams to be constantly aware and adept at the way their "babies" behave. "Baby" software can be steered and grown from the cradle, through the playground, until it flourishes and matures into a respected and highly profitable citizen on the Internet/Intranet.

In the context of continuous insight, teams need to know well the behavior and limitations of any given application across different screen sizes, devices, browsers, operating systems, end user workflows, complex functionality, and so forth. This means that they have to be able to monitor the app in all of its complexity at scale. Relying on insights filtered out from the outside (e.g. a central Ops team) adds noise and causes undesirable delays. If you were a parent, would you like to know that your kid was not doing well in school a bit in advance, or would you like to have a dedicated meeting with the principal to be informed about an upcoming expulsion? You get the point, right?

Agile approaches towards software development, as well as striving for continuous delivery, mandate that application/feature development teams are quite engaged with and empowered by what they do — all the way throughout SDLC. Talking about SDLC, we know it is significantly shortened in terms of time. There are websites and mobile apps that are being updated in every few hours. This is why the concept of "DevOps" is so hot now. The general idea behind this term is visually explained on the diagram in **Figure 136.**

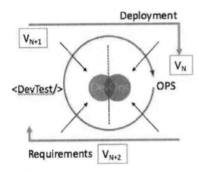

Figure 136: Agile Approaches towards Continuous Delivery and Operations — DevOps

This is a pace organizations can hardly follow with a central IT/ Ops team. Why?

1.   When your app is ready to be upgraded/updated in production (Version "Vn+1"), the central monitoring team will need to start writing scripts to monitor any new functionality. Time to create and execute them, troubleshoot and resolve discovered issues will be necessary. Does it mean that we postpone the release until all major issues are

resolved? Alternatively, if time-to-market is key, does it mean that we release a low-quality increment because we cannot really wait? Why should we be caught between Scylla and Charybdis over and over again?

2. Central monitoring teams need visibility into the quality of future releases in order to plan for their future capacity and scale. For example, there are cases when problematic features pass through the "Go/No-Go" decision to reach end users. This should be clear in advance, so that the Ops team can be prepared to handle more issues. Now, scaling teams up and down in a timely manner is far more difficult than adjusting the volume of the sound system in your car. In fact, this is one of the huge pains for hiring managers in our industry and it really hurts badly. If you are a people manager, would you like to go through the whole hassle of sourcing, hiring, and onboarding the experts you need just for the sake of operating and supporting this flawed release? You may not even have any time to do so. Perhaps the next delivery (in a couple of hours, or days, or a week) will not be so troublesome and you will need scale the team down? Hey, money talks, so we need to listen. Wouldn't it be more reasonable to immediately re-prioritize the current the scope of the development team, so that they could fix critical issues and get back to their normal development schedule then? Or just bring performance testing earlier in SDLC and sleep well during releases and deployments?

3. Then, when something fails in production (Version "Vn"), the monitoring team would need help from the developers and testers to troubleshoot and resolve it as soon as possible. What if development and Ops teams use different test and monitoring solutions? The time it takes to align these in order for someone to resolve critical issues could be very, very expensive. You have gone through scary stats translating major outages and downtime of busy websites and apps into money loss, haven't you? You may have already experienced such. Not cool.

4. Last but not least, when Product Owners work on prioritizing the requirements for next sprint/release (Version "Vn+2"), they have to take into consideration existing flaws in the user experience of applications running in production environments. They need to prioritize those according to business impact, so that serious issues can be addressed in the very next iteration. The truth is that such insights, transparency, and awareness

can often be difficult to reach across many teams in huge organizations. Forget about proper timing and daily/hourly deliveries.

USING QUALITY INSIGHTS AND DASHBOARDS THROUGHOUT THE WHOLE SDLC

Modern software, running in heterogeneous and siloed environments, is complex. It does not exist in isolation anymore. Applications rely on many 3rd party services and products in order to offer core value-added features to end users faster. The rise of Cloud technologies, Big Data, real-time data analysis, and artificial intelligence does not mean that it becomes any simpler; on the contrary — the complexity of software architecture is growing. This said, the ideal solution for monitoring and troubleshooting software in production environments shall retrieve and synthesize data from many application-relevant data sources/services in order to speed up the root cause analysis and timely resolution of critical defects.

A SINGLE TOOL FOR EARLY TESTING AND MONITORING IN PRODUCTION

Considering the above challenges, the general recommendation for any team would be to bet on one (the same) solution to perform their normal testing activities, as well as the necessary Ops monitoring in production.

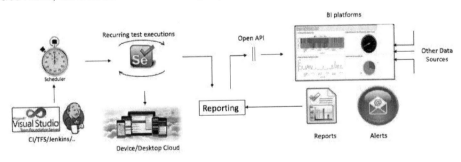

Figure 137: Tools and Workflow Recommendation for Continuous Insight

Assuming that you are committed to taking full ownership of the software released by your team(s) and even operating it in production environments, you can try out a simple concept of a workflow and the necessary tooling facilitating this process (illustrated in Figure 137).

The main building blocks of such a testing and monitoring solution are as follows:

* Schedulers — CI platforms such as Jenkins and Microsoft Team Services triggering regular, on commit, and as per request test execution

* Robust testing runtimes — used for repetitive execution of automated test suites, i.e. Selenium WebDriver, Appium, and more

* Device lab/ Cloud device lab — for the sake of device and web browser provisioning

* An easy-to-use and understand reporting solution made out of dashboards, detailed reports, alerts etc.

Essentially, this solution can be used both in production and pre-production. It can provide the required transparency to all interested parties within software delivery organizations. Being agnostic to the architecture of AUT, similar setups can become handy to test and monitor any piece of software. Yes, you will re-place building blocks here and there, but the basic principles remain the same.

SUMMARY

Within this chapter, we had a walk through the basic strategies and techniques used for monitoring and operating modern software in production. We elaborated on how crucial it is to do it right. Like it or not, the pace of industry innovation makes us shift IT operations of apps deployed in production as a core respon-sibility of the application/feature development teams releasing them. If done properly, organizations will achieve a reduced number of blocking issues in production, better timing, more cost effective diagnosis, and faster resolutions of critical issues. Last but not least, you were presented with an idea about unifying the test and monitoring infrastructure into a single solution.

APPENDIX I — FIGURES

APPENDIX II — TABLES

ABOUT THE AUTHOR
ERAN KINSBRUNER

I AM THE MOBILE EVANGELIST at Perfecto, one of the leading providers of digital quality solutions across the SDLC through its Continuous Quality Lab in the Cloud worldwide. Formerly a CTO for mobile testing and Texas Instruments project manager at Matrix, I have been in testing since 1999 with certifications such as ISTQB, CMMI and others. I carry experience that includes managing teams at Qulicke & Soffa, Sun Microsystems, General Electric, and NeuStar. I co-invented a test exclusion automated mechanism for mobile J2ME testing at Sun Microsystems — referenced in this book since it is still a valid method or concept in the mobile space. I have vast experience in the mobile testing world that includes ISTQB and CMMI certifications, as well as experience in leading testing teams, hand-on testing, speaking engagements in various global conferences, webinars, and meetups. I am also a constant blogger and author of white papers and other thought leadership content around mobile apps. You can find and engage with me on Facebook, Twitter @ek121268, LinkedIn, and my professional mobile testing blog.[1]

This Book, which also received valuable contributions from my brother Lior, is dedicated to my father **Marcel Kinsbruner** who passed away in 2006. He was a role model for me and my family in terms of perfectionism, dedication, and much more.

---

1   Eran Kinsbruner Blog — http://mobiletestingblog.com/

TECHNICAL REVIEWER
DANNY MCKEOWN

Danny McKeown, Lead Enterprise Test Automation Architect at Paychex

DANNY MCKEOWN has more than thirty years of technical and management experience in information technology. Contributing to the success of Paychex for thirteen years, Danny has spent the last seven of them as the lead enterprise test automation architect. In this role, he is instrumental in implementing a secure integration of the Perfecto solutions with the Paychex automation framework that leverages Selenium and other vendor technologies. In addition, Danny is an adjunct lecturer in the Rochester Institute of Technology software engineering department. He is a distinguished member of the advisory board of the International Institute for Software Testing.

Made in the USA
Middletown, DE
15 January 2018